# GUITAR

# Tim Brookes

# GUITAR

## An American Life

Grove Press
*New York*

*Published simultaneously in Canada*
*Printed in the United States of America*

FIRST GROVE PRESS PAPERBACK EDITION

Library of Congress Cataloging-in-Publication Data
Brookes, Tim, 1953–
Guitar : an American life / Tim Brookes.
p. cm.
ISBN-10: 0-8021-4258-3
ISBN-13: 978-0-8021-4258-0
1. Guitar—United States—History.   2. Guitarists—United States.   I. Title.
ML1015.G9B753 2005
787.87'0973—dc22      2004060877

Grove Press
an imprint of Grove/Atlantic, Inc.
841 Broadway
New York, NY 10003

Distributed by Publishers Group West

www.groveatlantic.com

06   07   08   09   10      10  9  8  7  6  5  4  3  2  1

*To the unknown guitar maker, the unknown guitarist,
and the unknown guitar.*

# Contents

# GUITAR

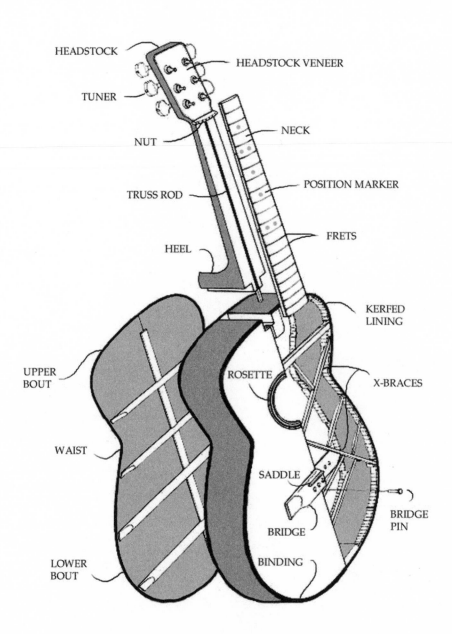

HEADSTOCK

HEADSTOCK VENEER

TUNER

NUT

NECK

TRUSS ROD

POSITION MARKER

FRETS

HEEL

KERFED
LINING

UPPER
BOUT

ROSETTE

X-BRACES

WAIST

SADDLE

BRIDGE
PIN

LOWER
BOUT

BRIDGE

BINDING

# Intro

On Sunday, August 18, I opened my guitar case, started to take out the guitar, and realized at once that something felt wrong. The strings were . . . floppy. Instead of that springy pressure against the palm of the hand, they were rattling and loose, splaying left and right across the fingerboard.

*That's weird*, I thought. *I don't think I slackened the strings.*

The previous day my family and my guitar had flown back from a vacation in Colorado, and now that I thought about it, someone had once told me it was a good idea to slacken your strings before putting a guitar on a plane. But these strings seemed to have slackened themselves. How could they do that? Very strange.

So I took the guitar out to tune it back up and to my utter horror saw that the whole head was *flopping*, falling back to its customary position and, as the strings tightened, bouncing back up again, as if it were hinged at the back of the neck.

Still not understanding, I turned the guitar over and saw what the baggage handlers had done. Where the neck joined the back of the head, a jagged crack ran so far up through the wood that the only thing holding head and neck together was the thin layer of headstock veneer that formed the face of the guitar. The head was all but snapped off.

For a moment, I could hardly breathe. Normally, I'm not that attached to my possessions. Things break. Things get lost. But this was my Fylde. This was my guitar.

I bought it in 1980, when I was an unfinished person, a collection of bits and pieces, surviving by my wits until a better idea occurred to me. I was still living in England, house-sitting for an Iranian woman who had come to England ostensibly to get an education but in reality to get away from her husband. She had asked me to look after her house and then, inexplicably, gone back to Iran. I was living on next to nothing, writing poetry and short stories, teaching English as a foreign language at a bogus institution that pretended to be an Oxford college, and playing guitar and singing at a couple of pubs and a wine bar.

It's astonishing to me now that, even though I could barely afford food, I sold my Guild dreadnought, a big, boomy guitar ideal for playing to noisy drunks, hitchhiked down to London, and bought the Fylde. Fylde is the brand name of a guitar maker named Roger Bucknall, who makes handcrafted guitars for people who want to play intricate, demanding fingerstyle work—that is, playing with the fingers of the right hand as if it were a classical guitar, rather than with a pick—and the top names in English folk music own Fyldes. It cost me four hundred pounds, all the money I had, and I hitched back to Oxfordshire with it that afternoon to play my evening gig. Standing by the road with my left thumb out and my right hand on my guitar case as it stood by my hip, I barely trod the ground. I was traveling, as Eric Clapton sings in "Crossroads," with my rider by my side.

Twenty-two years later, it was one of the few relics of my strange and erratic single life. It had moved to America with me and had continued in the background of my life, like an occasionally audible song from a distant room, through two failed marriages and one successful one, while I had shouldered a succession of jobs and started to raise two daughters. Now it lay across my lap, its neck broken.

Barbara, my wife, came in to see why I was making odd moaning and whimpering noises. She's a musician herself—a real musician, a classical flute player; a dozen times a year we play flute-and-guitar duets, mostly at weddings—so she understood at once.

"Look," she said. "Your fiftieth birthday's coming up. I'll buy you a new guitar."

This was, we both knew, mostly a gesture of moral support: neither of us had any money. But it gave me something to do apart from mope, so I started looking at guitars.

Guitar shops had changed a lot in the quarter century or so since I'd bought the Fylde. For a start, there were a lot more guitars on the walls, by a lot more makers: not only Martin, Gibson, Fender, Ovation, and Guild (plus a raft of classicals) but also Taylor, Takoma, Breedlove, Collings, Washburn, Montana, Santa Cruz, and a few more names at the cheap end. And much, much more variety: not only more variety in woods and colors but also in body shape and design, with the sound hole varying in shape, size, and position, the headstock flaring out into new configurations, and almost a quarter of the guitars in the showroom featuring various kinds of cutaway. Less obviously, perhaps a third also included built-in pickups for amplification, and even sliders for setting one's own EQ levels. The acoustic guitar, in short, had begun to merge with the electric.

I spent hours hanging out, fooling around with this guitar or that, and decided in passing that someone should write a sociology of the guitar store. Even when guitars were sold at more general music stores, or even at furniture stores or small-town general stores, the store offered more to the guitarist than just a new guitar. Guitar stores have functioned as message centers for local musicians, and as teaching studios. Field recordings often took place in music stores, and music store owners often acted as official or unofficial talent scouts for record companies. Many guitar makers learned their trade by doing repairs in a store's back room or basement, and the first consistent sets of electric guitar strings were put together and sold by a music store owner. Because guitar stores are often owned by guitarists, they've also become places where their mates can come and hang out, thus serving as so-cial centers and even old guitarists' homes. Most interesting of all, *a guitar store is the only place in the known universe where a guy will allow himself to shop like a woman*, spending half an hour, an hour, two hours trying a dozen guitars with only the faintest possibility of actually buying some-thing, playing a few licks, swapping a few lies, while in the background someone plays the opening bars of "Stairway to Heaven."

Yet all this diligent and selfless research was surprisingly little fun, and this was the first clue to the extraordinarily intimate relationship between a guitarist and his or her guitar.

I found I had strangely intense reactions to every guitar I saw. I hated sunbursts; I couldn't stand anything in orange; I despised dreadnoughts; I preferred light-colored tops to dark, and light-colored backs, too. The big-name makers didn't interest me; I wanted some-thing made by someone who cared about every instrument he or she made, someone living up a dirt road who made something slightly dif-ferent every time. I couldn't understand any of these prejudices, but I couldn't ignore them either. I despaired of ever finding a guitar I liked. Every instrument I played, no matter how fancy, just didn't feel right—not just under my fingers but in my hands, in its close and in-timate proximity to my body.

When the remarkable singer/dancer/guitarist Badi Assad looked closely at the classical guitar that had been passed down to her years previously by her older brother Odair, she saw it had a dark spot on the upper bout where he rested his bearded chin while practicing. "When we play," she wrote, "we *embrace* the instrument. We hold it close."

These shop guitars had the opposite effect on me: holding them was like being eighteen again, at yet another ghastly college party, sit-ting with a girl on my lap who had looked good a few minutes earlier but now was quickly becoming a dead weight, thinking, "Well, that was a mistake . . ."

I didn't want an expensive guitar, or even necessarily a beautiful one. I wanted a guitar that would feel at home, that would curl up on my lap like a cat.

I glued my Fylde's cracked neck as best I could, clamped it, let it heal for several days, and discovered that the glue job held. Now the Fylde seemed even more like me, lined and furrowed but still functioning. What a remarkable thing a guitar is, a small miracle of wood, vulnerable but oddly resilient.

After several weeks, two plans emerged, side by side. I was advised to check out a guitar maker named Rick Davis, living up a dirt road about fifteen miles away on the slopes of the Green Mountains. Wouldn't it be interesting, I thought, given that he lives so nearby, to watch the guitar coming together, and then write about it?

At the same time, my own unexpectedly strong reactions to the guitars in shops and on Web pages got me thinking. Why were there so many different kinds of guitars, when oboes, say, or violins had apparently reached a fixed state? Was it something to do with timing, that the guitar had arrived in a turbulent century, and changed with the times? Or did it have something to do with America, the land of endless inventiveness? Did the fact that the guitar varied so much make each one such a personal instrument? And—adding up all these questions—how did the guitar become wall-to-wall popular in the United States, and to a lesser degree throughout the world? Why had the guitar become the instrument of the twentieth century, to the point where more guitars are sold in this country than all other instruments combined?

So that's what I did when I wasn't looking over Rick Davis's shoulder and pestering him with questions: I set out to write a kind of chronicle of the American guitar, not a catalog of makes and models, nor a genealogy of celebrities, but an attempt to understand this curious relationship between the instrument and the people involved with it, and how that has grown and changed over time. A suite of unlikely stories. Part history, part love song.

# Meeting My Maker

It's a warm, sunny September day in the Vermont valleys, but in the hills above the bend-in-the-river hamlet of Jonesville it's already misty, looking like early fall. Stage Road, a dirt road that winds up toward the tiny village of West Bolton, is gulleyed by recent heavy rain, as is the long, steep dirt driveway up to Rick Davis's house, home and headquarters of Running Dog Guitars.

Rick's face is comfortably creased like soft leather, a warmth of line unusual in one relatively young. ("Our age," he says, referring to another guy around fifty.) Early maturity is, of course, a positive and sought-after quality in a guitar. He's wearing a black turtleneck underneath dark blue fleece, khakis, mocs—the classic thinking person's cool-weather gear in Vermont, the Subaru of clothing.

His workshop, in among the birch and pine trees just uphill from the house, is small, new, and crammed with band saw, router, sander, drill press, heater, generator, humidifier, dehumidifier, and shelves bearing all manner of hand tools and pieces of wood.

On one workbench a broad strip of Indian rosewood is being bent into shape for the sides of a guitar. On another lies a guitar top—that is, the face or front of the instrument—with strips of Sitka spruce running across it for bracing. On yet another workbench is a nearly finished concert jumbo in Hawaiian koa, a tigerish wood with an astonishing complexity of grain, depth, and variety of color.

On the fingerboard, he has inlaid his own mother-of-pearl designs on the third, fifth, seventh, and ninth frets: small maple leaves, all set at different angles to make them look as if they're falling down the guitar, as they've already started to fall outside. Then, at the octave fret, a snowflake.

"I wanted something that would show where the guitar comes from, and cutting out Subaru Outbacks and Saab 900s was a bit difficult," he says dryly.

From that moment, I am lost. Not because I know anything conclusive about his skill, or the compatibility between my playing and his guitars, but because of those maple leaves. The Fylde, as I now see it, stands for the first half of my life, the English half. I'll ask Rick to build me a guitar for the second half of my life, the Vermont half.

Much later, after the guitar is finished, Rick will refer to "the eternal and infinite capacity of the consumer to confuse making a purchase with falling in love." I should have known better, I suppose—but then again maybe not. First guitars tend to be like first loves: ill-chosen, unsuitable, short-lived, and unforgettable. I'm not sure I ever want to get to the point of making a rational decision about a guitar.

Rick is well aware of his place in history—or, to put it another way, he's well aware that thirty years ago he probably wouldn't have been doing what he does. The custom-guitar business has existed as long as guitars have existed, but thirty years ago the chance of finding a guitar maker in the next valley, or finding a school of lutherie in the same state, was essentially nil. (Lutherie originally meant "lute-making," but the term is now used more generally to mean the making of stringed instruments, especially guitars. It's to some extent a snob term; Rick says dryly that a luthier is a guitar maker who charges more than $1,000 per guitar.) At the start of the new millennium there are probably more stringed instrument makers in Vermont per capita

than any other state, Rick says, and as he is the president of the
Association of Stringed Instrument Artisans and compiler of the
A.S.I.A. directory, he should know. Some of the more notable are
Froggy Bottom Guitars of Newfane, makers of steel-string acoustic
guitars with a national reputation; Roger Borys of Shelburne, who
makes top-of-the-line jazz-style archtop guitars, whose customers
include the late Emily Remler; and Paul Languedoc of Westford,
who makes hollow-body electrics for a select clientele that includes
Phish. Vermont even has its own guitar-making school, Vermont
Instruments, in Thetford.

To my dismay, I seem to be part of a trend. All over America, former
guitarists, part-time guitarists, and would-be guitarists are looking
ahead to their fiftieth birthdays and asking for the really good guitar
that they could never afford back in their impoverished but musical
youth. And if the fiftieth birthday isn't available as an excuse, then
there's the forty-fifth, or the fifty-fifth, or just the next available
Christmas. There's even an upper stratum of buyers who have enough
disposable income to be able to call one of these high-end handmade
guitars an investment—an investment that, unlike a wad of shares in
Ben & Jerry's, you can pull out of its case and use to play a blues or
some complicated New Age instrumental in DADGAD tuning.
Guitar makers even have a word for these baby-boomers-who-always-
wanted-to-be-great-guitarists-and-now-have-the-money-to-indulge-
those-dreams: dentists.

Starting slowly in the early seventies, then, and growing rapidly from
the late eighties, an unprecedented number of guitar makers, some full-
time, most part-time, have set up their own businesses—between five
hundred and seven hundred and fifty in North America alone. These
makers, moreover, are being granted artistic license to build guitars that
not only are of the finest available materials but are also open to a fair
amount of creative freedom. Some are making guitars that are as good
as any ever made. It's the Golden Age of Guitar Making.

It's a sign of how open-minded the guitar market is becoming, and
how selective Rick can choose to be, that he won't even make a dread-

nought, the standard flat-bottomed, big-bodied guitar (named after a World War I Royal Navy battleship) that you see in the hands of country and bluegrass players. He says he's never heard a dreadnought with a good mid-range. Strong bass, loud clear treble, no middle. Instead he makes five models, most of them far less familiar. In increasing order of size, they are:

1. The Sprite. A tiny, twelve-fret guitar, also called a terz, for "third," guitar because it is tuned a third higher than other guitars. It is an old style currently gaining popularity as a travel guitar or a high-harmony guitar, which is more or less the role a guitar might have played in an ensemble of the sixteenth century.

2. The Parlor guitar. A small instrument based on the size and style popular in the nineteenth century, also twelve frets to the body, being bought by Celtic players and women who've always hated lugging around guitars that were too big for the lap, too thick for the right armpit.

3. The Chickadee, with its sloping shoulders, based on a unique guitar made by Martin in the 1840s. The Martin original was a tiny instrument; Rick has enlarged it somewhat. He tells the tale of a woman who brought this unique Martin guitar to a show in Los Angeles, her chauffeur carrying it around and showing it. She was asking an ungodly amount of money, and nobody bought it, but luckily a few people thought to take photos and measurements, because after she disappeared everyone looked at one another and realized that nobody had asked her name. And the guitar, a unique shoulder-sloped Martin, hasn't been seen or heard of since.

4. The Mini Jumbo—"the oxymoronic guitar." Based roughly on an old Gibson body shape, with a narrower waist than a dreadnought, plus a cutaway that in its earlier incarnations looked like a biting shark. (A cutaway is the scoop taken out of the upper bout that allows the player to reach higher up the fingerboard.) There are

two styles of cutaway, Rick tells me: the sharper Florentine and the rounded Venetian, the latter perhaps so called, he says, because it looks like a wave. These guitars may have smaller lower bouts than a dreadnought, he says, but a dreadnought has a flattened bottom, like a hippo sitting on concrete, and straight lines don't help acoustics—that's why speakers are round. So the flat bottom creates an acoustically wasted area, according to Rick.

5. The Concert Jumbo is his largest. Even this instrument, the koa one in Rick's workshop, seems delicate compared with the huge prewar Gibsons and even a standard Martin dreadnought. He hands me his concert jumbo. The sound leaps off the instrument, and I almost yelp. I had no idea how many things could be so different. Even the fret wires are different to the Fylde's, wider and more rounded, so my fingers seem to slither more easily over them up and down the strings. The case is half as thick again as mine. The custom work—the rosette around the sound hole, the decorative strip of binding that joins the top to the sides and the sides to the back, the inlay—all make the Fylde seem a little dowdy, even shabby: these were details Roger could have put work into, and didn't. On the other hand, yes, it's a little more ostentatious than the Fylde, but not aggressively so. It still doesn't feel like the cat on the lap, but it is a member of the cat family, at least.

The Chickadee, the Sprite, and the Parlor seem too small—stocky and strong, like pit ponies, but not nearly as rich and musical as I want. But they are a different breed from the mass-produced guitars in the shop. These have a sense of ownership and purpose. It's like seeing someone else's children in the school playground: they aren't my children but they clearly have identities and futures that appear to be nobody else's but their own.

He checks out the Fylde. I hold my breath, expecting veiled insults to the guitar, to me, to my bad taste and worse sense in buying such a guitar, to my irresponsible ownership in allowing it to get into such a condition. He lends me a catalog featuring a cartoon of a guitarist (glasses, long ponytail, long sideburns) on a small stage in a bar announcing, "This next song is about the feelings of an expensive, finely crafted instrument spending its life in the hands of a musical hack."

He *hmm*'s a little. He breathes through his nose. He picks up something like a large dentist's mirror on a stick and inserts it into the sound box to examine the entrails. He squints down the neck. He runs his hands over the top. I notice nicks and gouges I've never seen before.

His eventual analysis is surprisingly encouraging. My amateur glue job seems to have held, though the edges of the break are still jagged.

"Sand them down," he says. "Then fill in the crack. Mix up a little good epoxy—not the five-minute stuff. Add a little mahogany dust to give it color."

"Where do I get mahogany dust?"

"Mahogany," he says. He turns away, rummages around, and hands me a sheet of 120-grit sandpaper and a wedge-shaped block of mahogany that later I'll realize is cut off a guitar neck.

"I won't use all that," I protest.

He shrugs. "It's kindling."

I can't get over it. This is wood from thousands of miles away, wood whose name is almost magical. Mahogany. Teak. Ebony. The exotics of empire, like sapphires, rubies, diamonds.

"Mix up the epoxy. Add a little dust—less than you'd think. Trickle it into the crack here. Try to work the bubbles out. Use a piece of wood." He makes little prodding motions. Down to work, his sentences become crisp. This was what I should do, and can do. He does it every day. "Work it in all across these other cracks. Let it dry, then bring it down with a rasp. Or sandpaper. The epoxy provides a kind of finish of its own."

In general, he pronounces, the Fylde has the expected wear and tear but has held up better than I feared.

"This is not to say you don't need a guitar for your fiftieth birthday," he adds drolly. Rick, I will learn, rarely goes into sales mode, and when he does it's a little startling, like watching your best friend, meeting a girl for the first time, turn on a charm and intensity of focus you've never seen before, never suspected was in his range.

I laugh, and Rick starts to sketch out, from what he has just seen of my playing, the kind of guitar that he'd suggest for me. We settle on a concert jumbo—not a huge, boomy box but one with plenty of balanced sound, with a cutaway so I can get to those high Django chords. It'll be ready for my birthday in June.

And the price? Like most luthiers he has a base price, onto which he adds the extras: cutaway, special woods, built-in pickup, top-of-the-line hardshell traveling case. He clicks a mechanical pencil and writes tiny numbers on an order form. I hold my breath. Well, he says, it would come out to between two and three thousand dollars, depending on the extras. I release the breath. I've set myself a top limit of twenty-five hundred dollars—about the price of a new Fylde, as it happens.

We discuss the arcane specs I've started to hear about: scale length, nut width. These technicalities start making me uncomfortable. How can you call yourself a guitarist and not even know something as basic as the right nut width? I was happier twenty years ago being ignorant, picking out a guitar because I was besotted with the name, buying the only model I could afford. I've got to be on campus soon, I tell him, to meet a student who can't figure out what to do with her writing talent. It feels like a relief to be heading somewhere where I know I'll be equal to the challenge, to know that in this respect, at least, I can do as good a job as anyone else she might seek out for advice.

No problem, he says. Mind you, if we are going ahead with the guitar we'll need to decide on the wood. He pulls out from the bottom of a pile what he calls "the good stuff": two boards, 9 by 18 by ¼ inches, of coastal redwood, probably eighteen hundred years old, salvaged from a blowdown. The great advantage from a Vermont guitarist's point of view: they're unaffected by humidity, which up here gets high in the summer but then disappears down into the single digits when winter arrives and the home heat goes on. He knocks the board with the side of his thumb and it thrums, an utterly unexpected round, rich, deep sound, like a drum.

As I drive away from his cluttered-but-orderly workshop I keep seeing all the multifarious tools and bits and pieces, and it strikes me that there's no more mystery in building a guitar than in playing one. The pieces are like musical notes; it's all in the way you put them together.

# The First Guitar

The best place to understand what a guitar is, what it has been, and what it might have been, can be found in a windowless, half-hidden back room in a small house perched on a hillside overlooking Los Angeles: the Miner Museum of Vintage, Exotic, and Just Plain Unusual Musical Instruments.

Gregg Miner, a bright, chirpy guy who works in the aerospace industry and has taken the concept of guitar geek and run with it into entirely new dimensions, gestures toward the brightly lit display case running down the left-hand wall.

This, he says, contains "fretted Americana" from around 1880 to 1920: the "giraffe banjo," the banjeaurine (not a fruit but a five-string banjo with a short scale for playing the melody in banjo orchestras), and the giant five-string banjo with a sixteen-inch skin head to play the bass parts. Then the weird mandolin hybrids, like the piccolo mandolin, tuned a fourth higher even than a mandolin, and the vast mando-bass, like a gigantic musical frying pan.

"That was the normal case. Now things get a bit odd." He moves on to the wall opposite the door and points to something that looks like a combination of a guitar and a wooden shoulder-mounted grenade launcher. If Hieronymus Bosch had ever started making musical instruments, this is what he'd have made. It's a harp-guitar, a combination of a standard guitar neck and another harplike neck with as many as twelve bass strings.

That's just the start. Here are Hawaiian-influenced guitars with sloping shoulders and hollow necks. Guitars converted to be played by banjo players, and banjos converted to be played by guitarists. The theorbo, apparently the result of an amorous encounter between a lute and a garden rake. The tiny harp-ukulele, which looks like a baby hammerhead shark. You can't help suspecting that at least one of these is a fake, the Piltdown man of instruments, with something of one arbitrarily glued to something of another.

Even Gregg Miner's collection doesn't quite convey the range of instruments that the guitar left behind in its race to the top, especially those that show the extraordinary cultural diversity that existed as recently as sixty years ago. When the folklorist Sidney Robertson Cowell explored California folk music between 1938 and 1940, she found an incredible gaggle of instruments from Croatia, Dalmatia, Turkey, Armenia, and other distant shores that had arrived in the United States and hung on only in small numbers while the guitar survived: the *kamanche*, a miniature rectangular fiddle; the *qanun*, a zitherlike instrument; the *blul*, which looked like a recorder; the *daph*, a kind of tambourine; the *misnice*, based on a bladder like the bagpipe; the *gusle*, which looks like a bowed banjo, played between the knees; the *zurna*, something like an oboe; the *dumbelek*, not unlike the Irish bodhran; the *cimbalom*, built rather like a hammered dulcimer; the *svirala*, a cousin to the tin whistle; the *lirica*, like a bowed dulcimer; the *dvorgrle*, a double-barreled pipe; and a quintet of guitar-family instruments: the *saz*, a three-stringed plucked instrument looking like an ancestor of the thin "backpacker" guitar; the *tar*, an exquisite instrument with a long neck, carved tuners, and a body like a Japanese beetle; the *oud*, an Arabian ancestor of the lute (the word "lute" is in fact a contraction of *al oudh*); the *viola d'arame*, which could be mistaken for an eighteenth-century guitar but for having a curious coronet of tuners sprouting from its headstock and two sound holes, each carved in the shape of a heart; and the English guitar, its top like a perfectly halved pear or fig, which despite its name was brought over by Portuguese musicians from the Azores. American culture was unified, and the guitar rose to dominance at the expense of these fascinating oddments.

Thinking about such extraordinary instruments, I find myself wondering, *Why was it the guitar that survived, in the face of such multifarious and energetic competition? Why was it the guitar, rather than one of these contraptions, that became so popular that by the end of the twentieth century it outsold all other instruments combined?*

The conventional answer is that the guitar is portable, cheap, can be learned in an hour or two, and has range enough for both treble and bass voices. Yet the Miner Museum houses a host of instruments with some or all of these qualities.

Another important element, the glass cases argue, is adaptation. People change, music changes, musical instruments change, but not all instruments are equally light on their feet. It's easier and cheaper to tinker around with a ukulele than a concert grand, and it's well nigh impossible to tinker around with a violin when the heavy hand of the concertmaster is on your shoulder. When the most rapidly changing century arrived, in the most rapidly changing country in the world, the guitar would be available, useful, and so receptive to our evolving social needs that it would constantly be reinvented. By the end of the century it would have changed into a variety of forms, some of them barely recognizable as guitars.

In fact, the Miner Museum shows in every cubic foot of each case that no instrument has just one form at one time. What is a guitar? Not a single instrument but a syndrome, a collection of symptoms from a list. Six strings, played with the fingers. A hollow, wooden, hourglass-shaped body. A fretted neck. Okay, check your list. Six or more of these qualities and what you've got is some kind of guitar. Three or four and it's a balalaika, or a bouzouki, a baja sexto, or a banjeaurine. Fewer than four and it's something really bizarre, like a chitarrone ("an eye-popping archlute so ridiculously long that it's not safe to take it out of its case while indoors," writes Miner, adding that the open bass strings alone use nearly six feet of gut) or a tromba marina, a one-string instrument whose name translates as "a trumpet played by nuns." Yet even this syndrome approach breaks down almost at once: a pedal steel guitar doesn't meet *a single one* of these criteria. And what are we to make of a visionary one-of-a-kind instrument made by Fred Carlson called the Flying Dream, a thirty-nine-string sitar-harp-guitar whose shape was inspired by a dream of a chicken trying to fly?

The same difficulty arises when we try to find the first guitar in history. The first portable, hollow, wooden stringed instruments with fretted necks and hollow bodies that we know of appear in artwork produced by the Hittites nearly 2,500 years ago. Reinforcing this weak evidence, the word "guitar" also seems to originate in that region: the Persian word *tar* (meaning "three-stringed") seems to have given rise to the Indian *sitar*, the Hebrew *kinnura* or *kinnor*, the Chaldean *qitra*, and the Assyrian *chaterah*, which lead, in anything but a direct line, to the Greek *citharis* and *cithara*, and thence via the medieval European *gittern*, *qhisterne*, *guitarra* to guitar. In any case, a fretted hourglass-shaped stringed instrument, later called the *guitarra morisca* or Moorish guitar, entered Spain by way of the Moors, the North African Arabs, and the coronation of Alfonso XI (1311–1350) resounded with instruments, including the guitar. Over the next two hundred years it slowly spread north and east, probably varying in its guitarness with every instrument maker, carpenter, cabinetmaker, furniture builder, whittler, cooper, and sawyer who tried his hand at making one. Then it came to the New World.

It came remarkably early, perhaps more than half a century before the *Mayflower* set sail from Southampton. As early as 1513, Spanish explorers, many of whom brought instruments, were visiting the land area we now call the United States. A traditional belief among the natives of the Azores, who emigrated to California, held that the first European music to be sung and danced on the North American continent was the Chamarrita, supposedly taught by Cabrillo's men to friendly Indians when the Portuguese explorer Cabrilho (Cabrillo in Spanish) sailed up the coast toward Oregon in 1542. But this is all conjecture, and besides, these are visitors to the continent, not residents.

Astonishingly, we may actually know the name of the first resident of North America to own a guitar. The candidate in question was Juan Garcia y Talvarea.

The oldest continuously occupied settlement in the United States is Saint Augustine, Florida, founded in 1565. Wiley S. Housewright's *A History of Music and Dance in Florida, 1565–1865* says that in 1576 a soldier named Juan Garcia y Talvarea died at Saint Augustine, and among his possessions was a guitar.

What kind of guitar was it, this first arrival? It's hard to know for sure, because not a single example of the sixteenth-century guitar has survived, but it was almost certainly an hourglass-shaped instrument with four courses—that is to say, pairs—of gut strings. Very small by today's standards, perhaps a third the size of a modern classical guitar, with as few as seven frets. What did it sound like? It almost certainly had less sustain than a modern classical guitar, and less bass. (As much as two centuries later a writer would still be complaining about the "dead, lumpish, and tubby" tones of the bass strings of the guitar.) It probably had a chirpy, lutelike sound, and might have been played solo, or as the treble instrument in a small ensemble. What did he play on it? Again, it's a guess, because he was a soldier rather than a professional musician (the Spanish took professional musicians everywhere, and paid them remarkably well), but he probably played the same repertoire that the folk guitarist still plays—ballads, love songs, comic songs, complaints. Strummed music for dances. The garrison at Saint Augustine must have needed all the music it could get, three thousand miles from home.

I should have guessed Spain right away. Spain was the guitar's European home, as well as one of the launching points for journeys to the New World. Ferdinand and Isabella, who bankrolled Columbus, also carried out a program of ethnic cleansing against the Moors, Gypsies, and Jews that would lead, ultimately, to the outsider folk music called flamenco. By 1565 the Spanish had a wide and sophisticated guitar repertoire, and they brought it with them to the New World. Mexico City was a cultural hub. By 1574 the city had workmen's guilds. As early as the end of the sixteenth century, guitar strings could be bought on the Camino Real between Mexico City and Santa Fe.

Over the next two hundred years a huge range of classical music for the guitar was both imported from Europe and printed in the New World, and a wide variety of instruments, too, were imported and/or built. Missionaries and traders brought the guitar (by now the five-course baroque guitar, probably) into the regions we now call New Mexico, Texas, and California, where it was played by soldiers, civilian settlers, and even indigenous Indians, who picked it up quickly. Mexico gained independence from Spain in 1821, and declared Alta (upper) California a province of Mexico. Between then and 1848, Spanish California life flourished in what is often regarded as a golden age. Any special occasion was marked by a *baile*, or dance, with the violin and guitar leading the dancing. In *The Land of Little Rain*, Mary Austin, who moved to California in 1888, describes a typical small village:

> At Las Uvas they keep up all the good customs brought out of
> Old Mexico or bred in a lotus-eating land, drink, and are
> merry and look out for something to eat afterward; have
> children, nine or ten to a family, have cock-fights, keep the
> siesta, smoke cigarettes and wait for the sun to go down. And
> always they dance; at dusk on the smooth adobe floors,
> afternoons under the trellises where the earth is damp and
> has a fruity smell. A betrothal, a wedding, or a christening, or
> the mere proximity of a guitar is sufficient occasion; and if the
> occasion lacks, send for the guitar and dance anyway.

What happened to this guitar tradition, so much more advanced than what was happening among the Anglo population on the east coast? What happened to the well-developed agrarian civilization that fostered it?

In short, the answer was gold. The 1848 Gold Rush and the influx of 100,000 Anglo-Americans that accompanied and followed it changed everything.

At first, many of the Anglo easterners visiting California write as visitors who are seeing Spanish culture for the first time, and there's a marked difference between the rough-and-ready appearance and behavior of the miners and the civilized demeanor of the Spanish.

"Among the fresh arrivals at the diggings the native Californians have begun to appear in tolerable numbers," wrote Edwin Bryant in *Four Months Among the Gold-Finders* (1849).

> Many of these people have brought their wives, who are attended usually by Indian girls. The graceful Spanish costume of the new-comers adds quite a feature to the busy scene around. There, working amidst the sallow Yankees, with their wide white trousers and straw hats, and the half-naked Indian, may be seen the native-born Californian, with his dusky visage and lustrous black eye, clad in the universal short tight jacket with its lace adornments, and velvet breeches, with a silk sash fastened round his waist, splashing away with his gay deerskin [boots] in the mudded water.
>
> . . . Since these arrivals, almost every evening a fandango is got up on the green, before some of the tents. . . . It is quite a treat, after a hard day's work, to go at nightfall to one of these fandangos. The merry notes of the guitar and the violin announce them to all comers; and a motley enough looking crowd, every member of which is puffing away at a cigar, forms an applauding circle round the dancers, who smoke like the rest.

Many of the new arrivals were struck by the democratic spirit of the dances. "It was not anything uncommon or surprising," wrote the Santa Fe trader Josiah Webb in 1844, "to see the most elaborately dressed and aristocratic woman at the ball dancing with a *peon* dressed only in his shirt and trousers open from the hip down, with wide and full drawers underneath, and frequently barefoot." Music, in other words, was not a commodity, nor an exercise in superiority. It was a set of traditions that infused the whole of Spanish California society and brought it together. And as with any important tradition, it had engendered skill and complexity among those who practiced it.

T. A. Barry and B. A. Patten, who visited San Francisco in 1850, later wrote of a Mexican quintet consisting of two harps, two guitars, and a flute:

> The musicians were dressed in the Mexican costume . . . and were quiet, modest looking men, with contented, amiable faces. They used to walk in among the throng of people, along to the upper end of the room, take their seats, and with scarcely any preamble or discussion, commence their instrumentation. They had played so much together, and were so similar, seemingly, in disposition—calm, confident and happy—that their ten hands moved as if guided by one mind; rising and falling in perfect unison—the harmony so sweet, and just strange enough in its tones, from the novelty in the selection of instruments, to give it a peculiar fascination for ears always accustomed to the orthodox and time-honored vehicles of music used in quintette instrumentation.

Yet the same newcomers from the east who were struck by the music and the comportment of the Hispanic Californians were accelerating the erosion of that culture. Gold and the massive influx of prospectors changed the economy and the demographics, and the initial burst of Spanish hospitality was soured when penniless miners and travelers killed cattle and stole corn. They also brought Anglo prejudices.

"The families of the wealthier classes had more or less education," wrote William Heath Davis, another newcomer. "They seemed to have a talent and taste for music. Many of the women played the guitar skillfully, and the young men the violin. In almost every family there were one or more musicians, and everywhere music was a familiar sound. Of course, they had no scientific and technical musical instruction."

It's that last sentence that gets me, reeking of the smug snobbery of the Victorian easterner. It's hardly surprising to read that as soon as the newcomers reached a critical mass, the "old" Spanish guitar was pushed aside by the instrument that best embodied "scientific and technical" music: the piano.

"On our return," wrote the Right Reverend William Ingraham Kip, "we stopped at Don José's house in town to lunch, where we were most hospitably entertained. His daughter played some pieces on the piano for us, with great taste and skill. As American habits creep in, this instrument is, in many California houses, taking the place of the guitar, whose music they inherited from their Spanish ancestors."

What we're seeing is a form of low-level cultural genocide, in which the guitar is a kind of metaphor: many features of Spanish California life that delighted the new arrivals would come to be spoken of with disdain and seen as primitive and uncivilized. Individual Latino guitarists would continue to be respected, such as Manuel Ferrer (1843–1900) in San Francisco and Miguel Arevalo (1832–1904) in Los Angeles, both of whom played concerts of Mexican, European, and European-American music for both Latino and English-speaking audiences. To the increasingly dominant English-speaking population, though, the Mexican-American guitar heritage, with its broad repertoire and advanced skills, was quaint at best. It would come as close to extinction as the theorbo, the banjeaurine, the tromba marina.

# Choosing the Wood

Guitars begin with wood. On a sharp, brittle January day I'm back in Rick's shop, writing him a check for the $500 deposit while he pulls down samples of wood for the back, sides, and top.

Insofar as I've been able to picture my Vermont guitar I've imagined maple, the classic Vermont wood, but Rick pulls out a plank of cherry that he bought at Sterling Hardwoods in Burlington, and it is breathtaking. A series of ripples run through the grain in the middle section, caused (perhaps) by a virus, and the wood looks like crushed velvet. He dabs a little naphtha on a rag and polishes a few square inches, and the wood takes on what the French call *chatoyance,* the luminous cat's-eye luster that throws light out of the depth of the wood, creating the illusion of three dimensions that shift and move like a hologram. Cherry guitars are unusual, Rick says, but he likes the northern hardwoods—maple, cherry, walnut, sycamore—rather than the tropical exotics. They're his neighbors.

What he didn't know was that cherry is my favorite wood. My family bought me a young cherry tree for my birthday, and it's the first thing you see outside our front door. We'll go with the cherry.

Mind you, if there's one thing Rick has already started warning me about, in a series of more and less pointed asides, it's the danger of falling in love with a gorgeous piece of wood. At the moment, he says, there's a trend among modern high-end guitar makers to treat the guitar less as a musical instrument and more as a sculpture. Startling headstock shapes. Wild bridge shapes and positions. A body shape that is so nonangular that it seems to be in the process of melting, like Dalí's soft watches. The trouble is, showy woods may not sound significantly better than plainer ones, and they may not age well. As Rick puts it, in ten years' time they may explode. Electrics, meanwhile, are also becoming more wood-conscious, more three-dimensional, as if furtively ashamed of their utilitarian roots and trying to take on some of the rounded charm of the acoustic. High-end guitars in particular, such as the Paul Reed Smith line, are filling out, becoming "almost cello-like."

In the various online acoustic guitar discussion groups, a certain regionalism seems to emerge. In Florida, the talk is all of wood and pearl. In California, it's all of wood. "If they're from anywhere else in the country they may mention sound. It's very annoying to me as a builder. I'm sick to death of inlay and pearl," Rick says, sick of the look that says "fifty oysters died to make this guitar." A bumper sticker on the wall shows a sea otter swimming on its back, opening a shell, with the legend: SAVE THE ABALONE.

Nothing gets a guitar maker fired up more quickly than a discussion about wood.

For many luthiers, love of wood is why they make guitars, or at least how they got into making guitars—that combination of color, smell, and feel; the curious nobility-in-service of wood, like the farmer's love for a good strong draft horse; the unexpected luster deep in the grain; the surprise that comes with stripping off the bark, always an educated guess as to what is underneath; the way in which it responds to tools, always demanding and threatening catastrophe but rewarding the careful hand and the knowledgeable touch.

The wood used for a guitar top is fairly straightforward. Some prefer Sitka spruce or Engelmann spruce, some prefer cedar or redwood, but in any case it is (or can be) a native wood from a tree that grows fairly quickly and is in little danger of being logged to extinction. The sides and back are a different matter: here we find ourselves among the exotics of empire with a vengeance.

For more than a hundred years, the wood of choice was Brazilian rosewood for its combination of beauty and hardness (and the fact that when freshly cut it smells of roses), but this tradition created its own problems. On the one hand, the world's supply of Brazilian rosewood steadily dwindled, and by the late sixties Brazilian was becoming rare and expensive—so expensive that the major guitar companies started switching to Indian rosewood.

By then, though, Brazilian had become so closely associated with the best guitars that anything else was starting to seem mediocre, or perhaps it would be more accurate to say that the guitar companies were afraid that anything else seemed mediocre, and that it would be increasingly hard to charge top dollar for a guitar if its back and sides were made from anything other than Brazilian.

Since then, the situation has become increasingly polarized. Brazilian rosewood is now protected under the Convention on International Trade in Endangered Species (CITES), and since 1992 it's forbidden by law to ship from one country to another any wood that was logged since that date, or anything made of wood logged since 1992. This means, for example, that before it can be exported to Japan a guitar made in America needs to prove that its wood was logged before the ban.

(In theory, at least. A recent Knight-Ridder story reported slave labor being used in harvesting rain forest woods. Among luthiers and wood importers, the CITES laws are spoken of as if they contain as many holes as a dead tree assaulted by a colony of woodpeckers. Small, unexpected stashes of Brazilian rosewood have a habit of turning up in unexpected places. Luthiers talk of buying expeditions as secretive and shady as drug deals.)

One response is to cull Brazilian rosewood in a way that doesn't involve cutting down trees—in other words, to cut stumpwood. This is a specialty of Allied Lutherie in Healdsburg, California, where Todd

Taggart sorts through a pile of production-grade (i.e., bottom-shelf) wood and pulls out a surprise, a stunning set with the characteristic orange flame at the heart of the rich, dark brown wood. "That's AAAA," he says, pleasantly surprised and professionally impressed. "I'll charge eight hundred dollars for that."

Finding good stumpwood is not an easy job, though. It's a mystery where the best wood is to be found, and why the tree develops that spiderweb pattern that is most highly prized. Todd hints at corruption, and grumbles at the bureaucracy that defeats his best efforts. "We put a lot of local people to work," he says. "We even planted Brazilian rosewood seedlings, but they made us dig them up."

The shortage of Brazilian rosewood has driven up the prices of other exotics, such as the beautiful tiger's-eye koa from Hawaii. "Not long ago a set of koa was going for thirty-five dollars. Now it can cost you three hundred and fifty dollars." Todd shakes his head.

Another option is to explore and develop what are often called "alternative tonewoods." Unfortunately, "explore and develop" is virtually synonymous with "exploit" and not far short of "clear-cut." Talk of "opening up" Madagascar for ebony, mahogany, and other exotic woods tends to overlook the fact that an ecological catastrophe is in the making. When a maker describes the back and sides of his latest guitar with a love that stops barely short of salivation, it's possible that the matter of the origin and future of the wood is being willingly overlooked by both maker and buyer.

The next possibility is alternative tonewoods that are neither exotic nor endangered—native woods, in fact. Cherry. Sycamore. Maple. Oak. Birch. Poplar. These make perfectly good guitars, especially as at least 80 percent of the sound of a guitar comes from the top, not the back and sides, a point proven dramatically by the great Spanish luthier Antonio Torres, who made a perfectly decent-sounding guitar out of a spruce top and back and sides of papier-mâché.

The big guitar companies complain that the customer just won't go for it. A century of building with Brazilian rosewood has created a public that, in crude terms, won't pay $2,000 for a sycamore guitar. In this respect, the Martins and Gibsons of the world are all in favor of

the small companies and independent luthiers using alternative
tonewoods: if Rick can make America believe in the cherry guitar,
Chris Martin IV is among those cheering him on.

The whole question of wood is a dispiriting one, with an uncertain
and even gloomy future.

A certain amount of wood is being grown under programs for sus-
tainable harvest such as Smartwoods, but on such a small scale that
it makes little impact on either the guitar market or the world's
woodlands.

Wood can also be salvaged—from homes being demolished, from
old churches, from old pieces of furniture. One of my favorite stories
is that Roger Bucknall, maker of my Fylde, has built several guitars
out of whiskey casks. The sound is said to be pretty nice, but it's nothing compared to the wonderful smell when you open the guitar case.

Another potential source is so-called drowned wood—hundred-
year-old old-growth logs that have lain underwater in Lake Michigan
since the nineteenth-century fell-and-float days, now salvaged and
dried out, a painless harvest.

In the end, the future of the guitar and of the forests comes down
to a love of trees, and of wood. Ken Savage, a guitar maker in his fifties
with silvering hair and a ponytail who lives on Bainbridge Island in the
Puget Sound southwest of Seattle, tells his story.

"I was in my shop one day and this older guy shows up. This happens a lot. People are always saying, 'I've got some really great wood,'
and it's always crap. But I always look at it anyway, just in case.

"He showed me the wood and I couldn't believe it. It was definitely
guitar-quality wood. It was absolutely stunning. It was quilted maple,
very . . . puffy." The quilting is a ripple in the golden grain that makes
the wood look beautifully three-dimensional. Ken had seen quilted
maple before, but nothing like this—and the wood had been air-dried
(rather than kiln-dried) for twenty-five years, which made it not only
great wood but very rare.

The visitor turned out to be a recluse. "He's unmarried, and he
never leaves his house—his parents' house, which he was born in seventy years ago. He won't even answer the phone. Anyway, we talked.

He loved my shop, and loved what I was doing, and after a while he said, 'Well, I do have some more.'"

This is what Ken had been hoping to hear. Telling me the story, he chuckled and rubbed his hands together.

"So we drive off the island, and he takes me to a metal building, which is about thirty-five feet wide and about sixty feet long. He slides these doors open and half the building is taken up with these two-inch-thick planks stacked six feet high. You can't walk between them—it's just solid wood. There's enough wood there for five, six, ten thousand guitars. My knees went weak."

It turned out that twenty years previously, the reclusive neighbor had a friend who worked for a local lumber company that was logging fir. Mixed in with the fir were magnificent maples that the lumber company was simply grinding up for pulp. The friend said, "Come get 'em if you want 'em."

The neighbor spent five years rescuing the maples, going into the forest with a chain saw, cutting them into two-inch planks, carrying them as much as quarter of a mile out to the nearest road and then driving them back to his shed.

"Then he would restack them [in the same order] as he took them off the tree. He carefully numbered them and waxed the ends. He treated the wood perfectly. He had no intention for their use. He was just into it. He's very reclusive, as I said, and this is something that worked for him, to go out and gather wood.

"He loves his wood, and he covets his wood. He has enough money that he doesn't need to sell it. So he sells me one or two pieces a year that I can make several guitars out of. Right now I'm trying to get him to sell me, like, ten or twelve pieces." Ken chuckled.

"We've actually become really good friends. He comes over to my shop, and we chat. He's now building a shop for himself, and I've been helping him work on tool placement. And I'm still working on him to get those ten or twelve planks of wood!

"He really likes what I'm doing with the wood. As far as I'm concerned, it's the best calling for the wood."

# Other Colonists:
# French and
# English Guitars

O n the other hand, it's *just* possible that a French guitarist got here first.

The first Europeans in Florida were not the Spanish but French Huguenots, who in 1562 set up a colony called Charlesfort. This was short-lived, but in 1564 a French party returned and established Fort Caroline, near present-day Jacksonville.

Fort Caroline must have been a remarkable place. Compared to the Spanish, the French seem to have sailed to the New World not as conquerors but as civilizers. They took few soldiers (unfortunately, as it turned out) but a range of skilled artisans necessary for the establishment of high culture: a beer maker, dog trainers, shoemakers, and a coterie of musicians including a spinet player, a violinist/trumpeter, four horn players, three drummers, and a fifer.

There's no mention of a guitar, but as with the Spanish explorers, it's very possible a guitar might have been brought along without anyone thinking to mention it. France, where the instrument was called the *guiterre,* the *guiterne,* or the *guisterne,* may well have had a more developed repertoire for guitar than Spain. The guitar was used in French theater as early as the 1480s, and by the time Fort Caroline was founded French guitar music included all manner of songs and dances, and the small four-course guitar seems to have been played solo, or as an accompaniment to voice, or in consort, possibly as the high treble instrument. A reference in 1556 speaks of a recent guitar boom in France, claiming that there were now more guitarists in France than in Spain.

Sadly, Fort Caroline met a savage and bloody end. Once Pedro Menendez de Aviles had established his Spanish settlement at Saint Augustine, the French were doomed. Aviles took a raiding party up the coast, overran Fort Caroline, and slaughtered its inhabitants.

Well, almost all its inhabitants. It says something about the Spanish and the importance they invested in music that Aviles spared women, children—and the musicians. Did he see it as almost a form of sacrilege to kill a musician? Or was he simply trying to gather greater glory by having a larger fanfare to play in his own honor? All we know is that he took them back to Saint Augustine and added them to his ensemble.

The French would bring guitars with them to the New World, but they would arrive a century later, moving down from Canada along the great rivers to the French missions and settlements in present-day Detroit, St. Louis, Natchez, New Orleans, Baton Rouge, and many points in between, as well as Biloxi and Mobile on the Gulf of Mexico. Many of these settlements kept their French character until well into the nineteenth century, and likely kept their guitars, too. In his snappily-titled 1847 memoir *A Canoe Voyage Up the Minnay Sotor; with an Account of the Lead and Copper Deposits in Wisconsin; of the Gold Region in the Cherokee Country; and Sketches of Popular Manners; &c. &c.*, G. W. Featherstonehaugh wrote: "How different the tranquil existence of this primitive French village from the busy excitement of a populous city! At nine p.m. there was not a soul to be met in the streets; here and there the chords of a guitar, accompanied by a French voice, agreeably interrupted the general silence, whilst the only tread that was audible was that of cows slowly moving up and down the streets."

The British, meanwhile, went through two separate guitar crazes, with two distinct guitars. The instrument first arrived in England around the 1540s but made little impact until it was abruptly catapulted to the very summit of society when Charles II returned to England to take the throne in 1660.

During the period known as the Commonwealth, when England was a republic ruled by a severely Puritan Parliament, Charles had been living in the Netherlands. Like most exiles he had time on his hands, and when he was visited by the great Italian guitarist Francisco Corbetta he took up the instrument (by now the five-course baroque guitar) with enthusiasm and no little skill. When he returned to London, amid great celebration and an extraordinary flourishing of art, drama, and music, he took his love of the guitar with him—not to mention his new wife, the daughter of John IV of Portugal, and her household musicians, who likely included guitarists. This ensemble was supplemented by Italians, including Corbetta, who by helping to make the guitar fashionable in two kingdoms may claim to have been one of the most influential guitarists of his time. The guitar appeared regularly in masques and theatrical productions, and soon everyone in court was playing it.

"There was a certain Italian at the court, famous for the guitar," wrote Anthony Hamilton, somewhat caustically in his *Memoirs du Compte de Grammont*.

> He had a genius for music, being the only one who could do anything with the guitar; but his composition was so graceful and tender that he could have produced harmony on the lowest of instruments. The truth is that nothing was more difficult than to play in his style. The liking expressed by the King for his compositions had made this instrument so fashionable that everyone was playing it—well or badly. Even on the dressing tables of all the beauties one could rely on seeing a guitar as well as rouge and beauty spots.
>
> The Duke of York was a passable performer, but Lord Arran rivaled Francisco himself. This Francisco had just composed a sarabande which so charmed or desolated everyone, that all the guitar players in the court set about learning it, and God knows the strumming that ensued everywhere.

Many of the guitars of this era, especially those owned by the fashionably rich on the continent as well as in England, were inlaid and decorated with marquetry on every available surface. In his play, *Sir Courtly Nice* (1685), John Crowne pulled together the instrument's popularity, its showy decoration and its association with sexiness in a single brilliant sentence: "Oh! no, Madam, he's the general guitar o'the town, inlay'd with everything women fancy."

Both women and men played the guitar. A young lady would learn from a tutor (quite likely a Frenchman, an Italian, or a Spaniard), and as hiring practices in those days often involved the tutor being paid a small fee that was padded out with the offer of free board and lodging in one of the many rooms in the great aristocratic houses of the day, that tutor might well live in the same house as the young lady and see her every day. Not surprisingly, romance flourished often enough for the guitar-master to join the dancing-master as one of the stock characters in romantic comedy of the time. Sir John Vanbrugh's 1705 play, *The Confederacy*, includes a line that resonates through history to this day: "Psha! She's taken up with her impertinent Guitar Man."

The guitar's popularity extended as far afield as the colonies. In 1661 a Harvard student named John Foster was reported to have a "violl" and a "gittarue." He probably wasn't the Harvard man who in 1653 was overheard "in the forenoon with ill company playing music," but you never know.

The guitar craze died down in England, but it's reasonable to guess that whatever musical instruments arrived in the colonies were not readily thrown out, being hard to come by, so the guitar probably survived in a low-profile way in New England between 1620 and 1750. On or around the latter date, the English guitar picked up the tempo significantly, but by then it was a different instrument altogether.

In 1763 a visitor described the young ladies of Charleston as genteel and slender, with fair complexions and sparkling eyes. "They are fond of dancing, an exercise they perform very gracefully; and many sing well, and play upon the harpsichord and guitar with great skill."

The same bewitching company was to be found in Annapolis. Here is Rebecca Dulany writing to her sisters Molly, Peggy, and Kitty in 1764. "Mrs. Plater, the two Miss Tayloes, George Fitzhugh and myself," she writes, sounding like a character in a Jane Austen novel, "went upstairs where we were very merry as you may judge by the company, for Miss Tayloe is fully as lively and diverting as George Fitzhugh. . . . After tea the young ladies played on the guitar, and sung for us, and then we took a long walk in the garden, and after that, we had the guitar again, and a great deal of Mr. Fitzhugh's company. I never saw him in better spirits, or appear to be happier."

The guitars being played by the young ladies, though, were not guitars at all.

Back across the Atlantic, a guitar boom was taking place in London, starting shortly after 1750, but the instruments currently being called guitars (also "English guitars" or "common guitars") were citterns—wire-strung instruments, usually with six courses tuned to an open C chord, without the characteristic waist of the guitar and shaped instead more like half a fig.

The English guitar was a rather odd duck. Citterns had been around for a century or more in a fringes-of-society way, flourishing among low company in the usual downmarket trio of bars, brothels, and barbershops. In *The Honest Whore*, Thomas Dekker wrote, "Is she a whore? A barber's cittern for every man to play on?" Barbers throughout Europe (and later, even some barbers in the United States) hung musical instruments such as citterns, mandolins, and guitars on their walls, and waiting customers were tacitly invited to take them down and play away. Ben Jonson put almost the identical metaphor into his play *The Silent Woman:* "That cursed barber . . . I have married his cittern that's common to all men." The joke was so common that word "slattern" or "slut" may even have evolved from "cittern."

The suddenly fashionable English guitar had a deeper body and more strings. Nobody knows for sure where it came from or why it became popular, but the consensus is that it had something to do with Portugal. The Portuguese were in the process of adopting and adapting wire-strung instruments (a fact that would become very important in the near future), and there was a strong connection between the two countries as a number of wealthy British wine merchants and their families had what we would now call villas or estates in northern Portugal.

The wire-strung English guitar was tough on the fingernails and fingertips, which was not what some of the ladies wanted. Players may have used a plectrum or fingerpicks, which would have made it sound rather like a zither. For a while it was possible to buy an attachment that sat astride the strings and plucked them for you as you pressed its keys, like a miniature harpsichord, but that involved another piece of equipment and another stage of learning.

Nevertheless, it was louder and brighter in sound than the baroque gut-strung guitar, and riding on its surge of popularity it crossed to the colonies, as if entire drawing rooms or country gardens were being shipped wholesale.

Yet the English guitar suffered a sad and curious fate. In England, an unscrupulous spinet and harpsichord maker named Kirkmann, faced with the prospect of bankruptcy, made or bought up a large number of bottom-of-the-line English guitars and sold or gave them away to every publican, barber, and brothel keeper he knew. All of a sudden the instrument no longer seemed chic, the boom was silenced, and Kirkmann was taking orders for harpsichords and spinets again.

The English guitar probably survived longer in the colonies. By the end of the eighteenth century, all the major East Coast cities had active concert series. Guitarists, both professional and amateur, played solos and duets, sang to the guitar, or played instrumental pieces. Some East Coast musicians played English guitars, some Spanish, some both, but the introduction of the modern six-string Spanish guitar and, perhaps, the improved bracing of Spanish guitars must have made the cittern-style English instrument seem clumsy and dated. Early in the nineteenth century the first of the great Spanish guitarist/composer/teachers, Fernando Sor, arrived in London, along with other virtuosi from Italy, France, and Spain, all playing six-string Spanish guitars. The English guitar was doomed, though ironically it would reappear in California in the 1930s in the hands of settlers from Portugal.

What happened to those genteel English guitars, which provided the entertainment in those genteel English days? My guess is that they survived into the early nineteenth century for the same reasons that the melon-backed mandolin survived in the early twentieth. They would have been kept because they looked nice, if quaint, hanging on people's walls, or perhaps gathering dust on a bureau or relegated to the attic, drying and shrinking in the summer heat, swelling and warping in the winter damp, the strings turning brittle and snapping in the middle of a quiet night, the instruments returning to their constituent pieces, like musical jigsaws in reverse.

# The Chain-saw Phase

In mid-February, with the temperature outside his temperature-and-humidity-controlled workshop falling below zero, Rick gets down to work.

"The early stages tend to be loud. We're in the chain-saw phase." He's cut the best section out of the plank of cherry, a piece roughly 24 by 9 by 1½ inches, and today's job is to cut that lengthwise, the most difficult way, like trying to cut an oblong of cheese into slices. He takes the old blade off the band-saw, which is as tall as me, and as we chat he attacks the various nooks and crannies of the machine, cleaning out the sawdust, faintly sticky with the memory of resin.

Rick grew up in the suburbs of Baltimore and Washington. "I was a good sixties kid. The suburbs were dead on arrival, as far as I could tell."

Two weeks after graduating from high school he moved to lower Manhattan, worked with the peace movement for eighteen months, "and it was wonderful." Then the peace movement started to sour, and life in the city began to sour. In 1968 he took a bus to Vermont, and when he got out in Putney "it was a perfect fall night. Every star in the universe was shining on Putney, and I said, yep, this is what

I've been looking for." He signed up to study economics at Marlboro College, bought woolen long johns and a red flannel shirt . . .

Wait a moment. So he became a Vermonter. But economics? How did he become a woodworker?

Well, none of it was quite that straightforward. He actually learned his appreciation for skilled manual labor from his grandfather, an Appalachian jack-of-all-trades, "the sort of guy who would build his own house and furniture and trim and even the clock on the mantelpiece." Economics lost its appeal ("I discovered that all economists go to work for banks") and while he was at Marlboro he supported himself by woodworking, and then he was a mechanic for BMW in Brattleboro, and that led to a stint as a professional race-car mechanic in Montreal . . . But that's another story, a story of metal rather than of wood, a story of skills and machinery that are only a century old instead of a millennium. Still, it was another aspect of tooling raw materials, and it helps explain why, when he decided to buy a DIY guitar kit from Martin Guitars some time later (that "some time" encompassing other careers as ski instructor, kayak builder, arts administrator) so that he could fool around on a guitar of his own, he looked at all the little shaped wooden pieces in the box and thought, "I could have made all this myself." By the time he'd finished that kit he was already working on three other guitars he'd started from scratch. "After that," he says, summing up his career as a luthier, "it was like eating buttered popcorn: if one handful is good, two is better."

He twangs the new band-saw blade, which he has now fitted and tightened up to around F♯, I'd say.

He suggests I step outside, for he's about to make his first cut of the cherry and he has only one set of earguards. I step outside. Crows rush, shouting, over his house, which he didn't build but is full of wood all the same; it must be like living in an overturned canoe. Two pairs of cross-country skis are propped up by the door. All around, leafless birches and maples stand in the shallow, hard snow.

"You're surrounded by the raw materials," he says, explaining why he loves the north country, and as the band-saw starts up with its muffled shriek the sound penetrates barely a few yards into the raw materials before being absorbed.

The phone rings: it's Paul Asbell, a guitarist who grew up hearing and playing with the great blues guys in Chicago, who won two Indie awards with the fusion band Kilimanjaro, and is now known as one of the best steel-string fingerstyle acoustic players in the country. Rick has made guitars for Asbell as well as other well-known people—the Celtic guitarist Arty McGlynn and the Vermont singer/storyteller Rik Palieri—but also nonentities like me.

"You can't survive on professionals," he says. "They're the icing. You need a good supply of recreational guitarists."

"How do you make a living?" I ask, shaking my head. I know of guitar makers in Vermont who charge two or three times what he charges.

He grins sidelong. "Behind every successful luthier there's a spouse with benefits." His partner, Joni, is an internist; they have a tumbling golden retriever called Alta—the Running Dog of the company name—but no children.

When he has cut the boards, we hold a low-key client conference about which pair to use, and which way up they should go. The boards will be bookmatched—that is, one will be flipped over, like the opening of a book, so the two pieces are left-and-right mirror images, symmetrical on each side of the seam that will run between them up the back of the guitar. One pair of boards has tiny dark smears—resin pits. Not his fault, he says. Can't tell from the outside that they're there. Just a natural hazard of working with cherry. Both pairs have tiny pin knots that are actually rather attractive. We select the pair with lighter resin pits, which in any case may be removed by the sander. But which way up should the boards go? He holds them one way up, and the astonishing crushed-velvet ripple seems to run downhill and away from the central seam, like falling water or hair falling in ringlets. He tries them the other way up, and now the ripples radiate up and out, looking uncomfortably like fish bones. We go with the waterfall effect.

This is the mystery and fascination of guitar making: nobody knows how a guitar will turn out. Even these boards cut from the same plank will behave differently, and will sound different from one square inch to the next, and will change over time. The best luthiers have discovered, by trial and error, methods that seem to work for them, but there are no guarantees. Al Carruth of New Hampshire, widely respected as the dean of luthiers, has argued that the guitar appears to be so well evolved that any small change will make only a small improvement at best, and may actually diminish the instrument. Yet others believe it's quite possible that, one day, one small change will revolutionize the craft and make today's guitars sound, in Rick's words, like rubber bands played underwater.

The best luthiers, I'm beginning to understand, are always doing insane things that push at the edges of guitarlikeness. Linda Manzer has built a forty-two-string cubist guitar called the Pikasso that seems to head in five different directions at once. Grit Laskin has built a classical guitar shaped like a running shoe so the strings can meet the soundboard at a twenty-five-degree angle and thus gain some of the volume and resonance of the concert harp. Tom Ribbecke has built a guitar that is half flattop and half archtop. And there's Fred Carlson's sitar-harp-guitar that was inspired by a dream of a chicken learning to fly.

Every luthier worth his or her salt experiments and explores, and almost all of them, amazingly, share their discoveries to an extent that in any other business would constitute industrial espionage. It's a living art, like music itself. If it weren't, the music would feel the effect, and though it wouldn't die there would be a slight but perceptible drag on its rear end. The chicken would never get off the ground.

# Evanescence

Reading back over what I've just written—*Nobody knows how a guitar will turn out*—it strikes me that the same is true of music itself. Nobody knows how a performance will turn out: it differs every time, with the audience, the musician's mood, the humidity, the novelty, the familiarity. As soon as it's over, it's gone, vanished. The musician may get run over by a bus outside the hall or the bar. And this uncertainty, this evanescence, is especially true of a quiet, intimate instrument, a solo instrument, such as the guitar. Everything comes back to the moment, the intense and mysterious physics between the guitarist and the guitar, and the guitar and the listener.

Yet this is a truth that's rapidly being forgotten. At the beginning of the twenty-first century, music is everywhere: on the radio, on iPods and CD players, in elevators and supermarkets and chiropractors' offices, in movies, in little snatches as you turn on your computer or open Web pages, in aircraft headsets, when the receptionist puts you on hold. Yet none of that is live music. None of it has that risky evanescence.

Nineteenth-century America saw the Indian summer of live music, and guitars were a useful part of the instrumentarium of the age.

Farmers (and farmers' wives and daughters) played guitars at barn
dances and square dances. Miners took guitars to mining camps. Railroad workers brought guitars when building railroads. The painter
Thomas Eakins, with his usual nearly photographic precision, painted
a scruffy cowboy playing his guitar at his kitchen table. The showman
Ossian Dodge, according to his biographer, earned $11,000 in nine
months singing and accompanying himself on the guitar. Mark Twain
owned a guitar, an instrument that he bought secondhand in 1861 for
ten dollars and traveled with all across the country. Soldiers took guitars with them and sang around the campfire at night, and whalers
took guitars onboard whaleships. Basques bringing guitars settled in
Oregon, Nevada, and Idaho; Portuguese bringing guitars settled in
Massachusetts, Rhode Island, and California. A traveler exploring
the Minnesota River found guitars in French villages in the upper
Midwest.

The guitar even turned up at hunting camp according to Sir William Howard Russell, in *My Diary North and South*, thus shooting down
the canard that in the nineteenth century the guitar was a ladies' parlor instrument.

Gunpowder River, Saltpetre River, facing Chesapeake; on
either side lakes and tidal water; the owner, Slater, an
Irishman, reputed very rich, selfmade. Dinner at one o'clock;
any number of canvas-backed ducks, plentiful joints; drink
whiskey; company, Swan, Howard, Duval, Morris, and others,
also extraordinary specimen named Smith, believed never to
wash except in rain or by accidental sousing in the river. Went
out for afternoon shooting; birds wide and high; killed seventeen; back to supper at dusk. McDonald and a guitar came
over; had a Negro dance; and so to bed about twelve.

When it came to music, as with much else in life, nineteenth-
century Americans were used to taking whatever they could get, or
create, and making the best of it. When a San Francisco–Chicago
train was held up by snow in Percy, Wyoming, the passengers, who

included Susan B. Anthony, senators, Japanese princes, and a Russian count, held a "ball" in the back of a grocery store, with dance music "furnished by a guitar, a mouth-harmonicon, and a fine-tooth comb." By all accounts, reported the *New York Times*, "The pleasure was exquisite."

At the other end of the scale of fortune, a guitar was installed in the heart of the White House. Washington bought an English guitar for his step-granddaughter Nelly Custis, and Jefferson's wife, daughter, and granddaughter played, as did "Lemonade Lucy" Hayes and, probably, Dolley Madison, but Abigail Fillmore made it an essential part of the First Family's furniture and way of life.

"When Mr. Fillmore entered the White House," a visitor wrote, "he found it entirely destitute of books. Mrs. Fillmore was in the habit of spending her leisure moments in reading, I might almost say, in studying. She was accustomed to be surrounded with books of reference, maps, and all the other requirements of a well furnished library, and she found it difficult to content herself in a house devoid of such attractions. To meet this want, Mr. Fillmore asked of Congress, and received an appropriation, and selected a library, devoting to that purpose a large and pleasant room in the second story of the White House. Here Mrs. Fillmore surrounded herself with her little home comforts; here her daughter had her own piano, harp, and guitar, and here Mrs. Fillmore received the informal visits of the friends she loved, and, for her, the real pleasure and enjoyments of the White House were in this room."

Herman Melville, in his novel *Pierre*, not only wrote a stunning description of the sound of a guitar ("the room swarmed with unintelligible but delicious sounds. They hung pendulous like glittering icicles from the corners of the room, and fell upon Pierre with a ringing silveryness") but grasped just how intimate the connection might be between a woman and her guitar. The bewitching Isabel tells Pierre that she believes the original owner of her guitar was the mother she never knew. When she breathed *"Mother, mother, mother"* into the sound hole, the guitar's sympathetic overtones "responded with a quick spark of melody that long vibrated and subsidingly tingled in the room."

In case this fiction seems too fanciful, Sarah Morgan Dawson's memoir *A Confederate Girl's Diary* provides a clear illustration of the depth of affection one young woman has for her guitar and its richness of meaning for her. She grew up in Baton Rouge and was in her teens when the Civil War broke out. At first the guitar was something to take pride in playing well, a part of the decorous Southern mating game and, to some extent, a channel for introspection, but as she grew up and the war intruded more and more violently into her life, her guitar took on an increasingly rich importance and meaning. She played to center herself, as we'd say nowadays, as a form of meditation, especially as the war drew nearer. (Another young Southern woman, Kate Carney, at the same time wrote the amazing sentence, "[P]racticed on my guitar, & this evening practiced shooting with Sister's pistol.") When Baton Rouge was shelled, Dawson and her family were forced to flee.

"[A]fter hard work we got safely off at three, saving nothing but our clothes and silver. All else is gone. It cost me a pang to leave my guitar, and Miriam's piano, but it seems there was no help for it, so I had to submit."

When she took refuge in the nearby village of Clinton, she started to recognize all the small things that meant so much to her.

"The following is a list of a few of the articles that shopkeepers actually laugh at you if you ask for: Glasses, flour, soap, starch, coffee, candles, matches, shoes, combs, guitar-strings, bird-seed,—in short, everything that I have heretofore considered as necessary to existence."

A crucial change had taken place. The guitar had become something sadder and richer, not just for Sarah Morgan Dawson but for many young women, especially in the South where the English well-bred-young-lady-guitarist tradition seems to have been a little stronger, and the social devastation that much greater. Especially in memoirs and novels written toward the end of the nineteenth century, the guitar is drenched in loss—loss of property, loss of a settled agricultural society, loss of the clear, simple rules of courtship. The fragile evanescence of the guitar, and of music, seems to evoke especially strongly that sense of loss.

It's also possible that there was a kind of diaspora of guitars. With the breakup of leisured life in the plantation South, guitars like Dawson's must have gone somewhere—they would have been expensive and well-made instruments—and socially they had nowhere to go but down. I suspect that a good number of guitars were lost, sold, or looted, finding their way into the hands of the poor and disenfranchised.

Meanwhile, several other crucial changes were taking place in postwar American musical life. A growing influx of Italian immigrants included not only the instruments (violins, mandolins, guitars) they brought with them, but also a strong tradition of musicianship and instrument craftsmanship. By the time the twentieth century was a decade or two old, two-thirds of the East Coast makers of archtop jazz guitars, and nine-tenths of jazz guitarists, it seemed, were Italian.

The banjo managed to shed its wooden, fretless, handmade origins and was reborn around 1880 as the hip American stringed instrument, a triumph of industrialization with frets and a metal rim. Around the same time the Figaro Spanish Students embarked on an astoundingly successful tour of the country, playing guitars and folk instruments with double courses of strings that to the untrained eye looked like mandolins, and mandolin clubs sprang up everywhere. And while substantial numbers of community groups and orchestras banded together to play light classical music on banjos, mandolins, and guitars (later to become institutionalized as the BMG movement), the guitar was invariably diminished in this company. It was given the least interesting parts, was routinely attacked even in the BMG publications for creating a poor posture or being too hard to play well, and taught in ways that encouraged limited playing and bad habits. With friends like the banjo and mandolin, the guitar didn't need enemies, though faint echoes of the BMG era can be heard in some of the string band music of the southeast and in the remarkable popularity of guitar-and-mandolin duets—the most famous of which was the Monroe Brothers, the founders of bluegrass.

The guitar's greatest rival, though, was the piano. Advances in piano technology created a larger, louder, more durable instrument with strings mounted on a metal frame that would not warp. By the late nineteenth century, the piano had elbowed the guitar aside to become more than a musical instrument; it had become a symbol of the civilizing virtues of music, home, and family life, and of the woman's job (as most home pianists were women) to uphold those virtues. "Oppressive and opulent, the piano sat steadfast," wrote Craig Roell, "massive and magnificent in the parlors and drawing rooms of middle-class homes, serving as a daily reminder of a sublime way of life. . . . When Catharine Beecher and Harriet Beecher Stowe devised their floor plan for 'a Christian House' and published it in *The American Woman's Home* (1869), they were careful to provide space for the inevitable piano."

At the same time, the founding of the first American symphony orchestras, with their fanatical insistence on vast, epic performance and the orchestral repertoire of the European masters, devalued the importance of the intimate performance by the talented amateur and made the guitar seem small, limited, and old-fashioned. The adjective that turns up time and again in references to the guitar in newspapers, books, and magazines of the late nineteenth century is "old."

The revision of history was so habitual and complete that the nineteenth-century guitar is even now routinely dismissed as a "parlor instrument," meaning a small, quiet, trivial thing that if it was to make anything of itself would need to be beefed up with steel strings and amplification. This is a very American view of history, a story of triumph through technology, a series of changes all for the better leading to financial success, world dominance.

Codswallop. Parlor music—in other settings it might be kitchen music or porch music, and in my family it consisted of singing songs around the living room piano—was a wonderful tradition. Everyone was encouraged to take part, both men and women, from practiced musicians to visitors and children, and in the nineteenth-century home the quality might at times be excellent. Yet in a sense that was not the point.

"The parlor musicale was not a concert," wrote Edith Boroff. "A concert is a parenthetical one-shot event; a parlor was a continuing social institution. . . . The parlor musicale was a part of one's life, an activity that went on 200 or 300 times a year, or even, as in my grandmother's case, more like 365 times a year. A family with this interest—and there were many—played and listened to music as often as we watch television today."

The parlor embraced an extraordinary and unpredictable variety of music. It was an active, participatory tradition as opposed to the passive listening to radio or recordings. It wasn't produced for the profit of a flour company or a tire company or a life insurance company or an international multimedia conglomerate. It wasn't organized by an instrument company or publishing company trying to sell more instruments or sheet music. And it constantly created new musicians, who made music not to show off or to make fortunes but just because making music was second nature.

The nineteenth-century American parlor, though, was almost the last flourish of live, unamplified, unmediated, uncommercial music. The twentieth century was upon it, and very shortly anything as unplugged as the parlor would become unthinkable.

# Gluing and Voicing
# the Top

By the beginning of March two months have passed. What with working on other guitars due for delivery date in the next few weeks, Rick has done nothing on mine beyond cutting four rectangles of wood: the two pieces of cherry for the back and two more pieces, pretty much the same size, of red spruce for the top. When he first mentioned in passing that the top would be of red spruce I cringed, because I was afraid it would be a dark red, like cedar, which for reasons that escape me seemed unbearably dingy. I wanted something light, new, almost Japanese in its light-and-dark simplicity; even the café au lait color of the Fylde's top seemed old-fashioned and musty. I needn't have worried. Red spruce turns out to be very light, like cream with a dash of vanilla.

Rick chooses two pieces, bookmatches them to give a sense of symmetry to the grain, then glues them side by side. When the glue has dried he runs a curiously bent chisel up the join to remove the excess glue. He shows me a bottle of the classic yellow Titebond wood glue, then a white bottle of the stuff he uses: it's similar but it doesn't have yellow dye, and it dries to an almost crystalline consistency. Titebond dries slightly gummy, he says, which is not good for his sander, and not as good for sound transmission, either.

I'm astonished that a slender thread of glue, perhaps an eighth of an inch wide, is strong enough to join the two rectangles just by one edge. Rick is amused, and he waves the glued top by one corner to demonstrate its integrity. The whole guitar, it suddenly strikes me, will consist of pieces of wood, each with its own internal stresses caused by the grain, pulling in different directions even before the strings take up their tension and try to pull everything apart. The mystery at the heart of all this is glue.

One of the other guitars Rick is making is a replica of an Ashborn, a small-bodied American guitar of the mid-nineteenth century that he's making out of sycamore. He calls the one he's making an Ash(re)born.

It's a sign of how badly the small parlor guitar has been maligned that now guitars are customarily amplified, and big, boomy guitars are less essential, American makers are returning to the small body. Women and fingerstyle players in particular are falling in love with them. When Rick takes one of his small models to a guitar show along with a few larger guitars, the small one is often the first to sell.

The Ash(re)born's body is complete, but without the neck and fingerboard it's just an elegant box, yet with so much curve in the top and back it looks like a Japanese lantern.

This is the lungs of a guitar, a box of air.

A couple of days later, the glue has dried and the top is ready for the sander. Rick has cut the top too thick, for safety's sake, and now the first mystical step in the process is about to take place: "voicing" the top.

"Listen," he says. He takes the top between thumb and index finger, allowing it to swing, holds it by my ear, and taps the wood with the side of his thumb. It gives a dull *thunk*, as you'd expect.

"Um . . . what was I supposed to hear?"

"Exactly," he says.

He sets the top carefully on the broad belt of the sander, and when he switches on the machine the wood vanishes with a faint grinding noise. As it emerges on the other side I realize I've been holding my breath, half expecting the two halves of the top, joined by the single thread of glue, to fall apart. But no: he picks up the top, as light as a piece of cardboard but stiffer, and runs it through again. And again, and again. And again.

The top has to be stiff but thin. When the guitarist plucks the strings, so little energy runs through the bridge into the top that any excess weight will suffocate it. "It isn't going to be able to get the top to vibrate, pump that air, and move the sound around," Rick tells me.

On the other hand, if the top is too thin, the mysterious and complex harmonics of wood don't come into play: you have one sound but not the overtones and harmonics that make the sound fat and rich.

"I'm looking to get it down to about one hundred and thirty thousandths," he says. Thousandths of an inch, that is. After he's inlaid the rosette, he'll take it down to its final thickness of between 110 and 120 thousandths. The top will be thicker than the sides and back, because it has to withstand the tension from the strings, which pull on the bridge, which is glued to the top. Strings exert a pull of somewhere between 180 and 220 pounds, depending on the gauge of the string. I am stunned; this wafer of wood passing through and through the sander will have to withstand the equivalent of my weight.

Every few passes he takes a gauge (officially, a digital dial caliper) and measures the thickness. Closing in on his 130 thousandths, he picks up the top after every pass, flexes it in his hands, feeling the stiffness. Makers of archtops, the big jazz guitars with f-holes and carved tops and back, use a process called "candling." Not working with a flat top, they have a much harder time measuring the thickness, which in any case is supposed to vary, the thicker central "pan" of the top surrounded by thinner wood that lets the top vibrate more freely, like a loudspeaker cone. As they carve away at the top, they hold it up to a light—traditionally a candle, hence the name—and the shade of the peach-colored light filtering through the wood tells them how thin it's getting. It also gives a sense of how smoothly the wood is making the transition from thicker to thinner: archtop makers such as Tom Ribbecke and Linda Manzer think that the smooth gradient may be more important than the exact thickness.

Rick works with his hands and ears, tapping here and there and listening. "You can hear the top open up as you sand it thinner," he says. He gives a grunt of satisfaction, holds the top by my ear, and taps it for me. It's startlingly loud and resonant. *Thumm.* Then he taps around a bit and finds another spot—*thimm!*—an octave higher. "They're called nodes," he says and immediately denies knowing anything about the propagation of wood harmonics. Actually, nobody understands the acoustics of musical instruments, he says. The really smart luthiers are the ones who will admit it.

This is the theory, put simply. The fingers, or nails, or pick, strike the strings and create vibrations of certain frequencies in the strings. These vibrations have various complex effects, most of which are too insignificant to trouble us here. The set of vibrations that matters to a builder is the set that is transduced—that is, passed—through the bridge and the saddle into the top of the guitar, which responds by bouncing like a small wooden gong and creating almost all of the sound we hear. (This gong effect is mostly limited to the lower bout, by the way. The upper bout is relatively rigid, especially as there's a thick brace that runs across the upper bout above the sound hole to strengthen it against the pull of the fingerboard. That's why a cutaway has little effect on the overall sound of an acoustic guitar. "You can take a built guitar, run it through the bandsaw, make a cutaway, and most people wouldn't notice the difference," Rick says.)

The wood in the guitar top is not uniform, though, and adds sympathetic vibrations of its own, making the sound richer and fuller. What's more, as each note produces a different set of vibrations, which in turn create different responses in all the other parts of the system, it's very possible to make a guitar that sounds great over one cluster of notes (say, from B to D on the fourth string) but average or dull elsewhere. Getting a good response over the entire range of the instrument is the holy grail of guitar making.

A single note, then, produces what Rick calls "an almost meteoro-logically complicated system" of vibrations and countervibrations—not so much a gong as a carillon. There are so many variables, though (the total volume of air in the box, the depth of the guitar, the size of the sound hole, the position of the braces, the stiffness of the back and sides, and many others), that the physics goes beyond human comprehension, let alone human calculation.

The product of the guitar is invisible and weightless. It is among the most intangible of human achievements.

"Compared to the guitar," Rick sighs, "rocket science is a piece of cake."

# The Hawaiians
# Have Landed

I n August 1863, a 1,160-ton steam cruiser named the *Sea King* was launched in Scotland. Within a year, she was secretly bought by the Confederate navy, and once she was at sea she was equipped as a warship and commissioned as the CSS *Shenandoah*. Her far-reaching mission: to capture, burn, or sink Union whaling ships, driving up the price of whale oil and economically crippling the North.

The *Shenandoah*, captained by James Waddell, rounded the Cape of Good Hope and broke into the Indian Ocean, where she captured nine U.S. flag merchant vessels by the end of 1864. Pausing to provision, repair, and take on crew in Australia, Waddell sailed into the Pacific and seized four Union merchantmen in the eastern Carolines. At this point, the Civil War ended. Waddell, of course, had no way of hearing the news, as by now he was harrassing the whaling fleet in the Pacific. At some point, possibly in June 1865, the *Shenandoah* sank or drove aground a whaler whose survivors made their way ashore in Hawaii. Some of those survivors were Portuguese, and when their ship was destroyed they apparently managed to save their guitars.

Years later, the statesman Curtis P. Iaukea recalled the occasion.

Another noteworthy incident of my school days was the arrival
of a number of Portuguese to work on the Pioneer Sugar
Plantation owned by Harry Turton and James Campbell.
These laborers were said to be some of the shipwrecked crews
of the whaling fleet which ran afoul of the Confederate
cruiser *Shenandoah*, up north during the Civil War then raging
at the time. Husky fellows, they were; dark complexioned;
natives of the Azores, I've heard it said.

They brought their steel-stringed guitars with them, the
first of the kind we had seen. At night-fall when the day's
work was o'er, they would gather at one of their camps and
entertain the crowd that had gathered to enjoy the music and
see how these steeled guitars were played. Needless to say, it
took like wildfire.

Of all the steps in the history of the guitar in America, this is the
least likely, the most happenstantial. Yet the *Shenandoah* was directly
responsible for a chain of events that led to the first great guitar boom
in American history.

It's not clear when the first guitar landed on Hawaii, but if it wasn't
there already, it certainly arrived with a group of vaqueros—cowboys—
hired from New Spain in the 1830s by King Kamehameha III to bring
order to a herd of wild cattle. With them came the lariat, the poncho,
the saddle, the spur, the leather-goods industry in general, and almost
certainly some guitars. In time, the vaqueros left and their work was
taken over by Hawaiian cowboys, called *paniolos*, from the Spanish word
*español*. The *paniolos* also took over the guitar.

From what we can tell, the first thing the Hawaiians did with the
guitar was to experiment with the tuning, especially by tuning down
various strings to create an open chord—hence the term "slack key"
to refer to this style. This became such a feature of island music that
individual families had their own favorite tunings, which were often
kept secret within the family.

The second thing they did was to play harmony lines on more than
one string, echoing the rise and fall of the chanting that was such a

central feature of Hawaiian music and life in general. They were already starting to make a guitar music that was both haunting and unique.

The *Shenandoah* brought steel-string guitars, and because in the years following the Civil War more and more Portuguese were arriving to work on the sugar plantations, the supply of instruments grew rapidly. One novel instrument was the *braguinha*, also known as the *machete* or *cavaquinho*, a small four-stringed guitar, which gained the name *ukulele*, meaning "jumping flea" in Hawaiian.

Why was the steel-stringed guitar so important? Because of an eleven-year-old boy named Joseph Kekuku.

According to a story that has become legend, in 1885 Kekuku was walking along a railway line, playing his guitar. Struck by a thought, he bent down and picked up a bolt, part of the discarded industrial debris of the railroad, laid it across the strings, and slid it up and down the scale while playing, making the characteristic singing slur of the steel guitar.

Note: a steel guitar is called a "steel" guitar because it is played with a steel—not because it has steel strings; not because it is made of steel; and not because it is played with steel fingerpicks. They came later, after Hawaiians had been playing for years with their bare hands.

Kekuku went home and practiced with an assortment of slides: a penknife, a straight razor with the edge ground down, a comb, a tumbler, and then, working in the school metalwork shop, a steel cylinder about four inches long, which was easy to hold and, being smooth, made no rasping noise as it slid up and down the strings. He also, crucially, used steel strings. Anyone who has tried to play slide guitar on nylon or gut strings knows that you get little more than a dull whisper: steel strings, the legacy of the *Shenandoah*, gave volume and ringing sustain.

Kekuku practiced long and hard (he estimated that it took him seven years to master the technique) and gave demonstrations and concerts in school and out in public. Friends at school picked up the technique and, as the Kamehameha School for Boys was a boarding school, took it to their homes throughout the islands.

Playing with a steel transformed the guitar. At the most basic level, it enabled people to play on guitars whose necks had lifted so badly that it was no longer possible to push the strings down onto the fretboard—a valuable consideration in a poor nation with high humidity. More subtly, playing with a steel extended the fingerboard and allowed the guitarist to play over a long scale even on a cheap guitar. It allowed the player to harmonize, playing not just one melody line but potentially as many voices as the guitar had strings, which in turn gave the guitar a fatter and fuller voice. And by changing the tuning, the player could also produce a wide variety of increasingly complex harmonies. The steel broke the rectilinearity of the fingerboard: the player could now command an infinite number of notes or tones, rather than a finite number. The guitar lost its frets, and with them it lost an entire history of musical culture. The steel extended the guitar beyond the stylized twelve-tone keyboard of Western tradition into what might be called the broad range of supratonal sound. This in turn meant that the guitar became closer to the human voice, and could make all kinds of vocal effects. It could also create nonhuman music: Fleetwod Mac had an early hit with a slide-guitar instrumental called "Albatross." It could echo the rise and fall of waves, as the early mainland listeners heard in the Hawaiian music, and it could also harmonize in sound with the visual movements of the hula dancers. With the steel, the guitar became more supple, more expressive. It found a voice.

All the same, the steel guitar would probably never have swept the world if not for Kekuku himself. There are actually two other candidates for the inventor of the steel guitar in Hawaii, but Kekuku was clearly the right person for the discovery: he liked playing the guitar, he liked the new sound and recognized its appeal, he was prepared to practice a great deal, and he was technically minded enough to experiment with different slides and to invent an "adapter" that would act as a second nut and raise the strings so the slide wouldn't clatter against the frets. He was also prepared to perform, teach, and travel, touring not only the mainland United States but Europe as well. That's an unusual constellation of qualities. All of us probably know a guitarist who was a star in one respect but not in others, and shone briefly, or fitfully, or locally, or barely at all, and left the world pretty much as he or she found it. Kekuku shone brilliantly and everywhere.

In 1893, Americans living in Hawaii overthrew the Hawaiian monarchy. The United States officially took no position on the matter, but by the end of the century Hawaii—technically still the Sandwich Islands—became a U.S. territory. In some respects this was a disaster for Hawaiians, but it also opened a corridor to the mainland, and Hawaiian musicians took it.

Wave after wave of Hawaiian performers toured the mainland over the next thirty years. Posters and playbills of the day show Albert Vierra's Hawaiians ("Five Genuine Native Musicians"), looking elegant and earnest in white shirts, ties, cummerbunds, and thin leis; Kekuku's Hawaiian Quintet, led by the leonine and magisterial Joseph Kekuku himself ("The melodious strains of the songs and the accompaniment on native instruments, with the peculiar sliding of the fingers on the strings, is plaintive and fascinating"); Major Kealakai's Royal Hawaiian Sextette; the Ellis Royal Hawaiians ("His company comprises the best steel guitar player in America"); the Liliuokalani Hawaiians; the Hamakua Singers and Players, posed like many against a painted backcloth of exotic vegetation; the DeLano Hawaiian Steel Guitar and Ukulele Sextette of Los Angeles; the Honolulu Students ("The stage was arranged for a moonlight scene and when the two appeared in their white costumes, the man a tall romantic, swarthy chap with guitar and sash, the effect was charming"); and dozens of others, some dignified, some dashing, some all-Hawaiian, some a mixture of Hawaiian and mainlanders, some all continental imitators, some Filipino musicians, riding the same Polynesian wave.

And the instruments! Spanish-style guitars played in the standard position, though probably in altered tunings slack-key fashion. Other Spanish-style guitars laid flat across the lap. Ukuleles, held as if they aren't toys but Hawaiian mandolins, perhaps. A cello. A piano. Violins. Harp-guitars, some small enough to look at a glance like double-necked Spanish guitars, some enormous, like musical wardrobes.

So-called Weissenborn-style guitars, with their thick, hollow necks and sloped shoulders.

The Hawaiian guitar was exotic, fascinating, relatively easy to learn at a basic level, sexy. Professional mainland musicians took to the steel guitar with alacrity, and by the mid-twenties it had become a sort of musical seasoning, used to flavor almost every existing musical genre. The early ragtime jazz bands, especially on the West Coast, added steel-guitar players who abandoned the slow harmonic swoop of Hawaiian music for a faster syncopated style that often included double or triple picking of the same note in quick succession. Cajun bands, rural southeastern bands, and cowboy bands so commonly used steel guitars that they often had different identities for different gigs: on Monday, Tuesday, and Wednesday they might be the Barn Dance Troubadours; over the weekend they might change their name to the Hawaiian Troubadours. This is how the steel guitar came to be a feature of country music.

The Hawaiian groups not only introduced the concept that we now call "lead guitar"—that is, the guitar as featured instrument, with its own voice and a prominent place in both songs and instrumentals—but also the combination of lead and rhythm guitars in the same ensemble (thus employing twice as many guitarists).

The Hawaiian guitar became so popular it forced the most significant and far-reaching change in the history of the instrument, and arguably in the history of music: the invention of the electric guitar. More on that shortly.

The Hawaiian guitar boom lasted an astonishingly long time, starting to fade only in the fifties. In 1953 the Hawaiian Room in the Hotel Lexington, in New York City, the most successful and longest-lived of the Hawaiian theme rooms in hotels and restaurants in the United States, finally closed its doors for redecoration. It had opened June 23, 1937, with the music of Ray Kinney (a leading Hawaii, singer and bandleader) and three dancers, the Hula Maids, who soon were the toast of Walter Winchell's nationally syndicated newspaper column and radio show. In its first two years alone it earned over a million dollars from more than half a million guests and gave away 364,176 paper leis.

When the craze was at its height, a skilled steel player could find regular work and move in some pretty select company. Of course, select company in the thirties was not quite what it is today.

Ralph Kolsiana was born in Oahu in 1912. When he was six—this is all according to Lorene Ruymar's exhaustive research—the family moved to Philadelphia, where there was a sizable Polynesian community, as there was in Atlantic City, Cleveland, and Chicago. His father played woodwinds with none other than John Philip Sousa; he introduced his sons to the Royal Hawaiian School of Music in Philadelphia, where Ralph and his brother John were taught by Jimmy Kahanalopua and Henry Kamanuwai. At some point in the late twenties the two brothers entered a talent show, the Major Bowes Amateur Show, and won the first prize of $1,000—astonishing money on the eve of the Depression.

In the early thirties the two of them and Kamanuwai were invited to play at the Steel Pier in Atlantic City as part of a large group called Aldridge's Steel Pier Hawaiians.

> At the time the show consisted of the most popular dancers of the day, the Mansfield Sisters (Lulu, Telu and Luka), and there was also a Samoan dancer, Siva Siva style, Tutasi Salima and a Chief Satini, with knife dancers Chief Kuka Tuitama and Chief Bob Ross. Chiefs Tuitama and Ross had at one time been Jack Dempsey's sparring partners when he was in training, in his prime. . . . There was also a big water show in the back end of the Pier, featuring a Tahitian girl who jumped off the 85-foot diving board on the back of a beautiful white horse.

After a stint working with health food advocate and pioneer body builder Bernarr McFadden in what sounds suspiciously like a high-class medicine show, and then a mobile gig on the *Orange Blossom Spe-*

*cial*, the New York and Pennsylvania Railroad train that ran between New York and Miami, they were hired by Al Capone.

"[H]e had us come and play on one of his small islands that were all connected by small arch-type bridges in a group near the Miami area. You may find this as amusing as we did at the time, but he and his cohort were really hung up on Hawaiian music. We were to serenade his guests who stayed overnight in the master bedroom of his mansion. This room had alcove-like sections which were closed in by beautiful blue velvet curtains. We would serenade them while they made love after the big party downstairs was over. We did the same thing in his posh hotel suites in New York City. He called us his 'Boudoir Serenaders.'"

# Bending the Sides

Rick's steep driveway is glazed with sheer ice, but my Subaru cruises up. An article in the local paper says that of the five best-selling vehicles in Vermont, four are pickups and the other is the Subaru Legacy.

Rick has cut the back to the right shape, following a cardboard template, and has also cut the cherry sides and planed and sanded them down to seventy-five thousandths of an inch thick, each of them a long, reddish wafer of wood nearly three feet long and about five inches wide, not exactly rectangular as they have been trimmed to accommodate the taper of the back and its arch. Now he has to bend them to fit the shape of the back.

He takes the first side in one hand and a plastic bottle with a spray nozzle in the other, spritzes the wood with distilled water, and wraps it in paper towels. He clamps one end against a heated stainless steel slat that is bent to the 3-shape of one side of the Running Dog Concert Jumbo, and slowly starts to bend the wood down against the slat until they meet farther and farther along the curve. I can barely watch. It's impossible that so thin and brittle a piece of wood can be elastic enough to bend one way around the large lower bout, then in and out again, sharply, for the waist, and then around the small upper bout. And this is the most expensive, rarest wood that will go into the guitar.

Rick is clearly at home in a crisis. He keeps talking but stays very, very focussed. The cherry is unlikely to break, he says, choosing his words carefully, feeling the wood fibers as they stretch in his hands. Though it's always possible. The more highly figured the wood, the less the grain provides it with the longitudinal strength and stability it needs in order to bend. He once bought four sets of very expensive koa, the Hawaiian wood whose grain seems to dance rather than follow a straight line, and in bending the sides of what would have been a high-priced commission he exploded one after the other.

He has rounded the plump hip of the guitar and keeps spraying and bending, now pushing the cherrywood down bit by bit into the waist. All the while, the heated metal is drying the length of side that is already in place. The workshop fills with the smell of toasting wood.

When the cherry is, astoundingly, more or less bent to shape he sprays it again and clamps a second stainless steel form over it so that it is now sandwiched, moistened, heated, and under pressure between two metal 3's. By this point the danger is probably over, and the side will conform to shape over the next day or two. Then the really hair-raising job falls due: he has to take one side and, using exquisite care, bend it around a heated pipe, first sharply one way, then just as sharply the other, to form the cutaway.

The next time I see the sides, they have crossed a conceptual line. When they were still flat, albeit thin, boards, they looked like pieces of wood, once pieces of a tree. Now for the first time they embody human purpose and design. Like the rough hourglass shape of the top, they are still wood, but also more than wood. The two 3's demand to be brought together, face to face, to make an 8, just as the finished guitar will demand to be played. Imagination calls to imagination. Even the individual parts of the guitar have something of the whole, and when brought together they will have something of the power of music even when silent.

# The Starvation Box

The first, longest, and most detailed account of guitar lust was written by none other than W. C. Handy, sometimes referred to as the Father of the Blues.

Handy, who was born in 1873 in Florence, Alabama, seems to have been about fifteen when he saw a guitar in a store window and fell in love. He couldn't afford it, of course, so he set about earning the money to buy it, and in his autobiography, *Father of the Blues*, he tells us what that entailed.

He picked berries and sold fruit from the orchard. He gathered chestnuts, walnuts, and hickory nuts. He sold old iron and rags. He made lye soap by getting bones from the slaughterhouse, scouring them in rainwater filtered through hickory ash, removing the bones, letting the residue cool, and cutting it into cakes. He had less luck raising cattle, but tried plastering, shoemaking, and carpentry, and half a dozen other jobs with better luck. He worked for the white Baptists as a janitor. Out of his earnings he began saving for a guitar.

The name of my ailment was longing, and it was not cured till I finally went to the department store and counted out the money in small coins before the dismayed clerk. A moment later, the shining instrument under my arm, I went out and hurried up Court Street. My heart was a leaf. I could scarcely wait till I reached home to break the news to my father and mother. I knew how the other youngsters would gather around, bug-eyed with curiosity and admiration, and I had no doubt that I would be able to entertain the girls royally.

Ah, yes, there it is: every guitar ad ever composed, compressed into one sentence. Yet it's an odd sentence, stiff with self-congratulation and reserve. What kind of bluesman is this? Nothing about getting his mojo working or being a hoochie-coochie man, no black snakes, no lemon squeezing. What he had in mind was "serenading beneath the windows of our sweethearts and singing till we won a kiss in the shadows or perhaps a tumbler of good home-made wine," sounding for all the world like a white college boy of the late nineteenth century.

In any case, he was out of luck. When Handy finally did save enough to buy and bring home the guitar his father, a minister, gasped, "A guitar! One of the devil's playthings!" and ordered his son to exchange the sinful object for something useful—a Webster's unabridged dictionary.

At this point in the story we know a couple of important things: first, the guitar was despised by many churches, black and white, not just in 1890 but for decades. As such, it was shut out of the primary music-making experience in many black families' lives. Vocal styles, choral harmonies, rhythms, organ playing, even the fact that a horn section can approximate the polyphonic singing of a gospel choir—the black Baptist church would be a constant source of energy and phrasing for black music, but the guitar would be a perennial outsider, the instrument of wandering evangelists and jake-leg street-corner preachers on the wrong side of the tracks.

What we don't know—and it's an infuriating omission—is why Handy wanted to play the guitar so badly. We know his mother, like many Victorian mothers, was fond of the guitar, but surely nothing is less likely to make something seem cool to a teenage boy than the fact that his mother likes it. Why would the guitar make the other boys curious and envious? Why would it make the girls feel so royally entertained?

These are important questions, because nobody knows quite why the guitar became popular among blacks, especially poor blacks in the rural South, some time before the end of the nineteenth century. By studying ex-slave narratives from the 1840–1860 period, Robert Minans found that the instruments most frequently mentioned as being played by blacks were the fiddle and the banjo, followed by the quills (a set of reeds of different lengths tied together in a row) and various forms of percussion. The guitar was less than a tenth as popular, apparently, as the fiddle, though Minans found a curious clustering (six out of fifteen references) in south-central Mississippi.

Yet Handy was by no means the only African-American from the Deep South to take up the guitar before the turn of the century. Brother George Goings, a black Pentecostal preacher, played his guitar while his wife played mandolin or shook a tambourine, traveling as far as California by 1901. The oldest recorded black guitarist, Johnny "Daddy Stovepipe" Watson, singer, guitarist, was born way back in 1867 and had traveled with minstrel and medicine shows. And a *New York Times* correspondent visiting Florida reported seeing Negroes playing banjos and guitars before the Civil War.

Around the end of the nineteenth century, the guitar gained favor among blacks, especially in the area known as the Mississippi Delta. Some authorities have suggested that the banjo was too painful a reminder of "slavery time." Somehow, the guitar became an instrument of preference, at least among the poor, but Handy never thought to tell us why. Interestingly, the blues guitar would in its turn come to be rather too uncomfortable a reminder for many blacks of their impoverished rural roots: for most of the twentieth century, the music of choice for the black middle class would be jazz or soul—neither of which gave much time to the guitar.

Handy took the guitar back to the store, but secretly he bought and studied the cornet, became a natural organizer and leader, and soon he was teaching music and leading his own band. The times were changing, though, and in 1903 he began to realize that a new music was being invented. His first sight of it was on a railway station in Tutwiler, Mississippi, near Clarksdale, where he was waiting for a train that was nine hours late.

> A lean, loose-jointed Negro had commenced plunking a guitar
> beside me while I slept. His clothes were rags; his feet
> peeped out of his shoes. His face had on it some of the
> sadness of the ages. As he played, he pressed a knife on the
> strings of the guitar in a manner popularized by Hawaiian
> guitarists who used steel bars. The effect was unforgettable.

At least two features of this scene were new to Handy: he had never before seen anyone play slide guitar with a knife, and he had never heard the simple repeated-line lyric structure that we now call the blues. His line about Hawaiian guitarists, by the way, doesn't mean that he assumed this loose-jointed player had learned slide from Hawaiians; Handy was writing forty years after the event, and this observation is by way of explanation. Hawaiians had visited the mainland by 1903, but only in small numbers, and almost certainly not in rural Mississippi. The Hawaiian steel guitar and the African-American bottleneck or slide guitar, perhaps because of the growth in popularity of steel guitar strings, seem to have been parallel and almost simultaneous inventions. (This genesis isn't as far-fetched as it may seem. Everyone experiments. Fooling around with a straight-sided beer glass in a pub in 1971, I thought I'd invented slide guitar myself.)

Shortly afterward, Handy had a conversion experience. His band—he calls it an "orchestra"—was playing at a dance in Cleveland, Mississippi, when a (white) member of the audience asked if a local colored band might play a few dances. Handy, amused, condescended to agree, and out came a ragged trio carrying a battered guitar, mandolin, and bass. They began to play the kind of tune probably played by many string bands that were expected to keep a rural dance going all night; we might call it a boogie or a breakdown. To Handy's surprise, the crowd loved it, and began to throw coins—more money, Handy reckoned, than his nine-piece orchestra was being paid for the entire gig. That, he said, was when he began to see "the beauty of primitive music."

Well, yes and no. Despite composing what is generally regarded as the first published blues ("St. Louis Blues," 1914) Handy never lost his preference for the well-organized band and the well-organized life. Handy could play the guitar well enough to enter a white saloon in St. Louis when he was destitute, borrow another guitarist's instrument, and sing several songs so well that the crowd took up a collection and invited him to come back and sing there again. ("I did not accept the invitation, but I did buy a change of clothing.") To play well and be popular was not enough for him; he wanted to get out of that destitution as fast as he could.

And he did. He became a successful bandleader and music publisher, and even though he was never entirely unsympathetic to the black street guitarists he came across in his travels, he spoke of them as if they were an affront to the hardworking, education-seeking, self-improving spirit that the Reverend Handy had instilled so successfully in his son. When his band ventured into a house in an exclusive white neighborhood and found "a group of dark merrymakers, rocking with joy and singing the blues to the accompaniment of a battered guitar," Handy seemed peeved at the competition, and at their effrontery. And when he mentioned a crippled guitarist sitting on a curbstone on Beale Street, playing and singing the blues with his right leg up behind his neck, it was to make the point that the guy was a fraud: later that evening, Handy wrote, he saw him again and his *left* leg was behind his neck.

This, then, was the birth of the guitar blues. What Handy saw (and disliked) was the beginning of an astonishing evolution—actually, two entwined evolutions, like the double helix of DNA. African-American blues guitarists, starting from no more than bits of wood and wire, reinvented the guitar. In doing so they created a body of radical and original music from beginnings so rudimentary that it was often described as primitive, and in some respects not even music. The blues, as a lyric form and a loose group of musical stylings interpreted by white musicians, was almost immediately popular, but the American public wanted as little to do with the actual sources of the music as Handy did. For the next fifty years or more, African-American guitarists played in poverty and often in isolation, developing a form so exquisitely and powerfully expressive that it eventually became imitated all over the planet.

There's so much we don't know about this early blues period. We don't know why African-American blues players so often played fingerstyle, whereas relatively few white rural players did. We don't know why strong regional variations developed in guitar style, more delicate and pianolike in the Piedmont area, rougher and simpler with fewer chord changes out in Texas. We don't know where the basic characteristic guitar phrases came from. We don't know, though we can guess, how blues guitar stylings were affected by the fact that the guitarists were playing some of the most primitive and difficult instruments ever made. We don't know for sure that the guitar was the first instrument on which the blues was played, long before it was even called the blues. Finally, we don't properly understand the rich, profound effect of the tension between the blues scale and the standard Western scale on the guitar fingerboard that produces the yearning, hungering feel of the flatted third, forever unresolved, sliding upward with the steel or bent upward with the finger toward a major third it can never reach.

Blues guitarists were directly responsible for the development of R&B, for the British Invasion (apart from more obvious examples, Pink Floyd combined the names of two bluesmen, Pink Anderson and Floyd Council), and hence for the guitar's dominance at the end of the twentieth century. Yet they were insulted and ignored by both white and black Americans for two-thirds of the century. Household names such as Robert Johnson and Muddy Waters were unknown even to people in the music business as recently as 1960. Even W. C. Handy, who probably did more than anyone else to make the blues acceptable to white society, was trapped. By 1938 he had been asked to conduct his own work over both WLS and the NBC radio networks, and he had been the featured artist when CBS broadcast a Negro Achievement Hour, but when he was invited to a dramatization of his life and work in which he was crowned "King of the Blues," he had to drive there because the Carolina Air Line refused to carry black passengers, or, as the Memphis cabdrivers put it, "haul coal." If that was the way the Father of the Blues was treated, what chance was there for a chocolate boy or a dark merrymaker, walking the streets with his battered guitar?

This was the biggest difference between Hawaiian music and blues: Kekuku traveled widely, entertained royalty, became a respected teacher. Is it surprising, then, that Hawaiian music and its instruments were assimilated with amazing speed? Compare him with Eddie "Son" House, a great teacher of the blues. When the folklorist Alan Lomax tracked House down in 1941 he was living in a shack behind the home of a farmer who promptly called the local sheriff. The lawman arrested Lomax on suspicion of being an enemy spy, sent to stir up unrest among "our niggers." Is it surprising, then, that the blues and its playing techniques remained unassimilated and largely unchanged for decades, and as such becoming steadily richer and more complex?

Most blues guitarists were so poor the guitar was often described as "the starvation box." Their guitars were on a par with their income; Handy's "shining instrument" was the exception rather than the rule. A remarkable number of one-day famous guitarists, both white and black, made their own: Blind Willie Johnson, Lightnin' Hopkins, Charlie Christian, Carl Perkins, Jimi Hendrix, George Benson, Roy Clark, Albert King, Hound Dog Taylor, Robert Pete Williams, Buddy Guy, Albert Collins, Pee Wee Crayton, King Bennie Nawahi, Big Bill Broonzy, Eddie Lang, Josh White, Fenton Robinson, Sleepy John Estes, and Scrapper Blackwell, among countless others.

This information has been enthusiastically gathered by Shane Speal, founder and president of the Cigar Box Guitar Hall of Fame. Speal holds an annual Cigar Box Guitar Festival in Carrollton, Kentucky, in honor of this tradition, and on his Web site he lists a number of autobiographical quotes, like vintage guitars arriving with papers of authenticity.

"So I went ahead and made me a guitar," Lightnin' Hopkins told *Guitar Player*. "I got me a cigar box, I cut me a round hole in the middle of it, take me a little piece of plank, nailed it onto that cigar box, and I got me some screen wire and I made me a bridge back there and raised it up high enough that it would sound inside that little box, and got me a tune out of it. I kept my tune and I played from then on."

The Pittsburgh *Post Gazette* wrote, according to Speal, "Eight year old James Marshall Hendrix wanted so much to play the guitar to set his poems to music that he used a broom to strum out the rhythms in his head until he crafted a cigar box into his own guitar." Jimi's cigar box guitar had rubber bands wrapped around the box, serving as strings.

Blind Willie Johnson's father made him a one-string cigar box guitar at the age of five, which he played with a slide. When Carl Perkins was seven his father made him a guitar from a cigar box, broomstick, and two pieces of baling wire. Roy Clark first played an instrument his father made from a cigar box and ukulele neck with four strings. Albert King made and played several one-string cigar box guitars, and like many rural kids, especially African-Americans, he also made a diddley bow, an elemental, one-string guitar made by stringing a wire to the side of the house and playing it slide-style with a bottle. Robert Pete Williams taught himself how to play guitar by first building one out of a cigar box and five copper strings. Furry Lewis, Muddy Waters, and Buddy Guy made their own first guitars. Albert Collins started out on a down-home cigar box guitar and then graduated, according to legend, to a guitar made by a local carpenter with rattlesnake rattles inside to improve the sound. Before he was old enough to attend school, Eddie Lang played a cigar box guitar, though it was probably a top-of-the-line cigar box guitar as it was made by his father, an instrument maker.

My favorite attribution concerns Josh White. A Dr. Tony Hymas, according to Speal, said, "I promoted a folk concert at Colorado State back in 1961 which featured Josh White and one of the first appearances of Josh White Jr. He and his son attended a small private party in my basement. After the concert, I remember him telling me that he too played a cigar box instrument as a kid." Dr. Hymas, Speal reveals, is the curator of the National Cigar Museum.

\*   \*   \*

Even among blacks, then, the bluesman was a marginal figure, and among whites he was one of the lowest of the low. In William Faulkner's novella *Old Man,* based on events during the 1927 flood, "a small man with a gaunt unshaven wan face still wearing an expression of incredible outrage" says that while he was stranded on the roof of his cotton house he saw a rescue boat go by "and they never had no room for me. Full of bastard niggers and one of them setting there playing a guitar but there wasn't no room for me. 'A guitar!' he cried; now he began to scream, trembling, slavering, his face twitching and jerking. 'Room for a bastard nigger guitar but not for me—.'"

To him the guitar is the final insult, the last word in worthlessness.

Faulkner, though, sees the musician very differently. In the story, a group of convicts standing on the levee watch the same rescue boat tow a cluster of skiffs, crowded with rescued people, both black and white, toward them across the flooded cotton fields. When the engine is shut off, the watchers on the bank hear "the faint plinking of a guitar." As the other refugees clamber up onto the levee, a young black man, carrying no bundle, no rescued belongings, mounts the slope, still playing his guitar, which is slung around his neck with a piece of cotton plow line. "The taller convict," Faulkner writes, "was so busy watching this that he did not hear the guard until the guard stood directly beside him shouting his name."

The guitarist clearly has, and is intended to have, an extraordinary presence, a self-sufficient, invulnerable, and unafraid quality that sets him apart from, and even above, everyone else, above the white prison guards, above the natural disaster.

The blues guitar, then, follows in a tradition in which the guitar has often been an outsider's instrument, a companion to the friendless—especially in the first two-thirds of the twentieth century, before it became the instrument of cool. The outsiderness, though, could be abstract or very concrete.

I'm by no means the first to point out how many guitarists have been blind: not only the famous, such as Blind Lemon Jefferson, Blind Boy

Fuller, Sleepy John Estes, Riley Puckett, Doc Watson, Willie McTell, Sonny Terry, Willie Johnson, the Reverend Gary Davis, and Arthur Blake, but countless unknown street players and evangelists with guitars. Charlie Christian's father was a trumpeter, but when he was blinded he took to the streets with a guitar to support his family.

Yet blindness is only one means of separation. When New York's first public school for deaf-mutes opened in September 1908, the *New York Times* reported that "Almost the first equipment for the school will be guitars and a piano."

"To be sure," the director admitted, "the children cannot hear the sound . . . but they are to be trained, first to feel the vibration and then to see it."

Throughout the twentieth century, well-known guitarists started out as children who couldn't run out to play because, like Hank Williams, they were sickly or had other reasons to cleave to an instrument. The English guitarists of the blues revival were all loners, asthmatics, the last to be picked for playground football. Pete Townshend was called "a nose on a stick." Townshend himself said, "It's the reason I played guitar—because of my nose."

Nanci Griffith wrote in *Other Voices: A Personal History of Folk Music*, "I just couldn't learn piano because of my dyslexia. . . . I needed to be doing something where I couldn't watch my hands, where I could just let the hands do, artistically, what they need[ed] to be doing. So guitar was natural." Learning songs was so hard for her that "it became easier to write something of my own and go in and play it for my dad or brother or sister."

Johnny A had scoliosis as a child, and when he was in high school he had to wear first a cast, then a back brace. He learned to play guitar with his head upright and looking straight ahead, barely able to see the fingerboard, which "forced me to develop a feel for the fingerboard that I never would have otherwise achieved." Tony Melendez, born without arms because of birth defects caused by thalidomide, which his mother was prescribed during pregnancy, taught himself to play with his toes on a guitar tuned to open G. He subsequently performed for the pope and has composed and recorded several CDs.

If the guitar was the instrument of the poor, the disadvantaged, and the disenfranchised, Jimi Hendrix was the ultimate guitarist. He was so poor that when he showed an interest in the guitar, the only instrument his father could give him was a broken ukulele he'd found in someone else's basement. He was so poor he was denied even the community of the black Baptist church, which sent him home because his clothes were so ragged, and he was too humiliated to return. He was part white and part black and part Cherokee. One of his formative musical and stylistic influences was Little Richard, who was gay. Hendrix was left-handed, a major disadvantage to a guitarist. He was shy, he stammered, he suffered from asthma and acne. When he joined the 101st Airborne and began sleeping with his guitar, his fellow grunts stole the guitar and hid it until he knelt and begged to have it back. Then he hurt his back on a jump, was honorably discharged, and found himself in nearby Nashville trying to find work as a biracial journeyman guitarist in 1962.

When Hendrix did find work he was still constantly bullied: Harry Womack threw his guitar out of the tour bus window when Hendrix was asleep. Bobby Womack, Harry's brother, recalled, "[H]e took Jimi's git-tar to the bus window, and he threw it out. I heard it hit the ground and Jimi was laying there asleep. Boy, he got up to play his git-tar—because he play it all night long, all day long, every day, that's all he did—and he looked for it and boy, he cried, he got upset, he didn't know *what* happen. At first I thought it was kinda funny, too, but then I thought, *man*, I'm a guitar player too." Bobby Womack ended up lending Hendrix money to buy a new guitar.

With so much against him, and with only his guitar by his side, is it any surprise that Hendrix became the best guitarist of his kind?

# Vertebrae n' Roses

This is where things stand. The top and back have been cut, glued, planed a little, and trimmed roughly to the shape of a Running Dog Concert Jumbo cardboard template, allowing a little extra to be sliced off later, once the box has been assembled.

The sides have been bent and, since I was last here, Rick has joined them by gluing them together using two chunks of mahogany called the head and tail block, the bookends of the guitar box.

The tail block has to be sturdy because some people like screwing tail pins into it and hanging the guitar on the wall, or adding a strap to the tail pin and wailing on the guitar in concert. It also helps give the butt end of the guitar, so to speak, strength and definition of shape.

The head block is more important. It provides the mounting point for the neck, and what with the neck joint pulling on it in one direction and the fingerboard in another and the rest of the body in yet other directions, it must be stable and perfectly aligned with the center line of the guitar. If you tip the guitar head down slightly and peer in through the sound hole you can see the head block. Unless you have the kind of light-and-mirror-on-a-stick apparatus that dentists use, you'll never see the tail block—though that doesn't prevent some luthiers, Rick adds caustically, from doing all kinds of cute carving and inlay work on it.

Maybe it's because I have a dicey back that I find these blocks reassuring, these thick, chunky vertebrae.

Now I need to make two more design decisions: the wood for the binding and the design of the rosette.

The binding is the strip of wood, roughly ⅛ by ¼ inches thick, that covers the joins between the sides and the top, and the sides and the back. Rick also runs a strip of binding up the seam between the two halves of the back and the two halves of the neck, though other guitar makers vary in this practice. Some bindings are quite ornate, with a repeating pattern like herringbone or harlequin, or a braided rope effect. Some have a primary strip with one or more narrow strips next to it to give an ultra-finished cabinetmaker's look, like a Louis XVI armoire. Still thinking in my minimalist Japanese way, I pick ebony.

The rosette is a relic of the baroque guitar, which had a curious ornate parchment cap called the "rose" inserted in the sound hole. Inherited from the ud or oud, a medieval predecessor of the lute family, it acted as a baffle to help the small, bright-sounding instrument produce a mellower tone. Around the sound hole, luthiers added a series of concentric rings of decoration, perhaps to make the rose look more intentional and part of the overall design and less like an extremely elaborate plug for the drain in a baroque bath. This decoration around the sound hole was known as the "rosette," or lesser rose, and it survived the extinction of the rose to become the only more or less obligatory feature of the guitar that is purely decorative. Or so I suggest to Rick, who raises an eyebrow and replies, "I wonder. I think the concentric rings actually provide support and, most importantly, crack resistance to this area. I wouldn't make a guitar without some sort of rosette."

When I try to imagine what rosette design I want, I draw an utter blank. Can't visualize anything at all. This puzzles me until I look at the Fylde, which turns out to have a nothing rosette, three concentric rings that are, when I examine them closely, actually just a decal. So I go online and look at the guitar-porn Web pages of the country's best luthiers, salivary glands at the ready.

Sadly, the field of rosette design seems to be underdeveloped. Even the best luthiers simply work variations on a necklace of abalone, and perhaps another smaller or larger ring or two of abalone or colorful wood. Abalone has some kind of old-lady stigma for me; it seems both old-fashioned and somehow fake. I quite like a Celtic-knot design of Rick's that writhes around the sound hole, but it won't work with the rest of this guitar. I quite like the classical guitar rosette styles, which are restrained Spanish mosaics, some of them looking like woven rope in shades of orange and brown, but those won't work either. I'm much more interested in the color and grain—the life, really—of wood. A simple ring of ebony might work, but a luthier named, appropriately, Woodley White has done wonderful things with spalted maple, a fungal invasion that makes the maple look veined, like marble. I mention this to Rick and to my delight he says he'll look for some spalted maple by walking the shoreline of Lake Champlain and hacking off a bit of driftwood. Another Vermont element.

We're done for the day. As Rick pulls on his boots and we step out of the shop, a brisk wind picks up, blowing through the hills of raw materials.

# Guitars and Guns

Reading that Muddy Waters, among many other guitarists of his time, carried a gun, it strikes me that guitars and guns have long had a strange and intimate relationship. It's almost as if guns and guitars are brothers who grew up together, but at some point went down different roads. Both have been designed and retooled over time to feel perfectly at home in the human hand. Both can be highly ornamented and personalized, and may become objects for display when not in use. They may even be made by the same craftsman. The well-known luthier Dave Nichols did his first inlay work on a rifle for his father, who was a gunsmith. Guitars are often slung over a shoulder like guns, or pointed like guns. Leo Kottke used to be nicknamed "Machine Gun Kottke." Gene Autry starred in *Guns and Guitars*. One version of the story of how Elvis got his first guitar holds that he wanted a rifle, but his mother bought him a guitar instead.

Reporters at the beginning of the twentieth century loved yoking guitars and crime as if anyone who played the guitar might be capable of dangerous passions. In a sensational courtroom scene, Prince Felix Yousoupoff testified that yes, he had indeed murdered Rasputin. Cyanide had been sprinkled over cakes and into wine glasses, and while waiting for the poison to take effect Prince Felix had played a guitar and sung to Rasputin for half an hour. When the leader of the notorious Black Hand Society of Northern Westchester, Antonio La Rosa, was arrested in 1909 the paper reported that his alibi consisted of the testimony of his sweetheart, Lucia Sammarco, who swore that at the time of the robbery she was playing her guitar and singing to him. And Clyde Barrow, of Bonnie and Clyde fame, began his career in murder, it was reported, in April 1932 when he and an accomplice awoke a shopkeeper named John Bucher, saying he wanted to buy guitar strings. When Bucher turned his back, Barrow shot him and made off with $40. The concept of the all-night guitar store must have been set back by decades.

# Desperadoes

M any jazz writers shut the guitar out of early jazz by means of a cunning circular argument: the guitar was not used in early jazz, they say, pointing to early recordings by Louis Armstrong and other notables, and if the guitar was used, then what was played was not jazz. No, they say, the authentic rhythm instrument of the early jazz bands was the banjo. The guitar was too quiet; behind all that brass, it would never be heard.

Yet the wonderful book *New Orleans Jazz: A Family Album* shows that as jazz was emerging in New Orleans, the guitar was everywhere, in black hands and white.

It is present in a damaged photo of the Jimmy Palao Band, circa 1900, the band looking very dapper in derbies and trilbies, sitting on chairs in someone's backyard with two unnamed children in their Sunday best. Rene Baptiste, brother-in-law of Big Eye Louis Nelson, holds what may be a C6 chord and stares very levelly at the camera; the whole band has the air of desperadoes dressed for a photo after robbing a bank.

The guitar is also in the hands of Brock Mumford, reportedly one of the great jazz rhythm men of all time. It's there in the Woodland

Band (1905), also known as Kid Ory's Woodlanders, who perch on chairs apparently by the side of a road backing onto swampland, the guitarist being one Stonewall Matthews holding what seems to be a twelve-string, his hat on his left knee. (The hats are a running joke: one player has his hat on his foot; the bass player has his hung on the head of his bass as if it were a hat stand.)

The guitar shows up in 1906 in Stalebread Lacoume's Razzy Dazzy Spasm Band. The guitarist's name is unknown but was probably something fairly odd: members of this gang had such bizarre nicknames as "Warm Gravy," "Chinee," "Family Haircut," and "Cajun." With names like these, how could they have played music that failed to swing? (The term "spasm band," by the way, meant something like what we now call jazz. Jazz, a name that hadn't yet been invented, was a fashionable northern designation for New Orleans instrumental ragtime. "Jazz" was also slang for "sex," as was "spasm," as was "rock and roll.")

The faces are as memorable as the names. Look at Bud Scott, looking like a well-fed bank manager, who played with Buddy Bolden, John Robicheaux, and other famous jazzmen. Or the dashingly handsome Johnny St. Cyr, his face engraved rather than formed, who played on the Armstrong Hot Five and Hot Seven discs, and with both King Oliver and Jelly Roll Morton's Red Hot Peppers. Or Ed "Snoozer" Quinn, barely heard on record but considered by some prominent New Orleans jazzmen to have been the greatest guitarist of his time.

What stories have been overlooked here! What about Frank Amacker and Narcisse "Buddy" Christian, who played both piano and guitar in the brothels of Storyville, where Frank Delandry also played "virtuoso" guitar when no piano was available? Or Bob Aquilera, a guitarist who also marched with his trombone in Fischer's Brass Band in 1907–1910 even though he had a wooden leg? Or Danny Barker, guitarist/banjo player and author of a "widely quoted, as yet unfinished autobiography"? Did the Fewclothes Cabaret in Storyville, where Joe Brooks played banjo and guitar in 1905, really feature few clothes and, if so, did the dress code include the guitarist? And what was the show that the great Lonnie Johnson went to London with in 1917 as "intermission entertainer," rising out of the Storyville brothels to fame, only to come back to New Orleans and find that almost all his family had died in the Spanish flu epidemic?

Is Frank Ferrer, who played with the Invincibles and the New Orleans Owls between 1919 and 1923, the only guitarist ever to have quit and become a successful banker? Is Rene Gelpi, who curiously enough played with the same bands, the only guitarist ever to have quit and become a prominent architect? And is their success story more or less remarkable than that of Charlie "Sweet Lovin'" Galloway, born in New Orleans during the Civil War, who was partially paralyzed by polio, played on the streets in the mid-1880s for tips, but rose to lead his own ragtime band in the nineties? Or Clarence Gabriel, who spent the Depression working in nickel-a-dance places but still managed to live until 1973?

Looking at these photographs, especially those ragamuffin ensembles of ill-assorted instruments, it's clear that it didn't matter that the guitar was small and quiet. If you were a bandleader your band played whatever instrumentation suited the gig; and if you were short of cash, as many were, your band played whatever instruments they could lay their hands on.

# INTERLUDE:
# DARK RECTANGLES

Exploring this guitaropia has changed me from someone who plays the guitar occasionally to someone who plays the guitar. Last thing at night I get out the Fylde, poor cracked thing that it is, and play for Barbara as she grades papers or works at her sewing machine.

I went as far as doing something I've never done before: I ordered a book of Django tabs, that is, music written not in classical notation but in tablature, a means of notation designed to tell us mentally impaired guitarists which finger to put on which string at which fret. Like most guitarists, I hate being taught, hate being told that some other way is better. I bought this just for the chords, I tell myself, those wonderful, emotionally complex jazz chords with the complicated names involving not only letters and numbers but stage directions: augment this, suspend that. Flatten that fifth.

One of the most endearing qualities about guitarists is their humility in the face of their instrument. George Harrison: "I'm so dumb, really." Wes Montgomery: "I don't know that many chords." Pete Townshend: "My musical vocabulary is unbelievably limited. It astonishes me." Mark Knopfler: "I'm not even what I'd call a proper musician on the guitar. I feel as though I'm a student who's not going to school." Jeff Beck, when asked what he knows about the technical side of music: "Nothing."

I often feel intimidated just by looking at the fingerboard. A fingerboard is a curiously disturbing thing, and not especially inviting, a combination of inscrutable rectangular geometry, strings one way, frets perpendicular. What about those inlays on the third, fifth, seventh, ninth, twelfth, fifteenth, and eighteenth frets, refusing to conform to any regular sequence, more perplexing than a Fibonacci series? *This is perfectly easy,* the fingerboard says, *but you will never understand it.* And of course classical guitarists raise the stakes by refusing to have fret markers at all. Classical guitar is an instrument played by socially phobic overachievers under a brutal regime of constant discipline until the results begin to approach what a guitar is truly capable of. By then, all but the best are broken men and women.

Ever since buying this Django tab book, I've been finding chords higher up the neck, in that blank, unmapped territory of increasingly small dark rectangles—what one guitarist memorably called "the dusty end of the neck." My hand is starting to curl automatically into some of these jazz chords, and I imagine one of those big-band rhythm guitarists of the thirties, after so many nights of shifting *chunk-chunk-chunk,* falling asleep in the station wagon between gigs, his left hand lying across his lap reflexively twitching E flat major seventh / C minor seventh / F minor seventh / E ninth . . .

Playing guitar is as much about the hand as it is about the guitar, perhaps more. Which is one reason why it's a conservative art: the hand wants to conform to the shapes it knows. Advanced classical and jazz guitar ask the hand to make shapes it only ever makes during electrocution or in the last contortions of strychnine poisoning, which is why those guys develop spidery fingers—long, thin, oddly spread apart. The rest of us stick with shapes we know, shapes that feel right.

These are what make the blank stare of the fingerboard bearable. Yet even so the guitar can face anyone down. The great jazz player Jim Hall said that some days you pick up the guitar and it just seems to say, "No, you can't play today."

# Radio Castles
# in the Air

Radio took everyone by surprise, but nobody was as surprised as the guitarist Walter Howard.

"Glancing over the radio program in a local newspaper yesterday evening," reported the *New York Times* of May 24, 1924, which was already carrying a whole page of highly specific radio listings every day, "Mrs. Anna Howard of 1,994 Second Avenue saw that Dettborn and Howard, once of the Naval Hawaiian band, were to broadcast a number from station WJY at Aeolian Hall at 9:30 P.M."

The name Howard sounded familiar. "Armed with a warrant obtained several months ago on the ground of desertion Mrs. Howard went to Aeolian Hall to ascertain if the Howard in the team was her husband, Walter Howard, who had left her and two infant children about two years ago. Her suspicions were confirmed.

"Mrs. Howard called Patrolman Koch of Traffic A from his post at Forty-third Street and Sixth Avenue and returned to the broadcasting room. They waited until Dettborn and Howard finished playing their guitars. Then Howard was taken to the West Forty-seventh Street police station."

This is an important story because it shows that radio created a new instrument—a kind of early electric guitar, a guitar that could be heard an infinite distance away. The transformations effected by radio may seem obvious to us now, but they clearly didn't at the time. Even Howard can't have grasped the radical changes caused by the new medium, or he wouldn't have taken the gig. As it was, he was left begging the desk lieutenant to let him explain.

"Nix on the static," the lieutenant retorted wittily, and then, realizing he had the opportunity to extend his amusing metaphor, went on, "You can broadcast that number tomorrow morning in the Domestic Relations Court."

Radio took over America, and the American imagination, with astonishing speed. The technology existed considerably before the outbreak of World War I, but during hostilities radio was officially shut down for military reasons. The first regularly broadcasting commercial radio station in the United States took to the air in 1920. By 1921 thirty-one stations were licensed. By 1922 the number leaped to 576, which were picked up by something between half a million and a million sets.

It was more than a new technology; it was a new science, a new hope, a new sophistication, a new and vastly broader horizon. In the advertisements of the day, the excitement of radio crackles as it rushes afield to bring back the exotic, to operate at the borders of the imagination. A 1924 ad for United Electric Stores describes "Radio Castles in the Air." A thousand windows, it says, open on the radio universe. "Open one window—you catch the twanging of a guitar in Cuba! Open another—in drifts lively band music from Chicago!"

Some of the early stations were almost vanishingly local. Les Paul told the story of a fifty-watt amateur station in Iron Mountain, Michigan. "The engineer tells me to peek out the door and look to the left, toward the barber shop. The barber used to sweep the hair off the floor and put it in a pile in front of his shop. If he lit it on fire and the smoke went up, that meant we were coming in great."

Others, in the heady days before international airwave regulations, were extremely powerful stations just across the border in Mexico, such as XERF, which came to offer the spectacularly weird combination of performances by the Carter Family and ads for goat gland surgical implants that were supposed to have the effects now claimed by Viagra.

Still others extended their range by joining one of the two networks—NBC, formed in 1926, or CBS, created in 1927. Late in the previous century Walt Whitman had written, "This is not a nation, but a nation of nations." With the advent of radio Whitman's "nation of nations" began coalescing: over the next two decades, American popular culture was born, and in a sense America itself was born. By the end of the 1920s more houses had radios than record players, and record-player manufacturers were forced to add wall-powered radios to their sets.

By no means was all the programming musical. Even though listeners in the New York area could pick up only three or four stations in April 1922, they had their choice of agricultural reports, shipping news, string quartet recitals, lectures, performances by child entertainers, opera, bird and animal imitations, charitable appeals, books read aloud, glee club concerts, piano recitals, church services, bedtime stories, an inspiring lecture by a dean of engineering entitled "Engineering and Happiness," and a talk by Dr. Reuben Gross, M.D., called "Some Facts about Your Feet."

There were several crucial differences between radio in the mid-twenties and radio today, and perhaps the most important was that radio then was live. In 1922, the American Society of Composers and Publishers (ASCAP) and the Music Publishers' Protective Association (MPPA) made it illegal to broadcast records. This may sound odd, but in those days the very idea of broadcasting music from disc seemed not only cheap but trivial, and above all commercial suicide. Why would the radio want to promote sales of its rival, the record business? Conversely, why would the record industry want to help out the popularity of radio by allowing discs to be used for broadcast, giving the radio stations free programming?

Radio was not just a new medium; it was a new industry. Musicians could now hope for two sources of income instead of one, and the most popular artists, such as Bing Crosby, would have a live show but then also make recordings that would be stamped NOT LICENSED FOR AIR PLAY. As competition between radio and the record industry heated up during and after the war, some bands (such as Bob Wills and His Texas Playboys) would get around the ban by laying down huge numbers of tracks in mammoth sessions specifically for radio play. Some of these recordings would be pressed and sold to radio stations—but as the stations were still priding themselves on their live broadcasts, the announcer would often mislead the listener by calling out "Hi, Bob!" and then playing the disc to give the impression that the musicians were in the studio.

Radio gave jobs to hundreds, perhaps thousands of musicians. The high-profile names were the orchestras—at first classical orchestras, then the big jazz bands, which soon began to call themselves orchestras as well. They broadcast from the major cities, they were announced with fanfare and aplomb, and they became synonymous with sophistication.

Precisely because radio was live, this created opportunities for smaller ensembles and lesser musicians. Almost at once there were more radio stations than orchestras, and the guitar began sneaking in at the first opportunity.

The guitar was lucky: the first broadcasts of radio coincided with the height of the Hawaiian guitar boom, so if the station broadcast any popular music at all, there would be a spot for a guitarist, or even two. The *New York Times* began carrying daily radio listings on March 30, 1922; the first identified guitar performance was about two weeks later. When the first radio barn dance show was broadcast on January 4, 1923, on WBAP in Fort Worth, the featured group was Fred Wagner's Hilo Five Hawaiian Orchestra. The first radio station in Washington, D.C., to broadcast regularly was WRC, in August 1923. Three months later, Ernest Deale and William "Babe" DeWaters began a regular Hawaiian duet gig as the Honolulans. Also in 1923, WJR in Detroit participated in the first transatlantic radio broadcasts; one of the broadcast numbers was a Hawaiian song. In the new theater of the imagination, as radio billed itself, Hawaiian music, like flamenco, came with its own live music video. Both forms were and to some extent still are intimately associated with dance. They made the guitar playing, already exotic and full of zest, into something undeniably sexy.

The radio barn dance variety show, so early a feature of radio, would turn out to be a staple for more than three decades, whether under the names barn dance or hay ride, frolic, hoedown, shindig, opry, hayloft, roundup, jamboree, or jubilee. Because farm folk rose early and came home for lunch, barn dance shows often aired early in the morning, at noon, or at night, and were sponsored by products used in the working-class home: flour, syrup, work clothes, laxatives. The biggest were out of WLS in Chicago and WSM in Nashville, but other major barn dances were broadcast from Shreveport, Knoxville, Atlanta, Dallas, Fort Worth, Los Angeles, and Bristol, Virginia. Some of these shows were broadcast locally, some nationally, and virtually every major rural musician of the twentieth century—even Elvis—played on the barn dance shows, one of which, at WSM in Nashville, would change its name to the Grand Ole Opry.

Yet even outside these flagship shows, the difficulties of scheduling all-live radio meant that there was a great deal of "fill-in" time to be dealt with. Nick Lucas, the first singer-guitarist to be known to America at large, benefited from these nooks and crannies. He remembered, "Between sets with our band I used to go into the WEBH studio adjacent to our bandstand and fill in some time with my guitar and sing—kind of croon. That's when I started to get mail from all over the country. Now this wasn't a network broadcast by any means; it was just that people had crystal sets and would get me all through the night. I started to become very, very popular. . . . I wasn't getting any money from it; it was all gratis. [But] that was my first stepping stone to my success as a single performer." The Brunswick record company heard him and recorded him, the record was a hit, and it led to a gig at the Palace Theater of New York and a tour of England during which he played for the Prince of Wales.

This point is worth making very clearly: radio (and records, and television, and later the Internet) utterly changed the character of music, and of instruments. Loud and soft were no longer the native characteristics of instruments; instead, they were recording levels, or volume levels on the radio set. Over the radio, a guitar could be as loud as a sax. The media revolution of the twentieth century, then, preferentially favored the guitar. To put it another way: if some massive solar flare permanently fried every electrical circuit on the planet, no instrument (except perhaps keyboards) would be more disastrously affected than the guitar, none would fall so far from grace.

Radio was also intrinsically predisposed to help the guitar because it created a kind of universal intimacy. In fact, it promoted the value of intimacy. The brasses of the marching bands were now something of a liability. They had to be set up so far from the microphone, and they created such acoustic competition among themselves, that they were hard to broadcast. A guitar or two in a tiny studio was ideal for radio. To the listener, it was like hearing a private performance in one's living room. The guitar's greatest strength, its intimacy, was finally able to come to terms with the vastness of America.

The first person who seems to have understood this was Jimmie Rodgers. According to his biographer Nolan Porterfield, "Radio figured prominently in his career almost from the beginning." Rodgers invented whistle-stop radio, billing himself as a "National Radio Artist" and using it as a springboard to the lucrative vaudeville theaters.

"Touring the Loew circuit in 1928," Porterfield writes, "he'd wangle a broadcast or two in almost every city along the way, plugging his stage appearances and garnering special attention in the papers. . . ." In early 1929, Rodgers had continued the practice in smaller towns where there were stations, showing up at all sorts of primitive studios and offering impromptu—and usually unpaid—performances on the air. . . .

Once he had succeeded in getting himself booked onto the Loew theater circuit in 1928, he then reversed his tactics and used his vaudeville tour as a means of wrangling a broadcast or two in almost every city where he was booked in to play the theater. Radio, he realized, was a means of broadcasting himself—not just his music and plugs for his shows, but his image, his very presence. He turned up with his guitar, often unannounced, at even the small stations that had primitive facilities, and sang a song or two, told a joke, gave a few yodels. "In Fort Worth," Porterfield writes, "he sang 'In the Jailhouse Now' and got stacks of fan mail; his initial broadcast in Houston netted seventy-five phone calls and ten telegrams while he was on the air."

A new kind of public appearance was being invented, and all it took was a guy and a guitar. Rodgers wasn't just using radio; he was creating it. His affable, conversational intimacy was years ahead of its time, as was his music. Unlike the Carter Family, say, who were still singing old-time music on radio until the eve of the Second World War, Rodgers introduced the listening public to (his version of) the blues, with its double entendre lyrics and what would now be called adult content. He introduced Hawaiian, jazz, and pop combos as backup musicians. As Porterfield notes, he was creating a medium that wouldn't become widely familiar until the forties or even the fifties. He was inventing country radio, and the guitar was at its heart.

The musicians were also advertising themselves, of course. Radio provided a curiously overlapping set of working relationships, intended to support the band on the air, the band's live gigs, the station, and the station's sponsors. It was common for a band to do its daily broadcast at noon, say—perhaps half an hour of playing requests, promoting its own upcoming dances and plugging the station's advertisers—then jump into a band bus or station wagon and drive as much as two hundred miles to play that night's dance.

Yet they couldn't travel beyond the reach of the station for fear of leaving their fan base behind. A critical factor, then, was how far their station could broadcast. "Minor-league outfits like KTUL in Tulsa might have 250-watt transmitters that only reached a score or so miles," writes Duncan McLean in *Lone Star Swing,* "but its Goliath rival KVOO was a hundred times more powerful: when Bob Wills first played there, a free eight by ten photo was offered to the furthest flung listener; a man from Oakland, California, 1,800 miles west, claimed the prize."

In some cases, this radial touring was not optional. When Patsy Montana was playing regularly on WLS, the station set up a contract with International Harvester, which made tractors, to put on shows to promote the regional IH dealerships. Her contract obliged her to play these shows, which in January 1947 involved playing every weekday for a different dealership. One day the show might be in a high school, the next in a gym, a garage, an armory, a city hall, or somewhere called Kepler's Air Flow. On Saturday she had to be back in Chicago for the Barn Dance broadcast, and had to wash, iron, mend, and repack clothes for the next week's shows. The big radio orchestras, classical and jazz, were different: they owned their places on the air. The guitar, like all folk instruments, had to earn its place.

Over time radio created, if not a national colorblindness then at least a kind of color translucency. Increasingly after World War II, blues musicians were to be heard on small, independent radio stations. The most famous launching program was King Biscuit Time on KFFA in Helena, Arkansas, which premiered in November 1941 with Robert "Junior" Lockwood (Robert Johnson's stepson) on guitar and the second Sonny Boy Williamson on harmonica. The house band grew to include a drummer, a pianist, and Joe Willie Wilkins on guitar—an electric guitar, the first to be heard by most listeners within the station's broadcast range. Muddy Waters, B. B. King, and drummer Levon Helm listened to the show, which has a host of famous alumni and is still broadcast on KFFA.

Just as good an example, though, was WDIA, which was started in Memphis by two white businessmen in 1947. They tried a country format, then a mixture of pop and classical. Faced with immediate closure, Bert Ferguson called on "Professor" Nat D. Williams, who ran the talent night on Beale Street, asking for black talent. A young singer-guitarist named Riley King landed a slot plugging a tonic called Pepticon. He was on from 3:30 to 3:40 P.M. as the Pepticon Boy; he sang two songs, plugged the Pep, and that was it. He was sufficiently popular that the station expanded the show and moved it to Saturday afternoons. Riley King played on WDIA from 1948 to 1953, becoming the Boy from Beale Street, or Blues Boy, then BB. His identity was so connected to this interwoven series of commercial connections that a photo from the period shows that on his guitar he has painted RILEY, B.B. KING W.D.I.A. 5:30 P.M.

Like many radio performers, King wasn't paid for playing live, but he made a fair living from a modern version of the medicine show. He visited stores that sold Pepticon, and played guitar and sang while a Pepticon salesman sold as many bottles as he could to the gathering crowd. It was better than passing the hat: if more than a certain number of bottles were sold, the guitarist was paid a bonus that might run as high as a hundred dollars on a good day—as King said, very big money for the time and the place.

Subsequently, according to one of the station's founders, Lucky Strike "bought B. B. King fifteen minutes a day across the board," though that relationship ended when the sponsor discovered that King had been booked to play shows more than a half day's drive from Memphis and the station had been covering for his absence by using prerecorded shows.

By being a medium that thrived on sound and its suggestions to the imagination, radio was a constant enterpise in the making of myth. It enabled musicians to cultivate simultaneous and parallel careers, as Lester Polfuss did, playing on one station as Rhubard Red, hillbilly humorist / singer / guitarist, and another as Les Paul, jazz guitarist. It blurred the distinction between live performance and recording, and it evaporated the listener's sense of identity and place. As such it became crucial in breaking the color barrier and allowing black and white audiences to hear each other's music. Chuck Berry grew up listening to country music, Kitty Wells, Gene Autry, Kate Smith, Fats Waller, and gospel music—and all of them were synthesized, to a greater or lesser extent, in his music.

Perhaps the most extraordinary radio show was one that created its own artificial reality. All the barn dance shows were artificial, of course, but one of them was ostensibly broadcast from a real place in rural America rather than from a studio—and then went on to create that real place. Before Lake Wobegon, before theme parks, there was the Renfro Valley Barn Dance.

Around 1936 John Lair, the talent manager for WLS's National Barn Dance, suffered a crisis of conscience and decided to turn his family's

Kentucky farmland into a "valley where time stands still," preserving mountain culture for future generations. In part, it seems, he realized that he had been a key figure in the emigration of talent from Kentucky; in part he may have been growing disenchanted with creating the illusion of country life in America's second city. In the words of the Traditional Country Hall of Fame Web site, "He felt that what radio needed was a little realism."

Realism was a relative commodity. One of the first acts he hired at WLS with the intention of moving them with him to his imagined authentic rural barn dance was the Coon Creek Girls. One of the first all-female acts to broadcast regularly on national radio, these performers were Lily May Ledford on banjo (Lair's idea—she preferred the fiddle); her older sister, Rosie, on guitar; Evelyn Lange (whom Lair renamed Daisy) on fiddle, mandolin, and guitar; and Esther Koehler (whom Lair renamed Violet) on mandolin, bass, and guitar. The girls wanted to name the group the Wildwood Flowers, after the Carter Family song, but Lair thought the name "Coon Creek Girls" sounded more country.

Lair hired a number of other top-name acts away from WLS (Red Foley, Slim Miller, the Girls of the Golden West) but there was no Renfro Valley barn in which to dance. Raising the capital to build an entertainment center proved as difficult for Lair as it would for Walt Disney twenty years later, and a delicious paradox developed. Radio, which draws so heavily on the imagination, was perfect for barn dances. When television tried to create its own barn dance shows such as *Hee Haw*, the hokiness of the sets was embarrassingly obvious (though the show was, strangely, immensely popular). Radio contributed the music, the jokes, the affable chatter, and let the audience sketch in the background. In a sense, all the barn dance radio shows were creating a fictional facsimile of an America that might once have existed— except for the Renfro Valley Barn Dance, which was creating a fictional facsimile of an America that didn't yet exist. And the guitar was a central feature of this once and future country.

The Renfro Valley Barn Dance was first held in 1937, initially in the studios of WLW in Cincinnati, then at WCKY, then in an auditorium in Dayton. Paddling hard to keep the illusion alive while he tried to finish building Renfro Valley, Lair sent his performers out around Ohio, Kentucky, and Indiana. "I had the best rollicking guitar backup behind my banjo breakdowns I've ever had," wrote Lily May Ledford in her autobiography, *Coon Creek Girl*. "Sis, when carried away by a fast fiddle tune, would let out a yell so high pitched that it sounded like a whistle. Sometimes, when playing at an outdoor event, fair or picnic, we would go barefooted. We were so happy back then. Daisy and Sis, being good fighters, would make short work of anybody in the more polished groups who would tease or torment us."

In short, they were not only great entertainers, they were great mythmakers as well. Just as Gene Autry and Roy Rogers would help create a myth of the American West, the Coon Creek Girls and John Lair helped create a myth of the American farm, a frolicking, musical place of warmth and good humor. The group became so popular they were even invited to the White House to perform for the president and the visiting King and Queen of England.

By November 4, 1939, the Renfro Valley entertainment facility was finished. It bore precious little resemblance to turn-of-the-century Kentucky, yet it was atonishingly popular, a Field of Dreams for rural music. Not only did it continue as a popular radio show but people drove hundreds of miles to be part of the audience in this strange artifact that had become a tangible representation of the America of the popular imagination.

# INTERLUDE:

# THE WORST GUITAR

Making a rare and unwilling trip to Wal-Mart, I stumble across the ugliest guitars I've ever seen.

There's a small column of them in large cardboard boxes, between the telescopes and the backyard metal detectors. They're all made by First Act and are surprisingly expensive, ranging from about $60 (acoustic guitar, picture of neatly dressed teenage girl playing it), through a larger dreadnought-style acoustic shown in the hands of a boy, Ken to the other's Barbie, to two electrics, both being played by young guys in the classic clench-of-orgasm position, the fancier costing about $200 and coming with a ten-watt amp.

These are sad enough but the saddest sight, reminding me for some reason of a veal calf in a pen, is the guitar that stands alone on a small stand nearby, roughly between the checkouts and the dwarf-sized door where the carts are pushed into the store. It's called a Mark II student guitar, and it is horrible—only twelve frets, an oddly large head and small body, and an action so high it's bound to discourage any but the keenest student.

And one last touch, lurching into cliché: the display model has only five strings.

# Wrestling the Rosette

On April 10, I go out to see Rick with my daughters Zoe, sixteen, and Maddy, eight, along as advisers. In the car, Zoe—who is already an artist with her own style and very strong opinions—studies the stunning photos in the 1999 and 2001 Healdsburg Guitar Festival catalogs.

"Boring . . . boring . . . ugly . . . oh, that's good . . . boring . . . I like this one with a carp carved in it, but it should be a dragon . . . boring . . . oh, this one's nice." She dog-ears a couple of pages.

Her idea of an exciting guitar is something like the Paul Reed Smith electric Dragon guitars. Starting in 1991, the Paul Reed Smith high-end electric guitar–making company has turned out a series of limited edition guitars inlaid with dramatic and complex dragon images. By 2002 there was almost more dragon than guitar: the inlay covered more than 85 percent of the body and ran onto the neck and was made of 272 pieces of inlay including Mammoth Ivory, Green Ripple Abalone, Abalone Sparkle, Paua Select, Paua Heart, Green Heart Abalone, Brown Lip Mother of Pearl, Black Lip Mother of Pearl, Orange Red Spiney, Gold Mother of Pearl, Black Onyx, and Blue Chrysacola. I daren't let Zoe see even a picture of one of these. They cost up to

$20,000 apiece, and it would only be a matter of time before she wrote to me in debtor's prison to say that she had become an electric guitarist. Or, worse, an inlay artist.

In Rick's workshop, Zoe studies my guitar-in-progress politely, but I can tell she finds it pretty dull, and the only recommendation she makes is to add the finest line of blue alongside the black ebony bindings.

"You won't see it," she says confidently. "It'll just seem to add color to the black."

Blue for Lake Champlain, I think, nodding.

Rick has been spending much of his hunched time working on another guitar, a jumbo with a diagonal oval sound hole and amazing back and sides made out of olive wood. "I tell people that this is the olive tree that grew next to Django Reinhardt's outhouse," he says. A guitar joke: Django's famous guitars, designed by Mario Maccaferri and built by Selmer of Paris, had oval or D-shaped sound holes.

My guitar has been progressing conceptually, at least. The top has been ready for some time: it is glued, cut roughly to shape, the sound hole has been cut out, and a groove is routed out in the top for the rosette. The back is glued, with a reinforcing strip up the inside of the seam and cut roughly to shape. It's the rosette that's been holding him up. He shows me pieces of maple he's dug out of the woodpile and sawn open, all with delicate and contourlike spaltings, but none of them quite right. Instead of looking like veins in marble, they look like smudges. He's never made a spalted maple rosette before and admits freely to having called around to other luthiers for suggestions. Ervin Somogyi, the luthier who carved the guitar-top carp that Zoe liked, as it happens, told him only, "You have to start with a really good piece of wood."

"Thanks, Ervin," Rick said. "Any other advice?"

"Well . . . you have to start with a really good piece of wood."

Another possibility, Rick suggests, suitably unusual yet steadily gaining in popularity, is a rosette of crushed stone. He shows me tiny baggies of different colored fragments—malachite, jet, lapis. When he's making a stone rosette, he lays down a bed of epoxy in the routed-out rosette groove, sprinkles the tiny chips onto the epoxy, arranging them in what seems a pleasing manner, lets it all dry, and sands the chips down flush with the top. I'm intrigued, but hesitant.

The other conceptual front on which Rick had been advancing shows more promise. "I just came across these," he says. He moves the gypsy guitar aside on the bench and produces two slats of cherry— not simple and straight-grained like the sides he's already cut for my guitar, nor a simple diagonal waterfall like the back, but a law unto themselves, with the crushed-velvet chatoyance everywhere, like the skin of a stoned leopard. He wanted to ask my opinion, he says, but he thought they might make interesting sides and just went ahead so I could see what the result would look like.

But you've already put so much work in on the other sides for my guitar, I protest. They're right there on the bench, cut, planed, bent, glued, and in the press.

I'll use those for another guitar, he says. No extra charge.

"Go for it," Zoe says, and goes outside to play with Maddy and Alta.

For the girls, the high point of the visit is a game played by Zoe, Maddy, and Alta, Rick and Joni's golden retriever—the running dog of Running Dog Guitars. Rick gives Maddy one of those big, hollow plastic baseball bats and a Whiffle ball and stands her at the bottom of the footpath leading up to his workshop, facing uphill, where Alta is waiting. To my amazement Maddy, disdaining both the baseball swing and my own along-the-ground cricket drive, throws the ball up above her head and serves it like a tennis ball. That's amazingly hard. I had no idea she could do that.

Alta races after the ball, grabs it, trots to a point halfway up the footpath, just where she started, and carefully puts the ball on the ground. The ball trickles slowly downhill to Maddy, who picks it up and the next round begins.

Alta apparently invented this game. "You should see her when we play on a piece of ground that's perfectly flat," Rick says. "She can't understand why the ball won't roll back to me. Gets terribly confused."

All the luthiers I know have their own version of Alta, or of this game, or of this spirit, or at the very least of this rhythm: three hours hunched over a piece of wood, then twenty minutes outside, frolicking.

Three weeks later, in early May, Rick's road is that glorious Vermont mud-season combination of dry, hard, uphill stretches and soft, level sections that have been churned into the consistency of charcoal-colored oatmeal. The big pickups have left ruts a foot or more deep and a good ten yards long; a small car like mine is wisest to edge around these mud puddles with two wheels off the edge of the road, which may be a combination of stones and tree roots but is at least fairly firm.

With a certain amount of self-mocking pomp and *ta-daaah*, Rick shows me the spalted maple rosette, which he has constructed out of four quarter-circles of veined maple, bookmatched to add symmetry. This is the moment I've been dreading since he started work on the guitar: I don't like it. He has gone to an enormous amount of work, but I don't like it.

The Woodley White rosette had a delicate tracery of dark veins against a light but rich background. This one is much blunter and less delicate. It looks . . . sooty. The veins—let's face it, the fungus— are thicker, the whole is busier, the background more beige, less colorful. It looks like swirls of black tobacco smoke. Smudgy. I'm in agony. I dither.

He saves me. After all, he has seen clients look uncomfortable before; he's used to the first-time custom buyer who has never pampered himself to this extent before, doesn't want to look like a pushy asshole. He comes to my rescue, and even adds a wry observation about clients: when they start out, they want the best guitar they can afford. By the time it's finished, they want the best guitar ever made.

We go back to poring over the rosette. He suggests adding a ring of pearl—perhaps blue-green, perhaps white—in the middle of the spalted maple ring. He shows me another of his guitars in the Healdsburg catalog where he did just that.

"So you like that style," I say.

"That way I can avoid being imaginative," he replies dryly.

I point out a Judy Threet guitar with a single broad circle of koa as a rosette, a lovely thing. Koa won't work for my guitar, Rick says, because there's no koa elsewhere, so it'll seem slapped on.

We look at another maker's koa rosette, but Rick raises an eyebrow at the fact that the grain runs diagonally.

"I wouldn't be surprised if that rosette pops right out." The koa and the surrounding spruce, he explained, expand at very different rates, and when the rosette is glued diagonally, the two sections of wood will expand in different directions, too. "I'll bet that koa starts to buckle and rise."

I keep forgetting that wood is so alive. Every piece of a guitar is working against every other piece, like a bad jazz band, and the strings are working against the whole.

Back with the rosette, nothing seems to work. I toy with the idea of some extra bands of inlay around the rosette, blue-white-black, to pick up the water theme again, to remind me that the maple has come from the lake.

Rick countersuggests a rosette made of cherry, which will pick up the color of the back and sides, and that sounds at least worth a try. By this point I'm almost sick of the rosette. It seems to be about decoration, at a time when what I really want is a guitar I can play, that will become mine by being played, not by being pretty. Worse, it seems to be all about trying to do something right, and as a guitarist I wish I spent more time making interesting mistakes.

Afterward, I try to persuade myself that I need this imperfect spalted rosette on my guitar, right there around the dark, mysterious heart of the instrument, to remind me not to try to be perfect. To be smoky, even sooty. To be not beautiful but musical. But to tell the truth I'm just impatient and depressed.

Within a couple of days Rick has made three specimen rosettes of cherrywood, and it's almost disturbing to see the anatomy of unfinished cabinetry: two are circles, one an octagon, all made of sections of cherry glued together—it all looks a little raw, hard to see how the final ring will look, where its beauty will lie.

One of the circles has the grain running perpendicular to the radius in a series of tangents, like a complicated STOP sign. The other has the grain running out radially, like an exclamation. I prefer the latter: it will make the sound hole look like the heart of something opening up, radiating with energy.

The octagon I like just for its nerve. I think I've seen a baroque guitar with something like that, but then they often used straight lines a lot, like the checkerboard patterns on the backs. I'm tempted, but Rick and I agree that its angularity just doesn't suit a guitar that will otherwise be composed of a variety of smooth curves, especially with the cutaway.

Then, just like that, he says, "Of course, we could always do an oval." At once it seems right, the long axis of the oval running roughly one o'clock to seven o'clock, lining up with the cutaway. A bit unusual but I like that, and somehow it fits in with the rest of the guitar. "Let's do it," I say.

Only when I'm driving away does it strike me that the oval sound hole is Django's trademark. Yet Rick's oval, the askew oval, is a new variation, a riff of his own. A nudge to me, too: *Play your own way, for Pete's sake.*

# The Guitar Breaks In

"My grandmother was born in 1890," Rich Kirby told me, sitting in the suitcase-sized production studio at WMMT in Whitesburg, Kentucky, in the heart of strip-mining country, "but despite growing up in an intensely musical community, she had never seen a guitar until her teenage years."

Rich has graying hair and mustache, piercing eyes, and an intense, even fierce look. He was born near Lexington, Kentucky, and after a stint as a folk musician in and around New York he has worked in the mountains of southeastern Kentucky as a musician, a deejay playing traditional Americana, and a producer, recording a wide range of local musicians to capture the sounds of musical traditions in danger of dying. His experience has given him a remarkable viewpoint: he has been able to see the impact of the guitar breaking into an area where traditional music was previously played without it, and to see how the guitar changed that music, not always for the better.

The guitar came to Appalachia with the African-American railroad gangs.

"These folks showed up to build what was actually eastern Kentucky's first coal-hauling railroad, the Ohio and Kentucky. The [existing] railroad stopped at Jackson [some sixty-five miles north of Whitesburg], and the O and K was built to connect that railroad with a coalfield, a small field of extremely rich bituminous coal called 'candle' coal—so called because you could take a match to it and it would burn like a candle.

"I grew up hearing stories of the O and K, which was a railroad like WMMT is a radio station—a small, very community-oriented railroad. My grandmother told me one time she was riding on the train and there was a woman nursing a baby. The woman's milk clabbered—in some way, the baby couldn't take the milk, and was raising hell—so the conductor stopped the train, got off, and milked somebody's cow! And if they knew someone was hurt, for example, or injured, couldn't do their work in the wintertime, they'd throw coal off as they went by the person's farm, so they'd have some [way] to stay warm. That was part of the ambience I wanted to get into the records [I produced] along with the music."

One of his principal sources was his grandmother, a traditional ballad singer. "She told me stories that as they were building the railroad up the creek past where she was living they had a cook car, a mess car I guess you'd call it, and at night they would cook there, and build a fire, and sit around the fire and eat, and afterward they would sing. She would go and hang out on the far edges of the circle, listening and taking it all in. And that was the first guitars that she had seen. She was like a human tape recorder. She would sing some of these [songs] and you could just about hear the guitar."

Rural America in 1900 was almost inconceivably rural. It was still quite possible to find towns of only one or two dwellings, towns where everyone was related, towns where everyone went to the same church, towns connected to other towns by roads that were no more than tracks, towns that were regularly cut off by snows and floods, towns where everyone was Moravian, or Scottish, towns where nobody spoke English, towns without electricity, towns whose only point of contact with the slowly accelerating forces of what we now call American culture were the mail-order catalog, the piano and the piano roll, the Victrola and the phonograph record, and the tent show, medicine show, vaudeville show, or other one-horse act that might pass through the region once in a while. The music people heard and played, then, came from all these sources: dance tunes, minstrel songs, novelty songs, favorites from the old country, hymns, new ragtime, old ballads, marches—and much of it varied from family to family, region to region.

Some areas, then—even some areas in Kentucky—knew the guitar well; others had never seen it. A good many cultures—Irish, for example, or Cajun—were perfectly happy with other instruments. In Whitesburg's case, individual families had drifted (or fled) over the mountains from Virginia and settled in steep little valleys that were as inaccessible as anywhere in the nation. Most were originally from the British Isles, but they weren't from the leisured classes who had settled into that gay life of hunting, sailing, and soirees around the guitar. They were poorer, and their traditional instrument was the fiddle; in the more recent past they had picked up the Appalachian (in other words, homemade, usually fretless) banjo.

Whitesburg wasn't the only Appalachian town that saw its first guitar in the hands of African-American railroad workers in particular. Sam McGee got his start in the Fruit Jar Drinkers, one of the string bands that dominated the Grand Ole Opry between 1925 and 1935.

"The guitar was rare in the Tennessee hills before the First World War," McGee told *Guitar Player* in 1975. "Where we learned the most about the style was from the black people. My daddy ran a little store, and these section hands would come over from the railroad at noon, and they bought pork and beans, sardines, and all that kind of stuff. Well, after they finished their lunch, they would play guitars. Two of them—great big black men, their name was the Steward brothers—they played real good, and that's where I learned to love the blues tunes."

Some blacks became sufficiently well established to become professional musicians. As a child in western Kentucky, Ralph Rinzler has written, Bill Monroe learned mandolin and guitar, picking up both technique and feel from a black fiddler and guitarist named Arnold Schultz.

Monroe told Rinzler "The first time I think I ever seen Arnold Schultz, this square dance was at Rosine, and Arnold and two colored fellows come up there and played for the dance . . . People loved Arnold so well all through Kentucky there. If he was playing a guitar they'd go gang up around him till he would get tired. . . . There's things in my music that comes from Arnold Schultz, runs that I use a lot in my music . . . I tried to keep in mind a little of it, what I could salvage to use in my music. Then he could play blues, and I wanted some blues in my music too, you see."

As it happens, I get the chance to see pre-guitar folk music the following evening. As part of a series of activities to revive traditional arts and culture in the county, a local community center is holding a square dance.

I head off to the dance with three questions in my head: What was this rural music like before the guitar arrived? How did the guitar change it? And what skill did it involve—or, in other words, what was the guitarist doing when he or she was playing well? What was in it for the player?

As the shadows start to spread into the valleys, I drive down a road that follows a deep wrinkle in the hills, locally called a "holler," as in, "I'd rather be in some dark holler / Where the sun refuse to shine." Looking at these tight, steep folds of greenery, it becomes clear how cold and dark a hollow can be, and how it could make spring arrive late and winter early. A square dance, in these hollows, falls under the heading of mental health care.

Everything is defined by the river. Small houses and trailers, horse pastures and corn patches jostle for the tiny flat spaces beside the creek. The community center is an octagonal wooden building with an upper floor running around over our heads like a gallery, and the whole thing rises to a kind of low spire. The wooded hillsides of the hollow rising around it are stunningly beautiful, but already gathering dusk.

The banjo player, a large, calm man in plaid shirt and suspenders, is Lee Sexton, a legend in these parts and belatedly recognized as a

National Heritage performer. Now in his sixties, he's playing an old Gibson banjo, the skin of its head worn transparent on both sides of the strings by his fingers, especially the thumb. His first banjo was a wooden fretless instrument that cost a dollar. "It had a groundhog hide on it, groundhog skin, and they'd left the tail on it!" He worked in the coal mines during the week and on weekends played banjo at bean stringings, log rollings, and corn shuckings, sometimes playing all night until his fingers bled. Nowadays, he explains, he plays only thumb-and-finger, since he broke his second finger working in the mines.

He and fiddler Ray Slone, a retired math teacher, play a steady series of old tunes such as "The Battle of New Orleans" and "Old Log Cabin in the Woods." Neither plays dazzlingly, but their fingers look utterly at home on the frets. They have the relaxed competence necessary for musicians who play dance after dance, sometimes all night.

Thinking like a twenty-first-century guitarist, I assume that the fiddle will play lead and the banjo will play chords, but something much older is at work. They play neither in unison nor in harmony, nor does one back up the other. They play, in effect, in parallel. Each plays the melody in the idiom of his instrument, with the banjo adding extra notes here and there and the fiddle adding an open-string note when possible, like a dog and a cat walking side by side. A braided tune, maybe.

To my surprise, what they're playing is not bluegrass, which I've taken to be the traditional music of the bluegrass state. This is an older music, appropriately enough called "old-time"—the music that enjoyed a surging revival after appearing on the soundtracks of Ken Burns's documentary series on the American Civil War and the film *O Brother, Where Art Thou?* To many of those at the barn dance, bluegrass is the rock and roll of Appalachian music, fast and showy with its own cult of celebrity. Old-time is more low key, more about the music and less about the people playing it.

Later, Lee and Ray are joined by a younger guy called Sean on guitar. Immediately the sound is different: more bass, fuller, something more like an ensemble and less like a musical conversation. Virtually every tune is in G and consists of three chords, and it's Sean's job to strum along steadily and nothing more.

This, I realize, is exactly what old-time music is all about: knowing the tunes. It's about participation, not demonstration. Old-time music starts to make sense to me. Its musicians might seem old and slow compared to bluegrass or country players, but the necessary skills are more social than digital; their job is to keep the music alive and to keep everyone involved, regardless of talent. They were the entire entertainment industry in the days before electricity brought recording, radio, and television. Unlike the modern music business, the musicians willingly bore a social and moral burden for the well-being of their small community. That's what old-time still is: music rather than music business. And the guitar plays only a supporting role, as it did in bluegrass until Doc Watson began playing fiddle tunes on guitar.

In a strange way, this old-time spirit survives in all kinds of communal acoustic music. When I was at college, playing guitar around the dying embers of a party, nobody wanted flash. They wanted songs they knew and could sing along with if they felt like it: Cat Stevens, Simon and Garfunkel, James Taylor, Arlo Guthrie's "Alice's Restaurant"—everyone's repertoire in the early seventies heyday of fingerstyle acoustic guitar. It was a party, after all, not a performance.

Back at the square dance Charlie Whitaker, an unflappable man with an Abe Lincoln beard and an ambling, bearlike gait, takes up his duties as caller and we start dancing to a very, very long tune that the musicians play helpfully, obediently. All ages promenade and do-si-do with a fair amount of confusion, which is half the fun. It's all about joining in—though in the name of full disclosure I must say that while the little square dance band is taking a break Sean, the guitarist, starts playing fast Doc Watson lines as if to reassure himself (and anyone else who might be listening) that he's really a young dude with some juice in him, and all the old-time stuff is fine but if you show him an open road he can be out of the gate like a drag racer, like any other young bluegrass stud.

Curious to know how people around Whitesburg learn the guitar—in other words, how they learn to think of the guitar and its possibilities—I sign up to help with an after-school program taught out at the same community center by Roy Tackett. Roy is a wild man, fifty-one, with broad shoulders and chest, brush-cut gray hair, wild goatee, suspenders. He grew up in a nearby coal miners' camp; now he's a single father, living on disability. As a kid he'd go to a soda fountain across from the camp, and Dock Boggs, not yet an old-time banjo legend, would come and play outside the fountain. He himself played rock-and-roll guitar in a mountain speakeasy across the line in Virginia, where eccentric local laws made it legal to drink but illegal to drink and dance. "It was wild, man. I'd see women come in there fighting with their high heels. Blood gushing out."

Roy has a new student, a seven-year-old boy named James, and the first thing he shows the kid is not how to hold the guitar but how to hold a pick. Meanwhile, I've been asked to help an older boy named Jason, and when I try to show him something using fingerstyle, Jason's eyes grow wide and he calls out, "He's playin' it like a banjo!"

Jason's startled comment offers a way into one of the great mysteries of American guitar music: whatever happened to picking with your fingers?

The debate over whether stringed instruments such as guitars should be played with the fingers of the right hand or with a plucking implement goes back four hundred years or more, when a goose quill was often used as a plectrum. It has always surprised me that in contemporary America, more than anywhere else I know, a sharp division has grown up between the two parties. Flatpickers regard fingerstyle players as wusses. Fingerstyle players regard flatpickers as Neanderthals. On the whole, the Neanderthals have swept the field: even moderately proficient fingerstyle playing is far rarer in this country than in most guitar cultures abroad. White rural music in particular has thrown its lot in with the pick.

If there was one place that might be an exception, I thought, it would be Kentucky, because the most famous fingerstyle tradition in white rural music—the Merle Travis/Chet Atkins style sometimes called "thumb-picking" because it uses the thumb alternating on two low strings to provide a stride piano–style running bass—grew up here.

To figure this out, when I get back home I call Eddie Pennington, ace thumbpicker, Smithsonian Folkways recording artist, and president of the Thumbpickers Hall of Fame in Drakesboro, Kentucky.

Eddie isn't surprised at my Whitesburg story. Western Kentucky and eastern Kentucky are almost two different countries, he says. Besides which, Muhlenburg thumbpickers are such a rare and localized breed that they could trace their lineage player by player.

Merle Travis learned from Mose Rager of Drakesboro, Eddie tells me. ("Merle told me if it hadn't been for Mose Rager he'd have been picking up aluminum cans.") Rager (the *G* is pronounced hard) is yet another in the centuries-old line of barber-guitarists. Mose Rager learned from Kennedy Jones. Kennedy Jones, born in 1900, was the guy who wore a blister on his thumb playing a dance one night in 1919, went into a drugstore in Central City, Kentucky, that also sold musical instruments, and found a box of thumbpicks. He examined them this way and that, Eddie says, put one on, and asked the proprietor if he could try it out on a guitar. "The guy said, 'No, no, that's for *Hawaiian* git-tar.' The owner finally let Kennedy try one out, whereupon he said, 'I believe I can use these in my business,' and bought the lot." He went back to the coal camps and wherever he played a crowd gathered, one of whom was Mose Rager. Another was Ike Everly, father of Don and Phil, the Everly Brothers. Ike was such a Kennedy Jones fan that he started walking with a cane because Kennedy Jones used one, not realizing that for Kennedy it had nothing to do with fashion: he had hurt his back in the mines.

Kennedy Jones learned from his mother, Alice DeArmond Jones, who played parlor guitar but seems to have developed her own right-hand thumbpicking technique late in the nineteenth century. Beyond her the trail peters out in the low clouds hanging in the hollows. Arnold Shultz, son of former slaves and local musical hero who had played with Jelly Roll Morton, may have been involved somehow, bringing in some of the ragtime feel of thumbpicking.

If the past is something of a mystery, so is the present. Travis-style thumbpicking influenced Chet Atkins, the most influential man in mid-century Nashville, and it is central to the Sun Records Elvis-era

rockabilly playing: Scotty Moore, Elvis's guitarist, played Travis-
style. Johnny Cash's "I Walk the Line" is perfect Travis thumbpicking. Yet it faded from country music and is now little heard on
country records. Traditional songs that have been adopted by bluegrass bands are also out of the thumb- or fingerpicking realm. You're
as likely to see a fingerpicker in a bluegrass band as you are to see a
guy playing sousaphone.

Ironically, you're more likely to find fingerpicking in Britain, where
folkies picked it up from the American musicians who brought it across
the Atlantic in the fifties and early sixties. I tell Eddie this. He sighs.

After my excursions at the Whitesburg community center I go back
to Rich Kirby at the radio station to ask a question that perhaps can
be answered only in Appalachia, where the guitar arrived so late in
history: What impact did its arrival have on traditional American music
that had hitherto been played without it?

"People complained that the guitar ruined old-time music," he says,
"because it forced a chordal structure on it that it didn't have.

"In Letcher County in the 1920s," he goes on, "virtually every
household had a banjo. And to a lesser extent the fiddle. Not many
pianos except in a small area in the Blue Ridge. A lot of the traditional
music . . . was in either the unaccompanied voice or [used] musical
instruments that had no definite pitches built in—in other words,
no fretted instruments, and no keyboard instruments. Many of the
banjos and, of course, all of the fiddles were fretless. There was no
standard tuning for the banjo, and the standard tuning for the fiddle
was only one of many tunings that were, and to some extent still are,
used.

"So people had a wide-ranging, anarchistic sense of pitch, and many
of the intonations used were clearly not of the standard twelve tones
that you can find on a piano. I can remember listening to my grandmother's music, and she would sometimes hit what sounded like a
wrong note, but when she would hit it in exactly the same place twelve
verses in a row you would realize that it was not an accident, it was
just a different *scale*."

These days, we tend to think of music in terms of white notes and black notes, tones and semitones, three-chord rock and roll songs. When I look at the guitar fingerboard I see the rectangles formed by strings and frets as being like pigeonholes: everything must fit in here somewhere.

This view, Rich explains, is urban and modern. It doesn't take into account the fact that the human voice doesn't work in neat incremental steps. Nor did old-time fiddlers, who hit pitches that sound weird and wrong to modern ears because they landed somewhere in between an E, say, and an E flat. The guitar erased those subtle distinctions—as used in white rural music in America, at least.

"It's interesting. In Irish and Scottish music, the guitarists have improvised a lot more in terms of how they tune and how they play, a lot more toward open strings and dissonances, and so on. A lot of young musicians today are tending to reach more for the Irish approach, to recapture that—I don't know what you'd call it—that wild, lonesome sound."

In her book *Cajun Music*, Ann Allen Savoy makes a very similar point about the folk musics of Louisiana, where this unifying effect that might be called the industrialization of pitch was brought about by a different keyboard instrument: the accordion. "The loss of many of the old fiddle tunes can partly be attributed to the appearance of the accordion," Savoy notes. "The accordion's simplistic scale could not handle the delicate complexities and half-notes of [the] old melodies."

When the guitar arrived, then, it wasn't clear how it fitted in; or, to look at it the other way, it wasn't clear how the guitarist might fit traditional music into guitar chords. On certain Appalachian field recordings, Rich Kirby says, you can hear early guitar players fumbling to find chords on a guitar to fit a song that comes from an older, freer vocal tradition. Radio producers and record companies accelerated this process: the keening tones of the old-fashioned voices, the eerie wailing of the fretless instruments sacrificed for what sounded right to city ears.

By the time the bluegrass players seized the same tunes at the end of the thirties, Rich says, they had been reimagined, or perhaps reheard, so that they had lost all their old-time wandering and inexactitude.

"You'll hear a bluegrass band play that same song twenty years later and by then it'll all fit. It'll be tight." In other words, clean. Modern.

Driving away from Whitesburg, I listen to a hatful of old-time CDs and then, for a change, throw in a CD of modern guitar masters called *Guitar Harvest*. To my surprise, there is the Scottish guitarist Tony McManus flatpicking a medley of two tunes that illustrates everything I've been hearing about the arrival of the guitar in Appalachia but haven't quite been able to imagine.

The first, "A Shepherd's Dream," is a classic fiddle tune that McManus plays very fast and skillfully on two double-tracked guitars plus some open strings in the "braided" or parallel banjo-and-fiddle style. The piece consists of two voicings of the melody, plus variations, but no bass, no rhythm, no chords. The harmonic structure—the chords, that is—is implied rather than played. It has a spirited but delicate charm, not only old-time but old world.

When he moves into the second tune ("Onga Bucharesti," a klezmer tune from eastern Europe) he brings in another guitar, striking chords. The change is radical, and it surely gives a sense of what the guitar would have sounded like when it was first added to old-time music. As soon as the chordal guitar comes in, the piece starts *rocking*. The hard chunky guitar, with its big square chords, makes the tune sound like a series of rocks—stepping-stones, perhaps. It loses some of the subtlety of the previous movement, and the sense of solitary, naked endeavor, but it gets fatness, depth, and that pile-driver energy. It sounds modern. It sounds American. It rocks.

# INTERLUDE:

# BEATING CANNED MUSIC

I drive over to John Leo's to have my snow tires taken off and my summer tires put on. Thinking about the importance of playing a guitar rather than simply admiring it, I take the Fylde with me, and while they're changing the tires on my car I play for the receptionist (a lady in late middle age), another customer (a lady in late middle age), and myself, in the ambivalent heart of middle age: Django Reinhardt's "Tears" and "Nuages" in my slowed-down versions, Scott Joplin's "Silver Swan," "Moonlight in Vermont," some general rambling—the loose peregrinations of composition in progress. Out of the corner of my eye I can see a toe swinging as the other customer reads a magazine. Guys from the shop seem to pause on their way through reception.

When the tires are done and I stop playing, the two women break into smiles. "Very relaxing" is the verdict. I'm tempted to hear that as "very boring," but I think, no, live instrumental guitar music probably is relaxing in the context of work, artificial light, the smell of artificial carpet and Naugahyde, oil and gasoline drifting in faintly from the shop. They agree that it beats canned music.

"I've never had someone come in and play music in all the years I've worked here," says the receptionist, and I think, *What good is a guitar if you leave it at home?*

# Hogging Off Wood

Beside Stage Road, the fiddlehead ferns are coming up through the mulch of leaf debris beside the road and starting to uncurl. The grader has made a rare pass: the mud season ruts are gone, the road is exposed, littered with small stones, raw as rope burn. A stream runs down the emerald darkness beneath the trees on the right.

The oval rosette is made, and it looks plain but perfectly fine. I'm not sure what else I would want and I feel oddly neutral.

All this ambivalence vanishes, though, when Rick shows me the faceplate, also known as the headstock veneer—the decorative slice that will be glued onto the front of the head, like a face. It's stunning: two bookmatched wavy pieces of cherry from the scraps of the back, not exactly symmetrical but vaguely consonant, as unorthodox as all get out. I love it.

He has been working concurrently on one of his least favorite elements of the guitar: the neck.

"It's basically just hogging off wood," he grumbles. The neck is built in two matching longitudinal halves. It started as a single piece of mahogany cut roughly to shape that got ripped down the middle. He planed, leveled, and cleaned up the surfaces where the faceplate and the fingerboard will go. Then he inserted a slice or spline of ebony flanked by two slivers of the blue-dyed maple, glued this five-layer sandwich together, and cleaned the whole thing up. The result is what is called a neck blank. From the top and bottom it's a rectangle; from the side it's neck-shaped, but oversized. It looks like a neck for a Flintstone guitar.

At some point when he hasn't got anything else to do, he'll rout the channel for the truss rod, a metal reinforcing rod that runs the length of the neck (hidden beneath the fingerboard) and can be adjusted at either end to counter any forces that may be twisting the neck out of true. Then he'll cut the tenon at the end where it will fit into the block at the head of the body—between the shoulders, so to speak.

The whole neck phase bores him. There's no design involved, there's no interesting risk to take, there isn't the wood-and-air alchemy of the hollow box—it's like making a solidbody, in fact.

"Bascially, I ignore it as long as I can."

# Bargaining with
# the Devil

From its earliest days, recording was a bargain with the devil.
I see it as a version on the old crossroads myth, which said that
if a man stood at the crossroads at midnight, the devil (in some vari-
ants, a tall black man) would appear and tune his guitar, making him
a spectacular player but also making him forever the devil's servant.

In my version, the man was only half convinced he really wanted to
become a great guitarist. He was pretty happy jamming on the porch
with his friends, when they came over, and he was looking forward to
teaching his daughter to play, if she wanted to. Every so often he went
into the local school to give the teacher a break and sing a few songs
he'd learned from his father and his grandmother, and whenever there
was a square dance he sat in and played D, G, C, and A all evening and
shared a jar of moonshine with his friend the fiddler.

Part of him was curious about this legend of the crossroads, though,
and in the end he went anyway, just to see. What harm could it do, to
be able to play the guitar a bit better?

He went to the crossroads at midnight on a dark night at the end of
the nineteenth century. The devil was there, sure enough, but he
offered the man a bargain he wasn't expecting. The devil said, "You
give your soul to me, and I'll amplify your guitar."

Amplify? The man didn't know what the devil meant.

"Listen," the devil said. "There's a flood of changes coming, and you can sink, or you can swim. Something called electricity is on its way, and you can't even imagine what it'll do to the world. But I can, and this is my offer. You give me your soul, and I'll not only make you the best guitarist in the world but I'll make the guitar rule the planet. I'll make you so powerful that when you play one note, people in *China* will hear you."

The man's mouth fell open. China? How could that be? But he was still wary. "What's the catch?"

The devil chuckled. "I already told you," he said. He didn't tell the man that he intended to bring about the death of live music as people knew it, the shared, equal interchange of human spirit, generous, risky, vulnerable, mysterious. He didn't tell the guitarist that he was planning to reduce this divine miracle to a commodity and a fantasy. The man wouldn't have understood.

The man looked eager but still suspicious. "When do I need to give you an answer?" he demanded.

Then the devil made his mistake. He assumed that everyone was as greedy as he was, and that the man was already hooked.

"Take as long as you like," he said casually. "Take a hundred years if you need to."

And that's what happened. A hundred years later, electricity had taken over the world and live music was dwindling. Even acoustic guitars were being made with built-in amplification, like cyborgs that were half-human, half-robot. Yet the man had never given the devil his answer, and the guitar had also become the instrument of choice for casual, intimate strumming among people who otherwise might never have played a note. On good days, the devil was pretty satisfied with the way things were going. On bad days, he was beginning to wonder if he'd been tricked.

It's a sign of the ambiguous nature of the recording process that when the phonograph emerged in the 1890s, one of the people who spoke out most forcefully against it was someone who stood to gain from it.

John Philip Sousa, one of the preeminent voices in American music, foresaw that recorded music was a trap. In "The Menace of Mechanical Music" (1906) he predicted "a marked deterioration in American music and musical taste, an interruption in the musical development of the country, and a host of other injuries to music in its artistic manifestations, by virtue—or rather by vice—of the multiplication of the various music-reproducing machines."

Sousa saw that live performance made music grow, while recorded music encouraged passivity and stagnation. Several decades later, the great classical guitarist Julian Bream looked back wistfully and perhaps bitterly at the way recording had changed the relationship between the performance and the listener. "Until the advent of recording," Bream said, "music had a sort of mysticism attached to it—the music was played, and it vanished; you could never capture it. . . . It shows a sort of greediness on the part of people that they want to conserve something which should vanish."

The early recording industry had little interest in the guitar because there was no money to be made from it—or, rather, there was a lot more money to be made elsewhere. In the spring 1899 Sears, Roebuck catalog, for example, we find the Musical and Talking Records section featuring several categories: orchestra, band, Sousa's Grand Concert band, Gilmore's Brass Quartette, and Miscellaneous Instrumental Solos and Duets, the last category consisting of xylophone solos, clarinet solos, cornet solos, banjo solos, piccolo solos (apparently a big draw, given their own illustration), zither solos, and orchestra bells with piano accompaniment. Not a word about guitar.

As I've said before, America in the early twentieth century was so much less homogenized than today that there was almost no such thing as "American culture." The record companies, then, thought in local and ethnic terms: they recorded Italian music to sell to Italians, German music for Germans, klezmer music and cantors for Jews, even Finnish music for Finns. They didn't record African-American music for the bottom-line reason that they assumed only blacks liked black music, and blacks had no money to buy records.

Mamie Smith proved both assumptions wrong. In February 1920 Fred Hager of the General Phonograph Company agreed to buy and record two songs composed by Perry Bradford, a black music-store proprietor from Chicago: "That Thing Called Love" and "You Can't Keep a Good Man Down." Hager wanted to use Sophie Tucker, a popular white vaudeville diva, but Bradford persuaded him to use a black singer, Mamie Smith. The record was released on the Okeh label and, despite the lack of any special advertising, sold unexpectedly well. In August Smith was called back to record "Crazy Blues" and "It's Right Here for You (If You Don't Get It . . . 'Taint No Fault of Mine)," which sold over two million copies. To say this came as a surprise to the record business doesn't begin to describe the shock. A new market had been discovered, the so-called "race" market, along with a new form of music that would tap it. The man who would tap that market most aggressively was Fred Hager's assistant, Ralph Peer.

The first stars of blues recordings were women such as Mamie and Bessie Smith (no relation), often singing what came to be called "classic blues" in fairly sophisticated urban settings to the accompaniment of small combos with something of a jazzy flavor. In the countryside, though, the blues was associated most strongly with men, and with guitars. The first rural black musician to make a record under his own name was Sylvester Weaver, who recorded two instrumentals—"Guitar Rag" and "Guitar Blues"—in November 1923. Singer-guitarists came with the additional advantage that they were easier and far cheaper to record than the popular female urban blues singers, who came with a band and were becoming increasingly difficult to order around. The era of the field recording began. Frank Walker, who signed Bessie Smith for Columbia in 1923, as well as Hank Williams for MGM twenty-five years later, drove out to the smallest of towns and even rode horses back into the woods to look for a singer or musician whom someone had told him about. His was a full-service operation: not only did he recruit and record, he sold records in rural areas by renting a storefront, playing the new releases, and taking in the cash himself. As soon as word about recording went out, though, "field" producers simply rented a hotel room or a vacant storefront and the musicians came to them.

The most successful of these field producers was Peer. When Victor, whose sales of highbrow and nineteenth-century popular music were falling hard, hired Peer away from Okeh, Peer pulled a cunning and important entrepreneurial switch: he would work for no salary, he said, as long as he controlled the copyrights to all the songs he found. He also encouraged his musicians to take familiar material and make superficial changes so it could be regarded as new; he could then of course own the rights. In the first three months alone of this new business arrangement, Peer made a quarter of a million dollars in royalties. He later said candidly, "What I was doing was to take the profits out of the hillbilly and race business and spend that money trying to get established as a pop publisher."

From the viewpoint of a poor musician, the up-front money was good: Son House was paid five dollars a side by Paramount, forty dollars in all, more than the average plantation worker earned in a year back then. But the transaction as a whole was fraudulent. Royalties for rural or urban musicians, white or black, would be paid only at whim and would never be accounted. John Lee Hooker heard a record producer say, "You mean you're giving these artists *royalties*? You're going to ruin the business for all of us!" Memphis Slim said, "Most of the blues singers didn't know what 'royalty' meant. I didn't know until Roosevelt Sykes told me I wasn't getting any. . . . When I started asking for royalties, I got boycotted." As late as the fifties, Chuck Berry would be startled to discover that he had apparently cowritten "Maybellene" with the deejay Alan Freed and someone called Russ Fratto, who turned out to be a printer who made up the labels for Chess Records, and that they would be getting the majority of his royalties.

The record companies had only the most cynical interest in African-American music and culture. In drawing a distinction between hillbilly records and race records, for instance, Ralph Peer said that hillbilly records brought in a torrent of mail from potential musicians, but race records didn't. "Of course," he added, "niggers can't write."

*   *   *

In looking for more hits by black musicians, Peer accidentally created what we now call country music.

In 1923 Peer and Polk Brockman, an Atlanta furniture dealer and Okeh record distributor, went to Atlanta. "We went down there to get Negro stuff," Peer later said. "This fellow [Brockman] began scouting around but to my amazement he didn't know of any Negro talent . . . he went to the local Negro theater and he tried to find acts but nothing amounted to anything." In order that the trip wouldn't be a complete waste of time, Peer recorded Fiddlin' John Carson, a white entertainer already popular locally and on the radio, whom Peer described as "pluperfect awful." Peer okayed an initial pressing of only five hundred copies, which sold out instantly at a fiddlers' contest. More records were pressed; when sales hit half a million, nobody was more surprised than Peer. There was even more money to be made out of hillbilly music than race records. The Columbia hillbilly series alone sold eleven million copies between 1925 and 1932, at a time when a single two-sided 78 rpm record might cost the equivalent of a day's pay.

Peer's motives were anything but altruistic, yet his efforts had important consequences. Black and white rural musicians were recorded who might otherwise have been lost, and many of these recordings were rediscovered and reissued decades later, becoming enormously influential. And the sheer fact that he hoped to make such vast sums of money meant that he, and only he, had the incentive to get these reords out to as many people as possible.

In 1927 Peer made a recording trip to Bristol, Tennessee, a town that could be considered both rural and urban: Bristol was remote enough that prewar melodies and old mountaineer songs had survived in the region, guaranteeing a certain nostalgia value, yet it was developed enough to have a railhead, two daily newspapers, three colleges, and suitable facilities for field recording. Peer took over part of the second floor of a building sometimes used as a warehouse for the Cox Hat Company, setting up his recording equipment and a rented piano.

Peer began recording on July 25, 1927. On August 1 he recorded a trio that had driven over from Scott County, Virginia—a girl who sang old-fashioned songs and played autoharp, another girl, her cousin, who played guitar, and the first girl's husband, a tall, rather remote man who provided the songs but who had the odd habit of singing a phrase or two and then stepping out of the song altogether. This was the Carter Family.

Before she married A. P. Carter, Sara Dougherty had formed a girl group with her cousin Madge Addington, singing old ballads and gospel songs in the houses of friends and neighbors in the old-time way. Between them they played guitar, banjo, autoharp, and organ. Madge's brothers were known for their guitar playing, and her baby sister Maybelle started out teaching herself the family autoharp by ear, then winning a local banjo contest at the age of twelve. When she was thirteen her brothers bought her a guitar. Within the year she was accompanying them at dances, sometimes playing all night. At seventeen she married E. J. Carter, A.P.'s brother.

The Carter Family's first release, issued later in 1927, "Poor Orphan Child"/"Wandering Boy," didn't sell much, but in early 1928 Peer released "The Storms Are On the Ocean"/"Single Girl, Married Girl," which sold all over the South. In 1928 they recorded again, another dozen songs, with Maybelle playing Hawaiian-style slide guitar. This batch included songs that subsequently would be recorded by musicians as diverse as Flatt and Scruggs, Doc Watson, Johnny Cash, Bob Dylan, Joan Baez, and Manfred Mann, plus "Wildwood Flower," which has been recorded by so many musicians that NPR named it one of the hundred most important songs of the century.

Maybelle Carter provided white rural music with three qualities: a repertoire, an almost dynastic coherence that gave the vital sense of family to the emerging genre, and a guitar lick. The repertoire, though beautiful and performed by countless other musicians, now seems a little dated—Carter Family songs ("Wabash Cannonball," "Will the Circle Be Unbroken," "Wildwood Flower") are still widely sung but they have more of a nineteenth-century folk-song feel to them than the more spirited, bluesy songs of, say, their contemporary, Jimmie Rodgers.

The family dynasty stands like a pillar supporting American popular rural white music. Maybelle's daughter June worked with Elvis

Presley and married Johnny Cash; Carlene Carter and her stepsister Roseanne Cash are third-generation Carters. Maybelle herself was an active musician until she was in her sixties, and one of the Carter Family tour guitarists was the young Chet Atkins.

From our point of view, Maybelle Carter's most important legacy was that she gave America a guitar technique that was simple, effective, and open to innumerable new inventions from the easy to the stunningly tricky.

Most entry-level guitarists strum. The strum combines two useful elements: by playing a chord it creates a generalized tonal and emotional ambience that lies under the singing voice like a bun under a burger; it also provides a rhythmic and percussive *oomph*. Given enough variety in one's material, a strum alone can be all a solo singer-guitarist needs. You can get an entire bar jumping with just a flat pick and "Nineteenth Nervous Breakdown" or "Sympathy for the Devil." Elvis never needed more than a strum.

If the material is quiet, gentle, and somewhat uniform, though, the strum on its own can put everyone to sleep by the third song, as coffeehouse folkies discovered in their droves during the sixties. What can you do about it? You can learn fingerstyle, but that adds layer upon layer of complexity, and loses volume. You can try using the pick on the treble strings to add the kinds of phrases blues players use, but then you tend to lose your rhythmic accompaniment, and in any case the treble pitches coincide with those being used by the singing voice and by other instruments and so get muffled or drowned out. What Maybelle Carter gave us (though she never claimed to have invented it herself) was the counterintuitive solution, the bass-string lick.

She'd play one, two, or perhaps three notes on the thick, loud bass strings and then continue the strum across the rest to keep up the rhythm. The bass strings are easiest to see, easiest to reach in the downstroke—anyone can do it. Best of all, you barely even have to move your fingers out of the chord position. Faced by the eternal dilemma of the guitar—is it a featured single-note instrument or a rhythm instrument?—Maybelle combined the two by introducing the inverted lead. And everyone, but everyone followed her, especially in white rural music. The early rockabilly guitarists of the fifties were playing Carter licks on electric guitars even when they had a rhythm guitarist to do the strumming. Bluegrass acoustic guitarists all start out in first position—that is, with the hand covering the first three frets so it can play the basic chords—and move up from the bass strings toward the treble, taking the Carter phrases and playing them faster and faster and, eventually, higher up the neck. Maybelle Carter gave the rural-music acoustic guitar a voice that set it apart from the monochromatic background jangle of the autoharp. She gave the country guitarist something to do. Many guitarists still play nothing more complicated than Maybelle Carter did, and it works for them just fine.

Maybelle Carter also set a crucial precedent for rural music: she made it clear that it included women, young and older, both as singers and as instrumentalists. The Carter Family may have been a little old-fashioned by the later twenties, and Maybelle and Sara may have harked back to the porch/parlor/kitchen/church venues of music making rather than the emerging loci of the professional musician, but there was no denying their precedent. Unlike, say, jazz, which came to be dominated very quickly by professional ensembles (which in turn translated to male players), the Carter Family balanced out Jimmie Rodgers by emphasizing the at-home nature of rural music, with all that implied. Every woman guitarist who has played country music has credited Mother Maybelle, with good reason.

The Jimmie Rodgers Entertainers (a.k.a. the Tenneva Ramblers) arrived in Bristol on August 3, 1927, and at once, in the great tradition of popular music, fell out over who was in charge and what they were going to call themselves. Jimmie had always been something of an add-on to the band, and in any case, from Peer's point of view, "the records would have been no good if Jimmie had sung with this group because he was singing nigger blues and they were doing old-time fiddle music. Oil and water . . . they don't mix."

Rodgers was from Mississippi. Working on the railroad he had, by one conductor's recollection, played guitar with black railroad gang workers. As a would-be entertainer he had traveled widely across the

South in the teens and twenties and picked up what he could from an "amorphous brotherhood of small-time entertainers, medicine show pitchmen, singing hobos, bandsmen and part-time minstrels." He played in blackface; he played as part of the "Hawaiian Show and Carnival" that toured in 1925, two guitars plus Hawaiian steel guitar, all three players wearing white shirts and leis.

On August 4, the morning after the split over artistic differences, Rodgers recorded alone, singing the yodeling lullaby "Sleep, Baby, Sleep" and the sentimental World War I song "The Soldier's Sweetheart." It took him seven takes to get the two songs right even in a basic sense; though Rodgers had been playing the guitar for several years, he was not the most proficient guitarist.

In less than a year he was a star.

It's impossible to overstate the impact Jimmie Rodgers had on America. Nowadays he sounds absurdly raw and amateurish, and paradoxically he looks fake, wearing a dashing straw boater in one publicity still, a perfectly clean Singing Brakeman railway outfit in another, yet at the time he was the singing voice of rural America, giving people the songs they knew or songs about the lives they knew, and if his guitar playing consisted of a handful of chords, well, that was pretty familiar too. He wasn't the first to sell a million copies of a traditional song of rural America, but he was the first million seller to tour the small towns, the first to sing about his own life and afflictions (notably in "TB Blues"), the first who came across as a genuine entertainer from out in the small towns. He was the Will Rogers of popular music, and everyone, but everyone knew him. You could walk down a street and hear the latest Jimmie Rodgers record playing on Victrola after Victrola, the sound wafting out through open windows. General-store owners, even those who didn't like his music, acknowledged that the sales of his records got them through the Depression.

Looking more closely at the extraordinary events of August 1927, it becomes clear that the guitar was very, very lucky. If Peer had started his field recordings half a dozen years earlier, it's conceivable that Rodgers wouldn't have played the guitar, but instead the banjo or ukulele. Like many entertainers of his day, he played all three, as well as the mandolin, and the photographs in Nolan Porterfield's magisterial biography show that the instruments were changing at the same time as the recording technology. One photograph taken before the Bristol date shows Rodgers with the Ramblers, but he's playing a banjo.

The most remarkable photograph, though, shows one of the bands that accompanied Rodgers on some of his recordings, the Blue and Gray Troubadours. The Troubadours are seven men in evening dress, arranged four standing, three in front sitting. The three in front all hold guitars; in front of them are banjos, scattered across the floor like oyster shells. The banjo, which had been challenging the guitar hard for forty years, is slipping. Within a decade it will be cold mutton.

One of the biggest problems facing the record companies was the country's pervasive prejudice against African-Americans and the rural poor. Victor responded to this massive challenge in public relations by producing one of the most extraordinary images in the history of the guitar.

It was the cover illustration to the company's 1930 "race records" catalog: "Vocal Blues, Religious, Spirituals, Red Hot Dance Tunes, Sermons, Novelties." (Several of the major companies kept race records out of their main catalogs.) It depicted a young black man sitting at a river dock, playing his guitar, his back to a bale, a riverboat at the jetty in the background. The guitar is well drawn, not conspicuously new but not battered—a mature instrument, the kind that now would fetch a couple of thousand on the vintage market. The guitarist's eyes are closed, his head is thrown slightly back, his hands are delicate, his neck strong. His clothes are loose and casual but neither ragged nor dirty—he could be posed in a Travelsmith catalog. He is unaffected by the haste of those around him. He has the relaxed cool that every college student would like, taking a summer off to bum around the country. He is playing for himself. It's astonishing to me that the artist could take the grim prejudices of his day, step outside them, and imagine for his fictional guitarist qualities that would be popular and marketable for decades.

Sadly, this commitment to the blues was superficial and transitory. The record companies had only the most cynical interest in African-American music and culture. As the Depression got worse, and Victor's record sales dropped from 104 million in 1927 to 6 million in 1932, field-recording trips dried up. The companies were far more likely to record hillbillies singing their versions of the blues, some of which sold well, than blacks. The few blues singer/guitarists that were recorded tended to play a smoother, more urbane blues.

The guitarist/folklorist/musicologist Alan Lomax saw the change firsthand on the streets of Memphis in 1941. He interviewed David Edwards, an itinerant guitarist who reckoned he made two hundred to three hundred dollars a year hustling music on the streets. "Not them old songs like my daddy plays, we don't know nothing about them old numbers. What we play is what they records, the people like Mister Melrose up in Chicago." ("Mister Melrose" was Lester Melrose, a talent scout/producer for RCA, Bluebird, Columbia, and Okeh, who recorded Big Bill Broonzy, the first Sonny Boy Williamson, Memphis Minnie, Roosevelt Sykes, Lonnie Johnson, Big Joe Williams, Bukka White, Washboard Sam, Champion Jack Dupree, Jazz Gillum, Big Boy Crudup, Victoria Spivey, and Leroy Carr, among others, more or less singlehandedly defining the Chicago blues sound before World War II. Following Peer's example, Melrose often assigned composer credit and performance rights to himself.)

It's a sad, familiar paradox: the record industry was narrowing the range of available music and dictating what Edwards played, yet to have his name on a record was to be special, to be a part of a transcendent world removed in geography, economics, and glamour from playing on the street corner. Melrose and his like had created a trap, and Edwards and his like walked into it over and over again.

Talking about Melrose and "they new blues," Edwards explained: "He used to pay twenty-five dollars a side for a record, that fifty dollars a record, real good money. He don't give no royalty, not unless you're blind or afflicted, but he put your name on the record. Whomsoever sing the song, that's your record. Who owns the song? Well, all I know, your name on the record, if you sing it."

No sooner had he sounded that optimistic tone than he continued, "Here, lately, they cut that money down. They cut from twenty-five a side to seven fifty a side. I don't know why."

One final observation about Melrose and the music business: "The last time I went to Chicago for him I made eight records for ninety dollars outside of expenses," Edwards said, singing in his chains like the sea, "and all I want to drink."

# INTERLUDE:

# NAIL ANGST

Two weeks before a gig, I break a nail.

It's my strongest nail, the long finger of my right hand. For once my nails were just about perfect, but hubris caught up with me. I let them grow a fraction too long, and with every extra tenth of a millimeter the nail dries out a little more and gets brittle. I'm taking the laundry out of the dryer, the nail catches on the rim of the door, the top snaps clean off.

Players who use picks can use anything for a pick. Chet Atkins used his index fingernail as a pick. Carl Perkins used a tooth from a comb. Billy Gibbons of ZZ Top uses a quarter, or a peso. Jerry Garcia tucked his pick between his index finger and the stub of his second finger (his brother severed it with an ax when he was four) when he wanted to fingerpick. Dave "The Edge" Evans of U2 uses West German picks with dimples to help you grip them; he uses that end on the strings to produce "a certain rasping top end." John McLaughlin used to make his own picks out of plastic pie boxes that he cut up with wire cutters.

Playing with your fingertips and nails probably gets the most natural sound, and the greatest range of sound, from a guitar, but in the end it all comes down to Mohs' scale of hardness: steel strings are harder than fingernails. No getting around it.

Some guitarists take silica supplements. Some take a megavitamin called Appearex, or Biotin, which helps with splitting and brittle nails, and also with bovine and equine hoof problems. Some use Ultra Nails Plus. One guitarist tells me he once asked the British fingerstyle wizard Martin Simpson how he kept his nails hard and Simpson whispered, "Superglue, mate."

I e-mail Simpson to check.

"I did use super glue with tissue paper and baking powder, producing concrete nails," he writes back, "[but] I have for the last 15 years used acrylic nails from the beauty salon . . . much better. Previous to all of this I used to just paint my nails with lots of polish, vanity mostly."

You learn to do things with your left hand. You pay extra care when opening the flap over your gas tank in cold weather. You buff constantly, like a nervous habit. Most of all, though, you just feel helpless, and ridiculous for spending so much time on something so damn stupid.

Ed Gerhard, a fine fingerstyle guitarist from New Hampshire, tells a joke that is the truest thing I heard in two years of asking people about the guitar: "You start off playing guitar to get chicks and end up talking with middle-aged men about your fingernails."

# Bearclaw

Blackflies settle on us in fives and sixes. The roadside is now completely fleshed out: the fiddleheads are no longer individual curls on stalks, the only inhabitants of the verge; they have unfurled into eighteen-inch ferns standing above other ferns, dandelions, grasses, all kinds of weedy spring pandemonium.

The oval sound hole requires that Rick make a whole new top, which he has already done, and as a bonus this particular piece of spruce has a figure—that is, any variation to the grain—known in the trade as "bearclaw": several narrow lines, a quarter of an inch or so wide and several inches long, run sideways across the grain with a slight quaver to them. Uncharitably, they might look like worm borings; woodworkers choose the more attractive metaphor, and they do look as though a bear might have raked its claws across the trunk of the tree. It's the kind of variation that the big makers would toss aside regretfully as a defect, but the custom builders offer it as a premium, a sign of individuality in the guitar.

The sound hole–and-rosette area looks . . . scruffy. The individual arcs of cherry have little gaps between them, the blue veneer (English sycamore, Rick says, dumped in large dye vats in France), which he has used to encircle the cherry oval, is tufty, like badly cut blotting paper, with tiny blue crumbs scattered across the top. I am determined to take it however it turns out, having worked on too many projects myself where the client dillied and dallied back to first principles every single step, a treadmill of a process. So no complaints.

Chatting, Rick takes the top over to the sander. He runs it through a few times and casually holds it up. It is transformed. The blue crumbs have gone, of course, but so have the ragged blue edges. The dust has started to fill in the cracks between the pieces of cherry oval—even the bearclaw in the top has started to stand out in the weird luminous depth of chatoyance. The whole thing looks . . . intentional. By taking the rosette down to two dimensions, he has changed it from an event—two weeks of back and forth, dozens of attempts and wasted scraps of wood—to a pattern, an expression of purpose and taste.

Speaking of taste, something strange is happening to my taste in guitars. Last September, when I first started looking for my birthday guitar, I discovered that I couldn't stand archtops. They made me almost physically ill. As did sunbursts; that style of staining the finish so that it's lighter around the bridge, the raised heart of the archtop, and much darker around the edges of the top evoked a repulsive sense of staleness and claustrophobia. I was surprised and puzzled, and began watching for other cultural artifacts that produced the same response, such as the singing of Frank Sinatra; torpid lounge jazz; white guys with little mustaches playing "The Girl from Ipanema" as if they were cool. Of course! This was popular culture of my parents' generation, past its due date and grown stale, and the sixteen-year-old in me still felt the need to put it down.

Spending so much time around guitars, guitar makers, and guitar history seems to have changed something. I still can't stand sunbursts, but I'm beginning to like the beautiful maple and classical lines of the new archtops being made by the best of the contemporary makers—Linda Manzer, Tom Ribbecke, Bob Benedetto, and John Monteleone, in particular—and I'm curious to know why they throw their hearts and souls into archtops.

Rick doesn't make archtops, and he views them with mild skepticism, so I ask Dave Nichols, who lives across Lake Champlain in upstate New York and, in addition to being one of the top inlay artists in the world, also makes both flattop guitars and archtop mandolins.

There are two major differences between archtops and flattops, he says, plus a host of smaller differences. First on the list is that with a flattop, the strings are attached to the bridge, which is glued to the top. With an archtop, the strings pass over the bridge and are anchored in a tailpiece that is attached to the bottom of the lower bout. The tension in the strings, then, exerts a straight downward pressure through the bridge onto the top of the guitar. In a flattop, the string tension pulls the bridge toward the fingerboard in a way that rotates the bridge, pulling the back of the bridge up and forcing the front down.

This difference means that an archtop behaves a little like a drum head or banjo head, bouncing rapidly up and down with the string vibrations being transmitted through the bridge. This is also how a speaker cone behaves. And this is where the second difference comes in: the area around the bridge is raised, like a violin top, and where it curves down the maker carefully thins the top by a process called "candling." As the maker is scraping wood away from the underside of the top, he or she holds the top up to the light (originally a candle) and judges the thickness of the wood by the light coming through the grain. Standing in his shop, where shells of guitars, half-guitars, and unfinished guitars hang from the rafters, Dave holds a mandolin up to the light and squints to demonstrate. When finished, the archtop has a thicker plate supporting the bridge surrounded by thinner wood that will let the plate or cone "bounce"—and that flexibility is increased by the f-holes, which are cut into the wood surrounding the plate to further reduce the resistance to vibration.

This sounds fine in theory but, on the other hand, archtops spectacularly fail the Sound-hole Test. If the builders' theory holds water, the number, shape, and positioning of an archtop's f-shaped sound holes are crucial, but recent history proves otherwise. In the early 1990s, Jimmy D'Aquisto opened the f-holes out into shapes like Nike swooshes (Gretsch had tried something similar in the late forties, calling it the "cat's eye" sound hole) and John Monteleone took this fanciful work further, breaking each swoosh into pieces until they looked a little like car radiator grilles, intended to function like separate woofers and tweeters. (Some of these are among the most beautiful guitars ever made, though I shudder when sound holes start showing too much of the guitar's bracing and innards: it starts looking to me as if a transparent patch of skin had been transplanted beneath someone's stomach and you could see the muscles, the intestines . . . I don't want to go on.) Bob Benedetto broke still further from tradition by moving even the placement of the f-holes: one of his archtops had no f-holes but what might be called perforated lily-shaped flourishes on the upper-left and lower-right bouts. Yet none of this seems to have harmed their guitars, which if anything are even more prized than regular f-hole archtops.

Doug Green, historian, writer, Stromberg archtop devotee, and thinking man's guitarist, has an especially subtle view. The archtop—the outstanding archtop, that is, for archtops are harder to make well than flattops—projected a sound that was perfect for chording, and perfect for the particular window of frequencies open for a guitarist in a big jazz band. This was the golden age of the archtop, that curious half-explained period beginning in the mid- to late twenties when the banjo fell hard from popularity, possibly because its strident tones couldn't match the greater variety of music the jazz bands were playing. Its seat in the rhythm section was taken by quiet guitar guys playing *chunk-chunk-chunk-chunk* in sevenths and ninths, barely audible to the audience but providing the rest of the band with a steady beat and a kind of weblike sonic texture that pulled the whole tune together.

"When the archtop guitar was created and developed," Green wrote, "it was the rhythm heart of the big bands. The warmth and depth of a good flat top was fine with soloists or string bands, but those overtones turn to mush when playing the 3 and 4 note rhythm chords up the neck." In other words, the flattop sound was too bassy and too complex. "The midrange bark of an archtop fills a unique place in the sonic spectrum of the rhythm section, between the bass and piano, and gives life and flex and a heartbeat to the band as Freddie Greene proved with Basie."

I had to take all this on faith until I finally got to play a Linda Manzer archtop at a guitar festival. I'd only ever seen her work in photos, or heard people talk about it in the reverent tones usually reserved for very old Chinese vases with dragons on 'em. According to report, they fingerpick very well. They flatpick very well. They take jazz like a good lawn takes croquet.

Players play Manzers. Collectors collect Manzers. Bruce Cockburn has four. Pat Metheny said of one of her acoustics, "This is the best guitar I've ever played," but that was just the beginning. "When you first receive her guitar," Metheny went on, a man bewitched, "you will love it like you never loved anything before. But that same guitar will sound twenty times as good ten years later than it does when it is brand new. Do you think you will be able to stand it?" His latest CD, *One Quiet Night*, consists of him noodling at home all evening on his new Manzer long-scale baritone guitar—a process akin to elegant melodic salivating. The guitar sounds as if it comes with its own cathedral.

Linda had three guitars on display at her table: a steel-string concert-style model, a baritone—that is, a model with a longer scale and deeper sound—and a jazz-style archtop. A fourth was outside, being played by God.

The guitars resisted the urge to trumpet their expensive woods; they were elegant rather than showy. They had the unself-conscious symmetry of trees, or Bentleys. Her archtop had the clean simplicity of a classical guitar. Its f-holes were suggested rather than copied; they were like the lines around the mouth of an old woman who in her lifetime had smiled a lot.

All right, I thought, but how do they play? How do they sound? How is the intonation? How was the balance between treble, mid-range, and bass? How is the action—easy or stiff?

I started to play, but I'll never be able to answer those questions. It wasn't like playing a guitar. It was like being dipped in melted chocolate.

# The Modern Age

There are troublemakers who argue that everything important that happened to the guitar happened in the 1930s, and by the end of that decade the guitar had gone from being a nineteenth-century instrument to a modern instrument in just ten years.

This is wildly inaccurate. Everything important that happened to the guitar actually happened between 1928 and 1941, and the guitar went from being a nineteenth-century instrument to a modern instrument in just fourteen years.

## January 1928

Segovia played his first concert in the United States. The guitar had been largely absent from the concert stage for decades, dismissed as a trivial instrument, a kind of Spanish kazoo. Olin Downes, writing in considerable astonishment in the *New York Times*, described the guitarist as "the dreamer or scholar in bearing, long hair, eye-glasses, a black frock coat and neckwear of an earlier generation. He seats himself, thoughtfully, places his left foot on its rest, strikes a soft chord, then bends over his guitar and proceeds to play like the poet and master he is of that instrument."

Downes went back to see Segovia again, as if he couldn't trust his eyes, or his memory: "The guitar had a hundred colors, a hundred voices, including the human voice. . . . Now one heard a distant shadowy thrumming, from which a solo voice emerged, in dramatic recitative. Always the voice was a little subdued, a little ghostly, an echoing voice that might have sounded through the dust of the grave and the reveries of many ages. Or there was the spangled brilliancy and flicker, pride of race, pride of the body, the throb of the dance."

In 1928 there was no such phrase as "classical guitar," and it would be at least half a century before the instrument was taken seriously in classical music circles, but the fact that this slow rise to eminence happened at all was due to Segovia. He was not necessarily the greatest guitarist of his time (many consider Llobet and Barrios at least his equal) but he was the greatest evangelist for the Spanish guitar, especially in the United States, and over the next forty years he would take the country, and the world, by force.

## 1928

Eddie Lang started writing the book of jazz guitar. Every so often, you come across an extraordinary moment when you can hear someone mining, step by step, an entirely new gallery of expression for the guitar. Uniquely, Eddie Lang (whose birthname was Salvatore Massaro) did that twice—once with Joe Venuti, the violinist, and once with another guitarist: Lonnie Johnson.

Lang had actually invented jazz guitar back in 1922 in the men's room of a restaurant in Atlantic City when he and his childhood friend and partner in crime Joe Venuti took breaks from playing mazurkas and polkas on stage and began improvising in the privacy of the restroom. Starting around 1928, though, Lang became the first guitarist the jazz guys would listen to and respect. Marty Grosz, a guitar student of Lang's with a turn of phrase like a Brooklyn philosopher, said that although Lang's rhythm was a little erratic ("He sounded like a guy running with a pie in his pants") he was the first guitarist to bring all the sensibility and skill of the classical guitarists (he adored Segovia and recorded Rachmaninoff's "Prelude in C♯ Minor") to the popular art of jazz. He played, Grosz said, in the "simplest yet most eloquent manner, blue and melancholy as hell. It is very difficult to play lead as simply and directly as that and make it come to life, especially on guitar. Here is the real genius of Sal Massaro. This is the honest bread stick."

Lang's duets with Venuti were recorded on and off between 1926 and 1933. They begin almost painfully, but by the end a new musical form is up and running. At first Lang does little more than the other rhythm guitarists of his day, playing chords threaded together with little ascending or descending runs of only a handful of notes. By the end, though, he is playing solo phrases and passages, throwing in off-the-beat chordings and off-the-melody elaborations. He is the one giving each duet its conception and narrative, and his sense of harmony creates the emotional landscape of the tune. Some are little more than throwaway ideas, but as they go on Lang and Venuti are clearly starting to think less of a tune and more of a composition. The jazz guitar and jazz violin don't sound like the odd couple any more; they sound like childhood friends.

Lonnie Johnson, a dapper, almost delicate man with a pencil mustache, was an extraordinary figure in the evolution of the American guitar, both heroic and tragic. After his early success in New Orleans and London and then the loss of his family, he moved to St. Louis, where Okeh Records ran a blues contest at the Booker T. Washington Theater. Johnson entered and won—won, he said, every week for eighteen weeks. He became in great demand as a recording artist and accompanist, able to play clean, delicate blues lines that worked with the rawest of blues shouters and the most sophisticated of jazz players. In his recordings with Armstrong and Ellington it's fascinating to hear the space and the respect they gave him; it was said that he was the first guitarist to make the blues guitar more than just a backing but an instrument in its own right.

Johnson's duets with Lang have the slightly stiff air of two people inventing ways to overcome their differences, but as with the Lang-Venuti duets they are groundbreaking stuff. Lang mostly plays chords, and as usual his rhythm is slightly pedestrian (not so much running with a pie in his pants here as walking with a peanut in his shoe) but his ear for harmony is exquisite; he creates the orchestra within which Johnson can improvise. Lonnie is both light and a little careful, but his bluesy feeling is infectious. He loosens Lang, and by extension the jazz guitar tradition; Lang gives complexity and thoughtfulness to the blues tradition. At times, the best of times, each man plays away from his own strengths and takes more chances, and they lift each other so much you can't tell which is which.

Johnson went on playing his cultured nightclub jazz-inflected blues, but his was an up and down life. He went through good years of recording and admiration, and lean years of working for a railroad-tie manufacturer and later as a janitor at the Benjamin Franklin Hotel, Philadelphia. When he was "rediscovered" in 1960 as part of the folk/blues revival, he was a disappointment: instead of being a rootsy Mississippi howler he had remained as deft a nightclub jazz/blues player as ever; his favorite song was "Red Sails in the Sunset." In the end, he moved to Canada.

Lang's own end was more sudden and more absurd, in the existential sense, than tragic. He developed tonsillitis in 1933, by which time he was at the top of his tree, working with Bing Crosby. Crosby urged him to have his tonsils out; Lang agreed. Under anaesthetic he developed an embolism and died without regaining consciousness. The honest bread stick was gone.

# 1929

A banjo player named Perry Bechtel went to Martin Guitars and asked them to build him a longer-necked guitar. As a banjo player he was used to a lot of frets; virtually every guitar of the day had only twelve frets before the neck hit the body, and he felt cramped. The longer neck, he suggested to Frank Henry Martin, would make the guitar more versatile, more appealing to players in jazz bands who were doubling on, or making the switch from, banjo. Martin built him a fourteen-fret model, calling it the Orchestra model—jazz orchestra, that is, not classical. The fourteen-fret concept was so popular that it became the standard for American steel-string acoustic guitars.

## 1929

A wave of immigrants from Mexico revived Mexican-Californian music and culture. By 1929 over a hundred thousand newcomers from Mexico filled a vacuum in labor in Los Angeles; many were also escaping the turmoil of the Mexican Revolution of 1911–17. Their welcome was not a warm one: job discrimination was common, forcing them to work at or below subsistence levels. Death rates among Mexicans were twice those among whites; infant mortality was three times higher. To survive, Mexican *colonias* in rural areas and *barrios* in cities developed as centers for Mexican immigrants and Mexican-Americans, and in these cultural oases the traditional *corrido*, or ballad, not only flourished but was constantly adapted and updated to encompass contemporary hardships, very much like blues in black communities and folk ballads in poor white regions. Touring guitar professionals from Central America and South America made regular stops in Los Angeles, and Spanish-language radio and recording industries began to develop during the twenties and thirties.

In smaller towns, Latino and Latina musicians played wherever their compatriots gathered. Lydia Mendoza, who would go on to become a successful radio and recording singer/guitarist on both sides of the border, began playing twelve-string guitar with her family in restaurants and barbershops in the Lower Rio Grande Valley, and by the early thirties they found themselves in San Antonio.

"We kept on struggling for two years, singing in the Plaza de el Zacate. That [square] doesn't exist any more—they tore it down. It was a huge open-air market. In the evenings from midnight on it was the market

where all the produce trucks from the valley and everywhere would arrive. This went on from midnight until about ten or eleven in the morning. Then they'd leave, and the market would stay empty awhile. Then
around seven in the evening all the folks who were going to sell food
there would come in and set up restaurant tables. Each stand would set
up its tables and sell chili con carne, enchiladas, and tamales—there
were lots of them. There would be about twenty on each side, with a
space down the middle where cars would come with people wanting to
eat or hear songs, for there were a lot of groups singing in those years. . . .
That was where we made our living."

The recording companies began the same process of exploitation
among the Spanish-speaking musicians that was so successful for them
among rural blacks and poor whites. Lalo Guerrero, a guitarist/satirist/
singer/composer/bandleader who in 1991, at the age of seventy-five, received a National Heritage Award from the National Endowment for the
Arts, gave a depressingly familiar account of the business relationship.

> I got paid fifty dollars a side, one hundred dollars a record. In
> a session I'd do two records, so I'd make two hundred dollars a
> session, and they wouldn't pay us royalties . . . Hey, we argued
> about royalties. "No, no royalties," and rather than not record
> at all, we went along . . . because I was making a name, that
> was what I cared about . . . But what the heck, every time I'd
> get two hundred dollars I'd buy my wife a washing machine, a
> dryer; you know, it was good for me because we weren't
> making that much money. . . . I didn't realize how much
> money [Imperial Records] were making until years later when
> Manuel Acuna, who was the A&R man there, told me. He
> says, "You know how much they used to make on your records?
> One of your records would produce as much as two or three
> hundred thousand dollars."

When Fats Domino and T-Bone Walker became best sellers for
Imperial, the company shifted its emphasis to black music and deleted
its Mexican recording catalog.

"They canceled all of us Chicanos out," Guerrero said. "[T]hose guys made a fortune . . . to the extent that after they got the black groups, they went higher and dropped all the Latinos or the Chicanos, and then they sold the label . . . for a million dollars, something that started with us Chicanos."

# 1929

The first singing cowboys hit the road. Otto Gray was rising from his early career as a vaudeville-style trick roper to become the front man of what was probably the first full-time professional cowboy band: Otto Gray and His Oklahoma Cowboys. "Their fame spread rapidly," Doug Green wrote in his fine book *Singing in the Saddle,* "and from 1929 through 1932 they tirelessly toured and broadcast in the Northeast. Traveling in huge sedans outfitted to look like railroad locomotives, complete with cowcatchers, the group became a success on the theater circuits of the era due to their dramatic showmanship—with whip and rope tricks in addition to music—their flashy costumes, and the visual humor and wide variety of their musical material."

In 1930 the first singer-guitarist found the true spiritual home of the singing cowboys: on the air. A popular NBC radio series, "Death Valley Days," featured John White as the Lonesome Cowboy with his guitar. When silent films gave way to "talkies," the corral gate was open, and every bunkhouse had a hand who played guitar and sang. Even Marion Morrison, better known as John Wayne, was cast in a series of B westerns as a character called Singing Sandy, though Wayne couldn't sing to save his life, and so had his songs dubbed.

The singing cowboy's role in movies rapidly expanded, for the most Hollywood of all reasons: money. Cowboy guitarist Buck Jones explained, "They use songs to save money on horses, riders, and ammunition. Why, you take Gene Autry and lean him up against a tree with his guitar and let him sing three songs and you can fill up a whole reel without spending any money."

Jones didn't pick the example of Gene Autry at random. Autry wasn't a cowboy at all, but a railroad telegraph operator, fired for playing his guitar on the job. In the late twenties he began a career as a singer/guitarist/yodeler in the Jimmie Rodgers mold, and over the next decade he dominated popular culture in a way that is barely imaginable today. By the mid-thirties Autry was already starring on a Sears-sponsored show called "Conqueror Record Time," in which he played a singing cowboy. He appeared regularly on "National Barn Dance," broadcast nationally over the NBC network, and had a gold record with "That Silver-Haired Daddy of Mine." He also toured constantly, often playing at rodeos in which he prudently owned stock. By 1935 he was appearing in a twelve-part western–sci-fi cliffhanger radio serial called *The Phantom Empire* in which he—that is, Gene Autry, radio star and singing cowboy—descended every episode into the bowels of the earth to battle aliens and then made it back to the surface in order to do his weekly radio broadcast.

By then he had begun appearing in movies for Republic at the now unthinkable rate of roughly one a month. The theme song for his first full-length feature, *Tumbling Tumbleweeds,* became Autry's second million-seller—and this during the Depression. Between 1934 and 1954 Autry made ninety films. Later there would be yet more star vehicles, such as a radio show called "Melody Ranch" that aired on CBS from 1940–1956, presenting the familiar formula of music, comedy, and a brief drama in which Autry saved the day. In 1942, the producers even arranged that Autry would be inducted into the military as a sergeant in the U. S. Army Air Corps during a "Melody Ranch" episode.

As Doug Green says, Autry (and many of the other characters created for the movies' singing cowboys) "embodied a charming Depression fantasy—troubles and problems could be dispelled with songs, good cheer, and innocent honesty." If the singing cowboys (and cowgirls) in general gave the guitar a place in America's greatest mythic panorama, Autry gave the guitar something else it had never had before, even in the cultures where it was as commonplace as a table. Autry gave the guitar star quality. People bought guitars, or bugged their parents to buy them guitars, not just because they wanted to play music but because they wanted to feel like heroes.

One company that was very aware of this connection was Sears, Roebuck. Sears had already developed an interlocking enterprise that combined every aspect of musical advertising, production, marketing, and sales. Sears owned the powerful radio station WLS ("World's Largest Store") in Chicago, which broadcast the "National Barn Dance," on which Autry became a star. Sears also sold Victrolas, Silvertone records, and radios, so it could put its artists on the radio to be heard in homes on Silvertone radio sets, thus creating the demand for Silvertone records, which would be played on Sears phonographs. Sears, which also owned the Harmony guitar company, brought out the Gene Autry Roundup guitar for under ten dollars and helped publish two Autry songbooks. Other "cowboy" guitars followed, many with campfire or mountain scenes painted or stenciled on the belly. It was the image that was the point, after all.

When Autry quit Republic in 1937, his place as studio singing cowboy was taken by Len Slye, who changed his name to Roy Rogers. Autry and Rogers, though, were just the biggest draws in a crowd of singing cowboy stars: Eddie Dean, Rex Allen, Monte Hale, Tex Hill, Tex Ritter, Jimmy Wakely. The dry hills around Los Angeles were alive with the sounds of guns firing blanks, and music.

Specifically, guitar music. The photographs (most of which are publicity stills) included in *Singing in the Saddle* illustate how central, prominent, and ubiquitous the guitar was, how important to the identity of the singing cowboy. As far as I can make out the photos feature the following instruments.

| | |
|---|---|
| upright bass | 22 |
| fiddle | 22 |
| accordion | 10 |
| harmonica | 0 |
| mandolin | 0 |
| piano | 1 |
| clarinet | 2 |

| banjo | 3 |
| unidentified | 3 |
| guitar, Spanish-style or steel | 99 |

There may be some selection bias in the choice of photos—after all, Doug Green is a guitarist, with a fondness for the big old Strombergs of the acoustic swing era—but, even so, this is a landslide win.

It bears repeating that the guitar rose to preeminence in the United States partly because of physical changes in the instrument, partly because of developments in skill and repertoire, but largely because it became associated with popular and financially viable myths. The cowboy was invented, for the most part, long after the West was settled, which is why so many western songs, like southern songs, are tinted with regret and loss. The guitar was hitched on his back to help give voice to the myth, and as the myth had to do with mobility and a hardscrabble working life, it had to be sung to a folk instrument, portable, expressive, and cheap. It's fascinating to look at the guitar's competitor, the piano, in westerns: it's an eastern instrument, prissy, immobile, plunked by a comic character in a saloon and just waiting to be busted up when the barroom brawl breaks out. I can't think of a single western in which a song sung to a piano means a damn thing.

## 1931

Martin relaunched the dreadnought. The original dreadnought was an oddity, a big, strangely shaped, boomy creature codesigned by Martin and a manager of the Ditson music stores and introduced in 1916 under the Ditson brand name. Dreadnoughts, nowadays often called dreads, didn't catch on for years, and Ditson went out of business in the late twenties. In 1931 Martin incorporated the dreadnought into its line of guitars, and in time it became immensely popular in the hands of string-band players and cowboy singers. By the sixties it was a staple in country music, folk, and bluegrass.

In the same year, the first production electric guitars went on the market. Electric guitars are the grassy knoll of guitar history: everyone has a theory about what happened, in what order, many of them involving conspiracies.

The basic point is this: the Hawaiian boom produced a crisis for the guitar. For the first time, audiences en masse wanted to hear individual notes being played on a featured instrument that was too quiet for its venues. The guitar, it's worth saying again, is by nature an intimate creature, suitable for rooms of, say, four hundred square feet—smaller, if anyone is talking. Not only were dance bands of the twenties packing 'em in, but the hot instrument, the steel guitar, was played flat on the lap, singing upward toward the rafters.

All kinds of solutions were tried. Guitars with hollow necks, to increase the cavity size. Guitars with horns attached. Beautiful, weird, art deco, all-metal guitars looking like miniature versions of the Chrysler building, with resonating aluminum cones set into the body—the so-called resophonic guitars made by the Dopera brothers and the metalworker Adolph Rickenbacker under the National and Dobro brands, later revived as the bluegrass instrument called the dobro.

The first experiments in electrical amplification used microphones and the house PA system, if it had one.

"We were . . . the first [Cajun] band to use amplification," said Luderin Darbone of the Hackberry Ramblers.

I had a service station in Hackberry and I got a catalog from which I could buy things wholesale. . . . In the catalog there was a speaker and an amplifier . . . and a microphone. We had never seen this used. But when we played in these dance halls, we'd get big crowds, and a fiddle with two guitars and no amplifiers—you can imagine how it sounded if you had 100 couples dancing. They couldn't hear us on the other end— they could hear the beat of our feet. The guitarists had these guitars with these big steel plates to make them louder. And on my fiddle I had my bridge cut in the middle and I used number fifty thread on my bow to make it louder. And you talk about break some strings[!] . . . but it sounded loud. When I got this catalog, I thought an amplifier would help the singer. Floyd Rainwater didn't need an amplifier. He could sing in here and you'd hear him across the road. But the others—myself and Duhon and Sonnier—our voices didn't carry like his did.

The amplifier came in and we played a dance with it at the Evangeline oilfield. And man, the people couldn't understand that. Even the fiddle and the guitars were carrying. . . . [W]e played in Morse, in Mermentau, five places each week, and the people would really come to see that. They couldn't understand it.

The problem was, the electrified string band spread faster than electricity itself. Although nearly 90 percent of urban dwellers had electricity by the 1930s, only 10 percent of rural dwellers did.

"You had to play where they had electricity, and in those days it wasn't every club who had electricity," Luderin Darbone recalled. "I heard that a fellow in Rayne made these generators for automobiles so that we could play in some of these country halls and use the amplifier. I had to run the car . . . so he built me a generator and I had to loosen the thing up and use the belt from the car to run the generator. That was hard on the automobile."

A microphone set up right in front of, or even inside, the guitar tended to feed back horribly. What was needed was a pickup activated by the movement of the metal strings through a magnetic field, which unlike a microphone would remain unaffected by the background noise all around the guitarist, though it would turn out that any unshielded electric motor operating nearby would make the amplifier hum.

Several individuals and companies tinkered with pickups through the twenties—one was the victim of industrial espionage; one may have designed a working pickup but then applied it to that dodo of popular instruments, the viola—but when the dust settled, a Los

Angeles–based steel-guitar player named George Beauchamp took the pickup he had made on his kitchen table to Adolph Rickenbacker, who reportedly said, "If we make this one work, we'll make a lot of money and put the Dopera brothers out of business."

Accustomed to working in metal, Rickenbacker made the prototype out of cast aluminum, and in 1931 he unveiled the world's first production model aluminum electric steel guitar, a strange creature with an endearing ugliness that looked a little like a badly squashed banjo and was immediately dubbed the Frying Pan. It came with an amplifier barely bigger than a shoe box; amplifiers would remain the runts of the system for another thirty years.

The Frying Pan didn't sell well at first, but it immediately attracted imitators. These had the paradoxical effect of promoting Rickenbacker's instrument, which was launched nationally in 1935 as the Electro. It cost $150, a stunning amount at the time, when the hall of fame steel guitarist Jerry Byrd bought his in 1937, but to him it was "this beautiful instrument . . . shiny black with curved silver plates on the top. Brand new, with green plush lining in the case. That thing just knocked me backwards."

This is how popular Hawaiian music and, more broadly, the steel guitar were at the time: in 1950 Rickenbacker would claim that his company alone had sold a million instruments.

## 1932

Milton Brown formed his Musical Brownies, and when Bob Dunn joined them shortly afterward, that amazing blend of string-band jazz later called western swing was born.

Robert Lee Dunn was born in Oklahoma in 1908, developed an early interest in Hawaiian music, and learned by a correspondence course— a remarkably common and popular option at the time and more or less the only option for beginners living in rural areas—offered by the famous Walter Kolomoku. Two things made Bob Dunn unusual and, later, important. The first was that he also played jazz trombone, in the spirit of Jack Teagarden. The second was an encounter when Dunn was working solitary gigs on the Boardwalk at Coney Island in New York.

"While he was doing this," a friend said of Dunn, "he ran into this black guy who was playing a steel guitar with a homemade pickup attached to it. He had this thing hooked up through an old radio or something and was playing these blues licks."

Dunn immediately thought jazz. He was fooling around on guitar, trying to play a piece that he'd heard three saxophones play, then began experimenting with simple triad passages patterned after three saxophones or three of most anything, trombones for instance. He tried adding occasional single-note passages, then moved on to combinations of one, two, and three voices. The steel guitar, he realized, would add an entirely different color to jazz, just as the violin did in the hands of a Joe Venuti.

Like a trombonist, he played single notes very expressively in lower registers, avoiding the saccharine Hawaiian harmonies. Crisp, short phrases, almost breaths or blasts. Delicate little fills. Bluesy slides, but never clichés. It's often been said that Charlie Christian was the first person to phrase a guitar like a horn, but the people who say that are usually those who sneer at western swing as a hillbilly genre. Bob Dunn played phrases that sounded like all sorts of things; a horn was certainly one of them.

When Brown died in 1936 from injuries received from a car crash, Bob Wills became the default leader of western swing. (Dunn retired to teaching soon afterward.) Wills's cry, "Take it away, Leon!" introduced Leon McAuliffe, the second great electric guitarist.

Like Bob Dunn, McAuliffe had little interest in playing the lush harmonies of Hawaiian style, but he was perhaps less of a jazz soloist than Dunn. At times he sounds like a blues-rock six-string, at times like a ragtime banjo, at times like an ethereal whisper. One of his astonishing achievements was his precision. It takes a lot of experience and precise hands and ears to hit a note exactly right on a steel, given that it lacks frets, but McAuliffe played his as if it were a Telecaster, using the steel to create slurs that sound very much like the bent notes that the blues electric guitarists in Chicago would develop twenty years later.

The western swing guitarists wrote the first editions of the electric guitar book, the Dobro book, and the pedal-steel guitar book. They also provided crucial continuity between the Hawaiian boom, which first presented the guitar as the featured band instrument, and rock and roll, which deified it. Without Bob Dunn and Leon McAuliffe, the guitar might have shrunk back to the rhythm seat, the strummer's spot.

Still, the Western swing band had to work damn hard to get ahead, especially in taxi-dance joints like the Tokio Club in Hobbs, New Mexico. A taxi-dancer was a woman hired by the song to take a guy around the dance floor—an arrangement that meant it was in the management's interests for the band to play as many songs as they knew as quickly as possible. Almost no solos, no breaks between sets, only a four-beat breather between one ninety-second song and the next, and they were expected to keep up this frantic rate all night: at the Tokio Club, the band would make an extra dollar apiece if they were still playing when the sun came up.

## Depression Years

"The Depression," a guitar historian told me," was a terrible time for the guitar," adding that new guitar sales nearly dried up altogether. Yet the Depression was actually a landmark time for the guitar, even though high-end instruments sold so poorly that Martin might not have survived had it not also made ukuleles, which were riding a wave of popularity and also were considerably cheaper than their larger cousins.

The Depression was good for the guitar because people needed it and realized how much it meant to them. Woody Guthrie, riding the rails, and a series of folklorists, recording interviews and songs at the miserable, dusty migrant workers' camps, testified to the life-giving, soul-saving qualities of dancing to a cheap guitar and a battered fiddle, or two young girls with one guitar singing "It Takes a Worried Man" to a crowd of hundreds, desperate for the solace of live music.

Besides which, the Depression brought out the best of American ingenuity in many ways, one of which was instrument building. The *New York Times* reported that when a certain Mike Quint of Ness City, Kansas, had his hours cut back by the creamery at which he worked, he turned his hand to making violins, mandolins, guitars, and even a cello, using only a jackknife and a combined chisel/rasp. "He says a secret treatment," wrote the reporter, leaving volumes unsaid, "makes any wood usable for violins."

Musicians didn't fit the one-face-fits-all sameness of modern commercial musicians, either. When John Lomax was recording in Louisiana in the thirties, for example, he found Ovide, an accordion player who also sang; a blind Cajun minstrel; a four-foot hunchback—"a merry old maid of forty-five years"—and a guitar used in possibly a unique musical combination: "a rural quartet of accordion, violin, guitar, and 'iron,' the latter played (or struck) by a sad-eyed little boy."

## Circa 1934

Americans started to hear recordings by the first of the two great jazz guitarists: Django Reinhardt, possibly the most extraordinary musician of the century.

Jean Reinhardt, called Django (the *D* is silent), was the Paganini or the Liszt of the guitar, larger than life, larger than several lives. Immensely proud, generous, superstitious, utterly unreliable, a compulsive gambler, almost illiterate yet able to compose not only for the guitar but for an orchestra, at one point he abandoned the guitar and took up painting. He was born into a wandering troupe of Gypsy musicians/dancers/acrobats near Charleroi, in Belgium, in 1910. When he was twelve, already musical, already brilliant at billiards, he was given a banjo-guitar and played it constantly, learning voraciously. At one point he went off with a hunchback called Lagardere who played the guitar and didn't return home for three days. By thirteen he was playing duets in a dance hall with an accordion player, by now aware of American music, especially jazz. When Django was seventeen, playing in nightclubs and winning banjo contests, the famous English bandleader Jack Hylton invited the scruffy young Gypsy to join his orchestra, which might have been an interesting disaster, but it never happened. Django was trapped in his caravan when it caught fire, covering himself with a blanket he held in his left hand. He survived, but the hand was horribly burned and crippled and the right side of his body was burned from knee to waist.

Django was bedridden for eighteen months and had constant nightmares about fire, but he began playing the guitar again, even with his left hand still bandaged. By sheer willpower he taught himself to walk and to play again, though the little finger and ring finger of his left hand were permanently curled to such a degree that he could use them only for simple chords on the first two strings. By the early thirties he was playing with the best jazz players in Paris, or Cannes, or wherever he and his brother Joseph happened to wander next. In 1933 he began playing with the conservatory-trained violinist Stéphane Grappelli, who had been supporting himself by playing piano in pit orchestras and jazz violin wherever he could get an audience. In 1934 they combined with Joseph Reinhardt, plus a bass player and a third rhythm guitarist, to form the Quintet of the Hot Club of France.

The music they played wasn't squarely in the jazz tradition—there's blues in there but no horns, and the atmosphere of old Europe cafés mixed with eastern scales—but it was squarely in the jazz spirit of surprise and invention. Above all—and this is perhaps its most enduring quality—Django's playing was playful. Even with only two fingers he could play faster chromatic runs—in other words, runs that took in every single fret, rather than mere scales—than anyone on the planet, but he never played them for their own sake, just to be flashy. He threw them in as decorations or flourishes, even as jokes; they have a Spike Jones quality about them. He often seemed to be deliberately making fun of the solid 4/4 beat by playing another equally convincing series of off-beats. He flirted with expected resolutions. Like Fats Waller, or like a traveling klezmer band, his playing was irrepressibly cheerful, and even in the most melancholy or tender song he was likely to throw out an almost outrageous flourish, like a priest intoning a Te Deum and suddenly producing from behind his back a huge bunch of brightly colored paper flowers.

At the time, American listeners were struck mostly by Django's astonishing speed, yet he was also the most romantic jazz player. When he ran into Lucille Armstrong, the wife of Django's hero Louis Armstrong, in the south of France in 1951, Lucille's friend wrote "Django seemed nervous and over-anxious . . . probably because of who Lucille was. . . . He patted Lucille's arm and behaved almost like he was smitten with her. And when he played for her, the tenderness that came out in his music was like a man stroking a woman's breast."

## December 31, 1934

John and Alan Lomax brought Leadbelly to New York, effectively beginning the folk music revival.

In mid-September 1934 John Lomax, who had already made a name for himself by collecting and publishing American folk songs especially from the South and West, sent a telegram to Huddie (pronounced Hugh-dee) Ledbetter, whom Lomax and his son Alan had "discovered" and recorded in 1933 at Angola State Prison Farm in Louisiana. Ledbetter, better known as Leadbelly, was released for good behavior in 1934 and was interested in pursuing a musical career. The Lomaxes, too, were interested in Leadbelly's musical career, though it's unlikely both sides had the same thing in mind. In ways both intended and unintended, the telegram set the tone for the entire folk movement the Lomaxes threw into gear. It read: COME PREPARED TO TRAVEL. BRING GUITAR.

The modern folk boom was crucial because it put guitars in the hands of large numbers of white middle-class Americans for the first time in more than half a century. It was the product of two initiatives: the end-of-the-nineteenth-century vogue for folklore, manifest chiefly in "spirituals" and ballad collecting, and the fascinating Roosevelt-era programs under whose auspices American artists, writers, photographers, and musicians traveled in search of America—an America that had been neglected, abused, taken for granted. A folk.

The word "folk" had a kind of heat to it, a political agenda, to be sure, but also an evangelical passion. America's poor and its working people were in need of help. The question was, what could music do about it? Cataloging, recording, and publishing "folk" songs might be some kind of antidote to the popcorn of Tin Pan Alley, but in sad fact it didn't change much. No, the folk had to be brought to face the public—that is, the white public of the North.

To John Lomax, the noncommercial music of all rural southerners, including African-Americans, was folk music. From the beginning, then, what we now think of as "blues" was embraced by the folk revivalists along with noncommercial rural white music. (Oddly, Hispanic and Native-American music seem to have featured very little in the folk revival.) What an educational act it would be, then, to bring a powerful black singer of folk songs to New York to show people what was really going on in this vast nation!

After three months of travel in the South, using Leadbelly as an "in" to gather more folk songs from African-Americans in several states, Lomax presented Leadbelly to, of all gatherings, the Modern Language Association convention in Philadelphia, whose chair had "welcomed your generous suggestion that your talented aboriginal 'nigger' sing for the guests." Leadbelly, not to be suppressed, passed the hat and made $47.46—nearly $700 today.

In New York, people seemed more fascinated by the fact that Leadbelly was a murderer than that he was a musician. One observer wrote, "His way before an audience [was] to sit quiet and relaxed, this man of terrible energy, turning over in his mind God alone knows what thoughts; then at the signal, to let loose his hands and his voice. He crouched over his guitar as he played, . . . and he sang with an intensity and passion that swayed audiences who could not understand a single word of his songs. His eyes were tight-shut so that between his eyebrows there appeared deep furrows of concentration curving back like devil's horns." He drew audiences everywhere he went, and mesmerized them, but sold few records. He did, however, bring the twelve-string guitar to the broad public for the first time, playing it tuned down a couple of steps and getting a deep, booming sound that most people had never heard. Gene Autry, amazingly, dressed all in white, visited Ledbetter in New York to check out his twelve-string.

All in all, Leadbelly was more of a novelty than a world changer, but once white America had recovered from the initial shock, he played occasionally on the radio, appearing often with Woody Guthrie, and his songs began to be adopted by a new breed of musician: folksingers. In the late thirties and early forties New York started to become a center for folk musicians and people who believed in the political importance of folk music. Alan Lomax, politically much more radical than his father, settled there with leftish musicians such as Aunt Molly Jackson, Sarah Ogan Gunning and Jim Garland from Kentucky, Pete Seeger, Josh White, and Guthrie.

In 1940 Woody Guthrie released "Dust Bowl Ballads," and in 1941 Pete Seeger, Lee Hays, and Mill Lampell formed the Almanac Singers, soon joined by Guthrie. They sang in union halls and May Day rallies, moving the social activism up a gear. It was not enough to collect songs of solidarity in the face of oppression. You had to go out and sing 'em.

## 1936

Gibson began turning out the first production version of a hollow-body electric guitar. The company had made its first electric the previous year, and like all production electrics it was a Hawaiian-style steel guitar called the E-150: E for "electric," 150 for the $150 it cost. Now Gibson took its L-50 acoustic and added a single-bar pickup, calling it the ES-150, for "electric Spanish." The concept of an amplified Spanish (i.e., standard acoustic) guitar was such a novelty that for decades the line would continue to be called ES to distinguish it from the EH, or Electric Hawaiian, line.

The first well-known guitarist to adopt the ES-150 was Eddie Durham, who had been going crazy trying to get more volume playing jazzy/bluesy lead figures with the Kansas City Six and subsequently became the first person (it is believed) to record electric guitar solos, in 1938. He also talked up the ES-150 to a certain Charlie Christian.

## August 16, 1939

Charlie Christian, wearing a purple shirt and bright yellow shoes, a huge hat, and a string tie, met Benny Goodman. It was the great musical entrepreneur/producer John Hammond's idea. Goodman had famously growled, "Who the hell wants to hear an electric guitar player?" It was Hammond, too, who snuck Christian onto the bandstand during a break while Goodman was off having dinner. But it was Christian who listened once through to a song he'd never heard before and played twenty-five choruses until the Beverly Hills restaurant crowd was on its feet.

"Christian," wrote Whitney Balliett, the dean of jazz critics, "singlehandedly changed the course of jazz." He didn't have Django's zest and exuberance, but he had cool, a kind of overarching, somewhat detached intelligence that stepped back from the tune and from the entire history of jazz guitar and came back in at an angle, and it was that angle that changed everything.

On "I Found a New Baby," for example, playing with the Benny Goodman Sextet with Count Basie, he lets the curiously old-fashioned song set itself up, sounding almost twenties-era in its chords and changes, and in comes old-fashioned Benny still playing as if it's 1933, nifty and nimble but kinda safe. And just as you're expecting a horn to come in, there's Charlie Christian playing with that smooth, almost too smooth tone, sounding more like the vibes than a gutsy sax, and just rippling coolly through his solo, throwing out phrases that jazz guitarists in brunch restaurants still throw out today. He throws in some unusual early-bebop intervals and then repeats them just to show us that he knows what he's doing, that in effect he's cooler than us, and plays those legato lines that go on longer than you'd expect and take in half of the next phrase too, hipper than the song, hipper than Benny. Then while the Count plays a chorus, also sounding a little dated, Charlie throws in little horn calls on single notes to show that even when he's out of the spotlight he doesn't just go back to the chair and play those Freddie Greene indentured *chunk-chunk* chords, though of course he certainly could if he chose. He is a free man.

On "Breakfast Feud" with the Benny Goodman Sextet, as soon as Christian takes a break and the massed horn chorus comes in, they sound out of date. They are the big band, which has only a few more years to live; he is the nightclub combo, which will take jazz out of the century.

Christian developed tuberculosis, like Jimmie Rodgers, and like Rodgers he refused to slow down or shut up. He died in March 1942 at the age of twenty-five. He left little information about his life, and relatively few recordings. Half his biography, though, is in an extraordinary photo taken at a recording session at Blue Note. He's sitting with a maple archtop Gibson on his knee, tipped slightly toward him, and he's playing something on one of the top two strings. But it's the nonmusical part that catches my eye. For a start, he's dressed in a tweed sport jacket, a tie, and a white shirt with a wide collar, a white handkerchief sprouting from his breast pocket; he looks like a hip young stockbroker, especially with his hair cut short and his rimless glasses. But it's his eyes that are unforgettable. He's looking off to his right, playing while he watches someone else, taking it in and making it up at the same time. His mouth is slightly open with concentration, but his eyes show an extraordinary alertness and intelligence. Nothing escapes him.

# 1941

Working in the Epiphone shop on Sundays when it was closed, Les Paul reinvented the solidbody guitar. Known as "the Log," it was more of a rhetorical than a musical device: it proved that you could put strings, a neck, and pickups on a four by four-inch post and it would still play like a guitar. This was in the great tradition of Antonio Torres making a guitar body out of papier-mâché and Bob Taylor making one out of pallet-grade oak in order to prove what was important about guitar design, and what wasn't.

Maybe this ugly lump of a thing looked too weird, or was too much like a primitive steel guitar slung over a shoulder, for people to be impressed. "I took the log into a club and played it—and they all laughed at me," Les Paul said later. "Hardly anyone applauded at all. So I went back down to Epiphone and put two sides of a butchered acoustic archtop on it and went back and stopped the show."

# Vacuum Packed

W hen I'm out of town Rick goes through a stage in the building process that I wish I had had the chance to see.

The top is now down to its final thickness of 121 thousandths. Rick cuts the braces, places each one on what looks like a large, abrasive pizza plate with a twenty-five-foot radius curve to it, and sands it so that it has a gentle curve to the face that will be glued against the top. When all is said and done, then, the top will have a gentle arch to it, like the upward arch of an unladen flatbed eighteen-wheeler truck. This is simple, but pure genius: it's so that when the guitar contracts and expands with the rise and fall of the ambient humidity, the top will rise and fall rather than being rigid, and cracking.

Even the process of gluing has a neat gimmickry to it, the kind of device-invention that is so perfect and satisfying when it works that some luthiers get sidetracked for weeks or even months inventing the perfect gadget. Gluing is a bear of a job—holding the constituent parts in the right places and exerting the right amount of pressure in the right spot and the right direction is a headache all woodworkers know. And what if you have a dozen or more different pieces of wood of differing heights running in different directions? Sheesh.

As soon as the braces are glued in place, the top goes right-side up onto the pizza plate, a rubberized cover goes over it, and the whole shebang is vacuum sealed. This technology alone saves an hour over the old paraphernalia of clamping.

When he's glued the braces he'll let them age a bit while he goes down to Maryland to run the annual Association of Stringed Instrument Artisans symposium. The guitar, he regrets, won't be ready for my birthday. I'm not worried. Watching him at work has been present enough. But it will, repeat *will*, be ready by the beginning of August, when Rick plans on showing some of his guitars at the festival in Healdsburg.

# Postwar Ennui

At this point, for the first time, I find my interest in my subjective and selective history of the guitar in the United States starting to flag. After the astonishing fertility of the thirties everything seems to fall flat.

Western swing and the singing cowboys were losing steam. Folk music, guitar in hand, took its first steps, but they were timid ones. The most popular folksinger was Burl Ives, whose repertoire was anything but radical: "I Know an Old Lady (Who Swallowed a Fly)," "Big Rock Candy Mountain," "Blue Tail Fly," and "Froggie Went a-Courtin'." The Weavers, postwar successors to the Almanac Singers, were surprised to have several hits, singing "Goodnight Irene," "So Long (It's Been Good to Know You)," "On Top of Old Smoky," and "Wimoweh." These may seem inoffensive songs, but the times were dark ones: the House Un-American Activities Committee was hounding anyone with the slightest shade of pink in their wardrobe, and folksingers were tantamount to communist agitators. Alan Lomax left for England in 1950, and when the Weavers were offered a TV show in the same year, the right-wing rag *Red Channels* attacked the group and the contract was torn up. This unacknowledged censorship of musicians such as Pete Seeger would continue for nearly two decades.

Of the two most successful folk songs of 1955, one was a faux-traditional ballad written in about twenty minutes as promotional filler by a Disney script writer who had never written a song in his life, "The Ballad of Davy Crockett." The other was Tennessee Ernie Ford playing Merle Travis's "Sixteen Tons," a grim account of life in the coal mines of Kentucky, where Travis had grown up, and an indictment of coal company labor practices. It spent ten weeks at number one on the country charts and eight weeks at number one on the pop charts. Yet it wasn't a traditional song—it was a commercial country hit, keeping alive, at least for a while, the country tradition of singing songs about real life no matter who it annoys.

Jazz underwent an astonishing metamorphosis. No sooner had the guitar, the perennial background instrument, reached spotlight status when the big bands died, the swing era ended, and the cooler bebop phase began. Charlie Christian, playing with Benny Goodman, had taken the soloing guitar into the national spotlight, but almost at once the spotlight began to fade.

It was a very confusing time for jazz guitarists. A lot of jazz bands, especially those consisting of older players, wanted nothing to do with the new jazz, and a lot of jazz guitarists were rhythm guys to the bone. They were used to being the musical and social lubrication of the band, the quiet one who kept everything together. It took a different personality to even think of playing solos. Besides, horn players were likely to be more than skeptical about a guitarist's ability to solo, so in many cases business continued more or less as usual, except for two changes: the rhythm guitarist was now almost certain to play an electric; and from then on jazz had a radical and experimental wing, and everything else was in danger of sounding dowdy.

At the same time, some guitarists began to work as featured players in smaller jazz combos that might be advancing the frontiers of jazz little by little, instead of radically, so the guitarist was free to follow the steady prewar development of the instrument. Oscar Moore, for example, played with shimmering delicacy with Nat Cole's trio, exploring more of a piano identity for his guitar than a series of attention-grabbing horn lines.

At the most aggressive end of the continuum, Charlie Christian had lit a fire under a lot of young ambitious guitarists but they faced the problems of trying to break into a small, new field with a new instrument.

It's easy to overlook how new and different an instrument the electric guitar was, and how mixed a blessing. An acoustic guitar had to be *attacked:* anyone playing with a pick played from the elbow, trying to use as high a percentage of downstrokes as possible for both volume and definition. Now the amplifier did all the hard work, and the electric guitar could be played from the wrist, which meant the pick could be used more quickly and delicately. Jazz players in particular took this to heart, and in their hands single-note playing on the guitar began to sound cooler and much more fluid; but what was gained in mechanical efficiency was lost in both the sound of the instrument and the excitement and drama of the attack. The electric could play single-note runs much more quickly, but just as in the late sixties with the superfast blues/rock guitarists such as Alvin Lee, and then with the "shred" guitarists of the eighties such as Steve Vai and Joe Satriani, it was possible to have too much of a good thing.

"The run became fashionable in jazz in the forties," wrote Whitney Balliett. "Propounded by Art Tatum and Charlie Parker and Dizzy Gillespie, the teeming run, ascending or descending, was taken up by every pianist, guitarist, trumpeter, and saxophonist. Some players used so many notes their solos resembled enormous glissandos. The individual note was sacrificed for babble, and silence, which allows music to breathe, vanished. Jazz began to sound harebrained."

The other problem the electric jazz guitar encountered was its sound. "The jazz players were playing Gibson guitars through Ampeg amps," explained Aaron Newman, former vice president of the Guild electronics division and an engineer specializing in guitar sound systems. "The original jazz guitar sound had no top at all. It was all bass and mid-range. They had crappy loudspeakers. They had no concept at all of the full range of the guitar—but that's what they knew as the sound of a jazz guitar, and that's what they came to want." The characteristic "cool" tone lacked punch, range, penetration—almost any kind of expressiveness, in fact. One critic called it a neon drone. Even the most skillful, imaginative players sounded emotionally monochromatic, the fault lying not with the guitarist but with the guitar, and the amp. It was said of amplification that it allowed the guitar to be played like a horn—in other words, in bursts of single notes—but it didn't have anything like the emotional expressiveness of a horn. Its timbre was limited, its volume was limited, the shapes of the individual notes tended to be all too similar.

The wise, sad player Wes Montgomery was so aware of the thinness of the guitar's voice that in the fifties he developed a technique of fattening and enriching a line by playing it simultaneously on two notes an octave apart, thus essentially playing two solos at once, a technique so demanding that every time he played it gave him headaches.

Yet this monochromatic sound became the defining sound of the jazz guitar for years, even decades, and it took a brave player (John Scofield, for example, or Jimi Hendrix, or, arguably, Frank Zappa) to mess with it.

In three utterly different areas, though, the guitar did show signs of growth, experiment, and risk. Classical guitar was getting organized, especially in New York City around the now-resident Segovia and in Los Angeles around the venerable but untiring Vahdah Olcott Bickford. Bickford (1885–1980) was an extraordinary figure. She had been taught at the turn of the century by Manuel Ferrer, and was thus almost the only torch-bearer of the old Mexican-American guitar tradition. She became a concert guitarist. She moved to New York and for a while lived in the Vanderbilt mansion and tutored two generations of Vanderbilt women. She took the name Vahdah on the advice of her astrologer. In 1923 she moved back to California and founded the first American classical guitar society. She composed and transcribed dozens of works, and became known as one of the very few classical guitarists of the time who could sight-read any score put in front of her. When she died she left a collection of American and foreign guitar music prints, manuscripts, journals, and letters so vast it took alternating crews of fifteen men, working five full days a week, two and a half weeks to remove.

New societies sprang up almost monthly in the major cities, offering an increasing number of concerts and classes. The classical guitar quarterly *Guitar Review* was founded in 1946, and is still being published today.

In 1947 another self-taught guitarist, as original and brilliant in his own way as Segovia, left Rio de Janeiro on a thirty-eight-hour plane journey to New York, and then another twelve-hour leg to California. His name, like many Brazilian names, was long: Laurindo José de Araujo Almeida Nobrega Neto. Unlike many Brazilians, he abbreviated it to not one name but two: Laurindo Almeida.

Born in a small coastal town in 1917, Laurindo Almeida taught himself to play the guitar, fought in a revolutionary army (at the age of fifteen), was wounded, met Brazil's foremost guitarist, Garoto (Anibal Augusto Sardinha, 1915–55), who was entertaining in the hospital, got a radio job in Rio as a musician and arranger at the age of eighteen, had his first pay packet stolen by his tenor guitarist, worked in clubs, wrote his own songs and led his own groups, worked with Brazil's top musicians, and played *viola* or *violao* (Portuguese for a standard guitar), *guitarra* or *bandolim* (a guitar-family instrument with six pairs of metal strings), four-string banjo, and *cavaquinho* (a small instrument like a ukulele).

When he was nineteen he landed a six-month job playing on a cruise ship to Europe in 1936. When the ship docked in France he saw Django Reinhardt and Stéphane Grappelli at the Hot Club in Paris, and became so entranced with Django's playing and the music of the French impressionist composers that he went back to Brazil playing choro and samba music incorporating ninth, eleventh, and thirteenth chords that were so foreign to Brazilian music that people called them "Japanese" chords. One of his songs, recorded by the Andrews Sisters and Jimmy Dorsey, among others, earned him a royalty check for $4,000 from RCA Victor, and he moved to California.

California had never seen anything like Laurindo Almeida, who played his own arrangements of Bach, Brazilian folk/popular styles such as the samba, choro, and baiao, a hybrid of several types of folk music of the Brazilian northeast, and also something that sounded like jazz unless you added Brazilian percussion, in which case it sounded like samba. He played with a pick, but he also played fingerstyle, and more often than not he played a Spanish-style guitar with the new nylon strings, like a classical player. Almeida introduced the subversive notion that classical guitar and jazz might not be so far apart after all, and that jazz might be played fingerstyle, on nylon strings—an approach picked up by Charlie Byrd, among others. He joined Stan Kenton's orchestra as its guitarist/arranger/composer, a role virtually unheard of in the United States at the time, and gave jazz new energy and a new direction by pointing it toward Latin America. He called it "samba-jazz"—music rich in percussion, played on a semi-percussive instrument. It all made a dawning kind of sense.

At the same time a revolution was taking place in Nashville. A recording center was developing, and for the first time a guitarist, Chet Atkins, was in a position of influence and power. Rural musics were being unified under the new heading of country and western, and as the guitar had become indispensible to both branches, Nashville became such a guitarist's mecca that by 1967 the Lovin' Spoonful could sing that there were 1,352 guitar pickers in town—a symbolic rather than a literal figure, but certainly far more than were working steadily in New York or Los Angeles.

It's a sign of how much better accepted the guitar was in Nashville than in the rest of the country that as late as the mid-sixties the top Hollywood studio musicians played, in ascending order of popularity, French horn, flute, percussion, sax, cello, viola, and, the most widely used instrument of the day . . . violin. There certainly were studio guitarists, such as the multitalented Jack Marshall, but they were hired sporadically on a per-job basis, and they would probably have come from a jazz background because they needed to be able to read music. Other musicians made their disdain for modern guitar music brutally clear: "Rock and roll, that's the lowest," said an unnamed studio musician. "You feel like a prostitute doing those types of dates. You come in there, and you're playing garbage, and you know that man's out to make money and he's selling crap to the teen market. That's probably the lowest form, the worst music."

Starting in postwar Nashville, studio guitarists, already becoming known for playing clean as country water, began to put other musicians, arrangers, and copyists out of work. "A typical pop session of the day used as many as thirty or forty instrumentalists at $41.25 for three hours," wrote Colin Escott in his biography of Hank Williams. "Before the session, an army of copyists was required to write out the arrangements, and a contractor had to be engaged to call everyone in. Then, typically, only one or two songs would be recorded during a session. In Nashville, most sessions used no more than six or seven musicians, arrangements were cooked up on the spot, no contractor was needed, and three or four songs were cut in three hours."

In the early fifties players in Nashville began tinkering with the steel guitar, adding pedals and knee levers to raise and lower the pitches of the strings. The result was the pedal steel, the most complex and demanding form of guitar, burdened with an almost infinite number of strings set in algebraically complex tunings in an effort to make the instrument sound sweet and simple. A commonly used form of steel had two necks, one tuned to chromatic E9 and the other to an extended C6. "Learning a pedal steel," said Marc Horowitz, who played steel professionally in New York for several years, "is like trying to be a log-roller while juggling full glasses of cognac and whistling Dixie naked."

In Los Angeles, Aaron Thibeaux Walker (everyone called him "T-Bone," which he hated) was inventing a type of music all his own, a kind of sophisticated nightclub R&B. Walker was a dandy, impeccably dressed, smile a mile wide, pencil mustache, hair brilliantined. When he first hit Los Angeles he made his living as a dancer, dancing on the tables, seizing the corner of the table in his mouth and whirling it around, and once he got a guitar job he transferred that show-manship to the stage, playing the guitar above his head, behind his back, doing the splits—exactly the kind of act that worked so well ten years later for Chuck Berry, who also borrowed a lot of T-Bone's guitar licks. (Berry's originality lay in being the first great rock and roll songwriter.)

Although in early recordings his electric guitar sometimes sounds as if it's being played from the bottom of a garbage can, Walker was clearly an uptown guy. His lyrics have a witty, ironic take on the music he's playing: "I woke up this morning / and I was in an awful mood." He sounds almost like Cole Porter writing a tongue-in-cheek blues. "It's a terminal thing / When you're in this world alone."

He brings in drums, a jaunty rhythm, a jazzy piano, and a horn section, but unlike most jazz of the time, the guitar is the lead in-strument, playing the breaks, stretching its legs. The chords, those sliding ninths, are mixed up in the front of the sound; the introductory phrase may well be a guitar phrase or series of lines, and these are almost always in his advanced-blues mode; and the featured solo(s) always include a guitar break.

This is a reason why people see T-Bone as one of the principal sources of rock and roll. He's too smart to be a rocker, and too complex, but with T-Bone, as in Nashville, *the guitar is in charge.* At last.

# Giblets

I e-mail Rick.

Can you let me know when you start working on the innards of the guitar, all those struts and bracings and giblets and whatnot? I know nothing about that stuff, which strikes me as sailing dangerously close to mere engineering, so I should see it in progress if poss.

"No," he replies, "that's where the art of luthierie, or at least the romance, is hidden. All those struts hold the beast together and make it sing."

The ribs around the lung.

# Killing for a Dime

Reading Francis Davis's *History of the Blues,* I come across two paragraphs that say almost everything you need to know about Chicago blues.

In 1954, when Aristocrat Records, soon to be renamed Chess, recorded and pressed Muddy Waters's second single, "I Can't Be Satisfied"/"I Feel Like Going Home," the records were loaded by hand into the trunk of a Chess employee's car, then driven around to 180 South Side outlets, not only record stores but five-and-dimes, beauty salons, and barber shops. Records weren't a special commodity, they were part of daily life, especially in the black community, and were sold practically everywhere people conducted trade. When a new record was brought around, the store owner took it out of the box and slapped it right on the turntable.

Davis writes,

Many stores had speakers over their doors or in their arcades, and you could tell right away if a record was a hit by the number of people it walked in the door. By mid-afternoon, it was virtually impossible to find a copy of Aristocrat 1305, and the Chess brothers were being bombarded with reorders they couldn't readily supply. Stores with copies still on hand began to limit sales to one a customer, in an attempt to prevent Pullman porters from buying copies in quantity and reselling them at a markup on trains and in stations down south.

Singles generally sold for 79 cents in those days, but by nightfall "I Can't Be Satisfied" was going for twice as much. Muddy, who was by then driving a truck delivering venetian blinds and still didn't have a copy, paid $1.10 for one the following morning, then stalked away in anger when the shopkeeper refused to sell him another. He had to send his wife to buy him a second copy.

This gives such a vivid sense of the black community and the black economy, and why it was that such an amazing music, the basis for modern rock, could be emerging between 1945 and 1960 in Chicago (and other cities, notably Detroit) without white America knowing or caring. Everything is local, everything is hand to hand, even the sales down the southward rail lines by the Pullman porters. The bars where the blues musicians are playing are local—small, dingy, often barely more than a room in someone's house. The music they're playing isn't abstract; they're singing and playing to people four feet away. When the guitar player shows off his licks to a good-looking woman, her man might walk over and bust him right there, or smash his guitar. In Harley Cokliss's documentary *Chicago Blues*, a woman on her way to the bathroom walks right through the band, playing in the corner of the room that counts as the stage. Most musicians carry guns for self-protection and, if necessary, to demand their money from a promoter. Sonny Boy Williamson, the harmonica virtuoso, is stabbed to death after a gig. Even the music is hand to hand: when the harp player Junior Wells has had enough of Buddy Guy playing one of his astonishing, impassioned solos, the ones that Clapton dreamed of playing but never quite made it, Junior just leans over and grabs Buddy's guitar around the neck, choking the strings. My turn now.

As we've seen before, the blues wasn't even especially esteemed in the black community, especially among middle-class blacks, who preferred jazz or soul. Bobby Schiffman, the manager of the famous Apollo Theater in Harlem, set up an extraordinary blues bill, consisting of B. B. King, Bobby "Blue" Bland, T-Bone Walker, Jimmy Witherspoon, Sonny Terry and Brownie McGhee, and Odetta, but the show tanked.

Schiffman and the musicians sent out for coffee, doughnuts, and bourbon, then sat down and tried to work out why such a bill didn't sell tickets. Their collective conclusion, Schiffman later said, was that blues represented misery—a throwback to sharecropping and even slavery. They acted as a reminder of times when African-Americans were at a low point in their history, and modern blacks didn't want that reminder. They came to the theater, Schiffman went on, to be uplifted, to see four-hundred-dollar mohair suits, gorgeous gowns, elaborate hairdos, magnificent sets. The last thing they wanted was to look back.

The way ahead was by recording, but recording was just another trap. The Chess brothers were running something very like a plantation economy: not only were they siphoning off their artists' royalties but they viewed their artists with a devastating lack of respect. Malcolm Chisholm, Chess's chief engineer, was quoted as saying, "You've got to understand, blues is a music of bare competence. And that's what these musicians are. Barely competent."

Buddy Guy recalled that when Chess wanted to do an acoustic album to catch the folk craze (they had in mind *Muddy Waters, Folk Singer*) Buddy played for Leonard Chess. Chess listened for a while, not saying anything, then demanded, "Do you want a drink, motherfucker?" Buddy said nothing. "How the fuck you learn this shit?" Chess demanded. "You been here all this goddamned time? We didn't know you could play this shit."

The Chess brothers were showing their generosity by offering the musicians manual labor around the studio. In 1964, ten years after the episode Davis tells, the Rolling Stones, touring America, went to the Chess studios to record and with luck to meet some of their heroes—Muddy, Howlin' Wolf, Willie Dixon, Little Walter, the other Chicago giants. Bill Wyman wrote: "The next day we helped Stu unload the equipment from the van, when who should appear beside us but the great Muddy Waters himself. We were staggered, lost for words. What shook us even more was when he helped us carry our things into the studio." And in reading Davis's anecdote about Muddy's hit single for the tenth or eleventh time it finally hit me: *The Chess brothers didn't even give him a copy of his own record.*

There was one other way ahead, the way B. B. King took, but it was risky and very, very hard: the chitlin circuit. Chitlins—short for "chitterlings"—were fried hogs' intestines, a subsistence-level soul food. The chitlin circuit was the southern black live-music circuit, which was nobody's idea of a cruise. It was based on a spine that ran between New Orleans and Chicago, with ribs that ran west across the Deep South and east to the cities of the Atlantic coast. The idea was to work Louisiana and Florida during the winter and move north as the weather got warmer, playing into Texas, New Mexico, and Arizona, even out to the West Coast.

The circuit had different levels. The big-name acts might play urban lounges and theaters, but blues players weren't big-name acts: whites didn't know them, and sophisticated blacks preferred jazz. The majority of blues artists found themselves booked into some shady places. Big Moose Walker, a chitlin regular, explained, "We played in Lambert, Mississippi, we played Cleveland, we played in Brooksville, all in Mississippi. We played juke houses, all out in different places, barns and stuff cut in two, just anywhere. And I seen guys get killed for fifteen cents. They would kill you for a dime, you know, a dime!"

If the regulars didn't kill you, the promoters might. The guitarist Clarence "Gatemouth" Brown, sharing a bill with B. B. King, said, "I remember one time we had about 3,500 people in the house and this guy didn't want to pay off nobody. Had a big .45 sittin' on the table and he didn't know I had a pistol in my pocket. So I pulled my pistol and I laid it right up above his head. I told B. B. to count his money out and count mine, too. And he did and I backed out the door with my gun, just like the wild west days. I hollered at my driver, I said,

'Get this Pontiac rollin'!' He had the motor runnin', I got in that car and we burned rubber from there back to Texas."

King became a professional nomad. In 1956 alone he made 342 appearances in 366 days, not to mention three separate recording sessions in Los Angeles.

The photographer Ernest C. Withers shot an unforgettable photo of King's bus "Big Red," looking like a large mechanical caterpillar, at a curb outside King's Palace Cafe on Beale Street with King's entire touring crew, fifteen well-dressed men and a well-dressed woman, lined up in front of the vehicle in their best suits and clean shirts. Well-wishers are leaning out of the windows of the rooming houses above the bus. Just as an actor might dream of taking the bus to Hollywood and being discovered, B. B. King was taking to the road in his bus, with his name and the contact information of his booking agent painted above the windows.

Nobody worked harder, traveled more miles on hard roads, or stayed more faithful to what he did well than B. B. King. Yet he might have died on the road, broke, if it hadn't been for those rip-off recordings making their way one by one across the Atlantic and starting a fire among a frighteningly small number of blues fans with bad guitars. "If it wasn't for the British musicians," he said, "a lot of us black musicians in America would still be catchin' the hell that we caught long before. . . . When white America started paying attention to the blues, it started opening a lot of doors that had been closed to us."

In one sense, Chicago blues spread out and saturated America, flavoring almost everything played on the electric guitar. In another sense, it ended at the B. B. King show at the Fillmore West in San Francisco in the summer of 1968. The last time he had played at the Fillmore, in 1963, he told an interviewer that the audience had been 95 percent black. Now Mike Bloomfield, the white American kid who went into the clubs and dives of Chicago to learn how to play, was introducing him as the greatest bluesman alive to an audience that was 95 percent white.

"I didn't know if I should walk out there. When I finally did, they gave me a standing ovation. I wanted to cry. Words can't say how I felt."

# INTERLUDE:

# BRIAN BULL'S GUITAR

In my friend Bill Kinzie's studio to record a short essay for NPR, I stumble upon Brian Bull's guitar. Brian is a guy who has lived around Vermont for some twenty years, but before that he apparently really made it to the show—played with Lowell George, the Spoonful. Had his chance. But something just wasn't tuned right in his temperament and he bailed out, ended up in Vermont like a stick circling in a small bay at the edge of the river.

He's not here at the moment, but Bill's studio is in its usual constant upheaval of rearrangement. The no-name hardshell case has been hauled out of a closet, where he apparently stables it, and left on a shopworn armchair. No stickers, no slogans.

I throw open the catches and there it is, the guitar that made America.

It's a working guitarist's guitar. The pickguard, if it ever had one, has vanished, and where it might have been are the signs of years of pounding: cracks, bruises, scratches, sundry little abrasions caused by picks and gawd knows what else. It doesn't look scratched as much as impacted: it looks as though a Volvo, a very small Volvo, has backed into that quadrant of the guitar and then driven off while the guitarist was still asleep on a threadbare couch in a corner of the studio, one arm flung over his eyes against the morning sun. The rest of the body isn't quite as beaten up, but nobody could mistake this for a piece of cabinetmaker's art.

Speaking of which—who did make it? Well, it's a dreadnought, no clue there. The headstock is in the classic Martin shape but bears no name. It's just plain brown, as if the instrument were made one weekend out of barnboard. No label inside. This guitar is nothing more nor less than an honorable tool, defined by function, in the same way that a spade says "spade." It has been doing its job—well enough, presumably—for years. It might have been a much nicer guitar, prettier, more expensive, more full-throated, I suppose, but you know what? If that had been the case it probably would have been stolen.

On second thought, it's not just a tool. It's an old brown dog of a guitar. I put it back in its case carefully, as if laying it in its bed, or its grave.

# Love Me Tender /
# The Worst Trip

The story of rock and roll has been told many times, but as usual it has been told by the winners. As such, it is often presented as a guitar revolution, which was by no means entirely the case. At the time, the guitar was fighting for daylight along with a number of emerging musical forces. When interviewed about the music that first fired his enthusiasm for rock and roll Alan Freed, the white deejay said to have invented the term, spoke of the tenor sax of Red Prysock and Big Al Sears and the blues singing and piano of Ivory Joe Hunter. Guitarists didn't feature.

Rock and roll was a loose, catchall phrase for several emerging sounds: the Bill Haley school of country-string-band-meets-R&B; the R&B piano school of Fats Domino, Ray Charles, the wild Little Richard, and the still wilder Jerry Lee Lewis; the Memphis rockabilly-guitar school of Elvis and Carl Perkins; vocal, doo-wop, and a capella groups, both black and white; and various unique figures such as Chuck Berry and Bo Diddley. In this mix, the featured, sexy instrument was just as likely to be a piano or a sax, significantly more so among the black musicians.

Rock and roll was about black music and white rural music finding an audience in white urban teenagers, but the resistance to the guitar in particular was based on class rather than on race prejudice. Rockers like Elvis, Jerry Lee Lewis, and Carl Perkins were viewed—not only in the North—as white trash, and the fact that many of them were playing guitars only added to the evidence that they were no better than hillbillies. A vivid illustration of this stereotype turns up in the cartoon *Huckleberry Hound.*

Huck was first syndicated in 1958, and by 1959 it was a major hit. It was broadcast in two-thirds of all major TV markets, in many cases in prime time for adults rather than kids, and claimed an international audience of sixteen million. Huck, his voice spoken in relaxed southern drawl by Daws Butler, had as his theme song "My Darling Clementine," and he occasionally played guitar. Not just any guitar. In one image, he has a guitar that seems to have only three strings and two tuners. Huck, then, is a parody of Elvis: nothin' but a hound dog.

A musician who understood the racial lines exceptionally well was Chuck Berry. In early 1953 Chuck Berry, who had grown up in a middle-class black home listening to a highly diverse range of music on the radio, was playing a regular gig in East St. Louis as part of a four-piece piano/guitar/bass/drums band at a nightclub called the Cosmopolitan Club.

"The music played most around St. Louis was country-western, which was usually called hillbilly music, and swing. Curiosity provoked me to lay a lot of the country stuff on our predominantly black audience and some of the clubgoers started whispering, 'Who is that black hillbilly at the Cosmo?' After they laughed at me a few times, they began requesting the hillbilly stuff and enjoyed trying to dance to it. If you ever want to see something that is far out, watch a crowd of colored folk, half high, wholeheartedly doing the hoedown barefooted."

The "black hillbilly" was at a peculiar crux in race relations. In addition to his country and western songs, he was playing Nat Cole and Muddy Waters tunes, effectively covering the entire racial spectrum, and altering his accent and delivery with each song. Out of this curious impishness came the kind of crossover thinking that led to "Maybellene," Berry's breakout hit in 1955. "Maybellene," far from being straight R&B or Chicago blues, is a revision of a country song called "Ida Red"—a car song, of all things. It wouldn't be out of place in an episode of *The Dukes of Hazzard*.

Word of his performances crossed the river into St. Louis and sometimes, Berry wrote, nearly 40 percent of the club's clientele would be white. As usual, the geography was crucial. East St. Louis didn't suffer from the restrictive early-closing blue laws that were in effect in St. Louis, and racial attitudes were different: "The state of Illinois in the beginning of the 1950s was a bit more liberal than Missouri in regards to relations between blacks and whites," Berry wrote in his autobiography. "A traveler might notice a considerable difference in the community just across the Mississippi in East St. Louis. For one thing, if a black and white couple were stopped by a squad car there they did not have to go to a police station and get a mandatory shot for venereal disease, as was the custom across the river in St. Louis."

Chuck Berry had one foot in each world, and that was part of his success: he was a great rock and roll songwriter, a great entertainer, a decent guitarist who was unafraid to make his guitar a prominent feature of his music and his act, and over the radio he could pass for white. Even some of his publicity stills and posters implied the skin tone of, say, an Italian. On tour, he was booked into venues in the South that never hired colored entertainers; sometimes he went ahead and performed anyway; sometimes he was paid off with apologies from the promoter. If Elvis was a white boy who could sing like a black guy, Chuck Berry was a black boy who could sing like a white guy, and who added the crucial and unexpected element of T-Bone Walker guitar licks and stage show. It's a sign of his unique position in rock and roll history that he was one of the few singer/guitarist/songwriters to be covered time and again by both the Beatles and the Rolling Stones.

Berry was also one of the few songwriters who had a particular vision of his potential audience. In singing "Maybellene" and "No Particular Place to Go" he allied rock and roll with cars, just as he would soon ally it with kids dying to get out of school ("School Days") and the desire of teenagers to have their own music ("Roll Over, Beethoven"). He was starting the process of enlisting the sympathy, even the fervor, of America's teenagers with the stuff of their lives.

Guitars had had virtually nothing to do with the youth market (in fact, there wasn't as yet a youth market) but now they were one of the essential props, along with cars, radios, record players, and a certain degree of rebellion. This, if nothing else, would give Berry's music astonishing longevity, as his songs would pull together the landscape of a generation discovering its own identity. His signature guitar riff, one of the most copied musical phrases in history, would say it all.

Growing up in England, first becoming aware of popular music around 1961, I never had much time for Elvis, who was already softening, already being left behind. I had no idea what an interesting character he was, especially as a teenager, especially in the way he treated his guitars.

He probably got his first guitar for his eleventh birthday. Some versions say he really wanted a gun, and his mother persuaded him to get a guitar instead; other versions say it was really a bicycle he wanted. Either way, he ended up with a small, cheap guitar.

Right away he was pulled in two directions. An uncle who played honky-tonks taught him a few chords, but so did his pastor. For the rest of his life Elvis would have one foot on each side of the tracks.

He was a shy boy, often bullied, with a distant father and a protective mother. Among girls and women he was comfortable, but polite. The guitar alone—and yes, this is Elvis we're talking about—brought out his tenderness and caring. This is Red West, a friend from high school:

> The way I found out he could play the guitar—I never remember seeing him have it in school, but one of the projects we had in wood shop was to bring an article from home that needed to be repaired, and our wood shop instructor, Mr. Widdop, would look at it and evaluate what had to be done, and that would be our project for a six-week time period. Anyway . . . Elvis brought a guitar. And he fooled around with it, sanded it, used some rosin glue and fixed a crack in it, stained it, varnished it, then he took this real fine steel wool

to get all the bubbles out of the lacquer and bring it down to a satin finish so it looked really good.

What an extraordinary passage. What a statement of inarticulate, inexpressible love! Then, as if in a scene from a movie, one of the boys demands he play something on the guitar, and when he does an aw-shucks no, they steal his car keys. So he plays.

"And it just blew me away," says Red West, who was a football player, not a musician. "I didn't even know he could play that guitar— I just thought he was fixing it for somebody else."

As far as I can tell, this was the same "child-size" guitar Elvis took into Sam Phillips's recording studio, nervous and shy, and kept asking if anyone needed a singer. When given the chance he sang gospel and old-fashioned sentimental country songs. It was the guitar he was play-ing when he suddenly let himself go wild with Scotty Moore and Bill Black, singing an uproarious, high-speed version of "That's All Right." He kept on playing it until late 1954, using it on the Grand Ole Opry and the "Louisiana Hayride," taking it everywhere as if it were his childhood, as if it were the child in him. I have a theory that this is why women fall in love with men who play the guitar: it may be the first or the only time they see into the guy's feminine side, suddenly manifest in such an unexpected vulnerability, such focus, such deli-cate touch.

At the same time, though nobody who knew him expected it, Elvis had an entirely different side, an R&B side to balance his gospel side, and again it was the guitar that brought it out. Before the gold lamé– suit days, he never appeared on stage without his guitar, and now he used it in an entirely different way.

"This cat came out in red pants and a green coat and a pink shirt and socks," recalled Bob Luman, a seventeen-year-old high school stu-dent who would go on to become a country singer/guitarist, "and he had this sneer on his face and he stood behind the mike for five min-utes, I'll bet, before he made a move. Then he hit his guitar a lick, and he broke two strings. I'd been playing ten years, and I hadn't broken a *total* of two strings. So there he was, these two strings dangling, and

he hadn't done anything yet, and these high school girls were screaming and fainting and running up to the stage, and then he started to
move his hips real slow like he had a thing for his guitar."

Elvis's guitar was no longer a musical instrument, a device by which
a working stiff made a living, a kind of musical plumber's wrench. At
a single stroke, Elvis made it something else: his prop, his drum, his
penis, the girl in his arms. The guitar would carry the beat for rock
and roll, and take the heat for rock and roll, too. It would become dangerous, repulsive, and, at long last, cool. This is why men fall in love
with men who play the guitar: the power, the freedom, the screaming
girl fans. The invulnerability.

For the rest of his troubled life Elvis would have difficulty reconcil-
ing his gospel and R&B selves, but he found a fascinating way of rec-
onciling his opposite and antagonistic uses of the guitar, a solution that
again is surprising in its tenderness: he bought a leather sheath, a kind
of bodysuit, for his guitar. Hank Snow had given him the idea, he told
a wire service reporter, and there was only one other like it. "It keeps
the guitar from getting splintered when I swing it around and it hits
my belt buckle."

The sheath still exists; it can be visited at Graceland.

The rise of rockabilly, and rock and roll in general, was so turbulent,
its audience so unpredictable to promoters and record companies, that
all the usual bets on popular music were off. This confusion offered a
small epistemological chink, through which dashed a number of rock
and roll guitar heroes that history seems to have forgotten. They were
women.

Most came from small towns via the great barn-dance and hayride
radio shows, which had a long history of featuring women performers,
not merely the decorative chick-up-front but accomplished women
playing a range of instruments, the guitar included. Wanda Jackson,
from Oklahoma, had a moderately successful string of rockabilly and
country hits from 1954 until 1961. Cordell Jackson (no relation) played
rockabilly guitar, sang, and ran her own record label in Memphis. She
appeared in a 1991 Budweiser commercial in a guitar duel with Brian

Setzer. Martha Carson (formerly a member of one of the first all-female sister string bands and later described as the First Lady of Country Gospel) played and sang in the Sister Rosetta Tharpe tradition, and according to Peter Guralnick impressed the up-and-coming Elvis, who was sharing a Memphis bill with her: "She broke several strings, danced ecstatically at the end of a long guitar chord, and in general created the kind of smoldering intensity and infectious enthusiasm that he sought to achieve in his own performance."

Perhaps the first was Bonnie Buckingham. Born in 1924 in the Pacific Northwest, she played in western and pop bands and might have been the first woman hired as a studio guitarist, in 1955. (Mary Ford had certainly played a great deal in Les Paul's studio, but the circumstances were somewhat different.) She adopted the name Bonnie Guitar in 1956, had a hit with "Dark Moon," appeared on *Ed Sullivan*, toured with Gene Vincent and the Everly Brothers. Quitting the road, she went back to Washington and became one of the first female record producers.

Peggy Jones, born in New York in 1940, was the first female guitarist to be hired by a major recording act. At the age of seventeen she was already a singer, dancer, and part-time model and had won a talent-night contest at the Apollo Theater. She planned to go to Juilliard when she ran into Bo Diddley. "I was always a subject of someone coming up to talk to me; you're automatically different anyway when you're walking down the street with a guitar." She was invited to play in Diddley's band and became known as "Lady Bo."

"Even though a lot of people thought I wasn't playing, you know, that I had a tape recorder or something and was not really playing!" She continued to play with or lead a variety of soul, pop, and R&B acts through the turn of the century.

I have a two-part theory about women guitarists in the twentieth century, a theory provoked by the number of men who have said or implied that every great guitarist has been a guy. This is, of course, not true—the best young classical guitarist in the world and the best slide guitarist in the world are both women—but looking at the long list of male guitarists made me wonder.

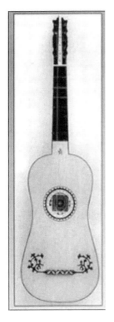

It's impossible to know what the earliest guitars in America looked like. Few specimens from the era have survived, and they differ from one another in many ways. These beautiful copies of period instruments, by Stephen Barber and Sandi Harris, give some clues. (*Clockwise from top left*) A reproduction of a baroque guitar made by Jacopo Checcucci in Livorno 1623; an "English guitar," or cittern, like those popular in the second half of the eighteenth century; and an amazingly elaborate "rose" made of parchment that was inserted into the sound hole as a mute. (Images courtesy of www.lutesandguitars.co.uk)

Probably no other instrument has been the subject of as much tinkering as the guitar. This patent, issued in 1873, was for a pedal-operated capo, an absurdly complicated version of the little device that is clipped or clamped across the fingerboard so you can play in different keys using the same chords. The late nineteenth century was an age of mechanical improvement through industrialization, but, even so, it's amazing what people will go through to avoid learning a few more chords. (U.S. Patent and Trademark Office and Capomuseum.com)

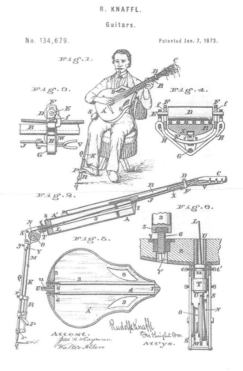

The class of 1902. The vast wooden instruments like musical aircraft carriers are harp-guitars, built to enable the guitar to double as a bass. Not all of these musicians would have played at the same time but, nevertheless, the guitar and mandolin ensembles of the turn of the century were often as large as small orchestras. Imagine trying to pile all those harp-guitar cases into the buggy. (Gregg Miner)

By the age of twenty Elsie Tooker, born in 1879, was a guitar virtuosa, arranger, and teacher. Among the works she arranged for guitar, according to *Cadenza*: Beethoven's "Adagio"; Schwarenka's "Polish Dance"; Thome's "Simple Aveu"; Paderewski's "Minuet a l'Antique"; Robyn's "Manzanillo"; and "a few duos and two quartettes for four guitars." (Paul Ruppa)

The nineteenth-century guitar was by no means only a ladies' instrument. This specimen is in a miner's cabin at the Camp Bird Mine in Ouray County, Colorado. (Denver Public Library; reproduction number: X-61351)

Picnics, tennis parties, canoe trips, days at the beach, outings of all kinds—in the nineteenth century people took their instruments with them. This particular excursion may have been on Lake Keesus in 1915. The mandolin player in the white shirt is Adolph Waech, for three decades the leader of the Bonne Amie Musical Circle, which later gave birth to the Milwaukee Mandolin Orchestra. Note the giant mando-bass in the stern, taking up half the boat. (Paul Ruppa and Bob Waech Sr.)

One interesting difference between the Spanish and later traditions in America was that in Spanish-influenced areas the guitar was more likely to be played outdoors, and was more likely to have a ceremonial role—not only in dances but in processions, funerals, and a wide range of celebrations such as weddings. This is a fiesta in Santa Fe, where custom and instrumentation had barely changed in two centuries or more. (FSA Photo by Russell Lee; LC-USF33-012870-M4)

Joseph Kekuku, arguably the most influential guitarist in American history, invented and championed a new way of playing the guitar, which in turn led to the Hawaiian guitar boom, which in turn led to the electric guitar. (University of Iowa)

Hawaiian music was so popular that it took the steel guitar and, in many instances, the rhythm guitar as well into all types of non-Hawaiian music. This is a Cajun Hawaiian guitar player at the National Rice Festival, Crowley, Louisiana, in October 1938. Note the National-style guitar playing rhythm, itself another by-product of the Hawaiian craze. (FSA Photo by Russell Lee; LC-USF33-011736-M4)

A Salvation Army worker playing guitar and singing to Mrs. Oscar Mortonson in Swede Hollow, St. Paul, Minnesota, ca. 1915. There's something timeless about this photo—the posture of the guitarist, the position of her left hand (is that a D minor chord?), the radiance in her face, the way her eyes are focused somewhere beyond this world, and, equally, the way the older woman is looking up at her, she herself transformed by the transformation in the singer. This is the alchemy of live music, and the intimacy of the guitar, and as such it transcends time and even gender. (Minnesota Historical Society)

A white migrant strawberry picker playing guitar in his tent near Hammond, Louisiana. The Depression was a terrible time for the music industry and the high-end guitar makers, but the cheap guitar, played with the most basic of skills, was a priceless possession when most had so little. (FSA photo by Russell Lee; LC-USF34-032875-D)

A prisoner dances while another plays the guitar at a prison camp in Greene County, Georgia. The identity of the black guitarist was reshaped by John Lomax, who took Huddie Ledbetter (a.k.a. Leadbelly) to New York, made him play blues and ballads instead of his repertoire of popular songs, and played up Leadbelly's time in prison for murder. In doing so Lomax and Leadbelly gave the guitar a new magnetism and potency, and that revitalization was repeated in the late fifties and early sixties when the old blues recording artists were "rediscovered" and brought north to play for educated white audiences. (FSA photo by Jack Delano; LC-USF34-044766-E)

When the ethnomusicologist Sidney Robertson Cowell investigated folk music in California in 1938–40, she found all manner of curious guitarlike instruments: (*clockwise from top*) the saz, the romantic viola d'arame, with its twin heart-shaped sound holes; and the tar, and the oud. (Library of Congress, American Folklife Center, WPA Sidney Robertson Cowell Collection)

Charlie Christian inventing modern guitar jazz at a *Profoundly Blue* recording session, with Edmond Hall (clarinet), Meade Lux Lewis (celeste), and Israel Crosby (bass). (Frank Driggs Collection)

Farm boy playing guitar in front of the filling station and garage, Pie Town, New Mexico, June 1940. Is there anything else that needs to be said about country music? (FSA Photo by Russell Lee; LC-USF33-012756-M2)

One of the great originals, Sister Rosetta Tharpe, single-handedly invented nightclub gospel jazz. Seen here with Count Basie at Carnegie Hall in December 1938 as part of John Hammond's "From Spirituals to Swing" concert. (Frank Driggs Collection)

The guitar has been taken into combat for perhaps 450 years, offering solace and company—sometimes in unexpected ways: the Hawaiian guitarist Johnny Kolsiana took his guitar with him when he entered the air force, and ended up in Paris sitting in on a session with Django Reinhardt. This is the First Antilles battalion embarking at Hampton Roads during World War II. (Library of Virginia)

The guitar may have become a symbol of political integrity in the sixties, but before that a guitarist was likely to hire out to the highest bidder. The band yowling for Fuller Warren in his successful 1948 campaign for the governorship in Florida chose an especially slippery political figure to back up. Warren has become notorious in the history of political double-talk for what is now called an "if-by-whiskey" speech. When asked if he was "wet" or "dry" on the subject of a ban on whiskey, he replied: "If by whiskey you mean the water of life that cheers men's souls, that smooths out the tensions of the day, that gives gentle perspective to one's view of life, then put my name on the list of the fervent wets. But if by whiskey you mean the devil's brew that rends families, destroys careers and ruins one's ability to work, then count me in the ranks of the dries." (Florida State Archives Florida Memory Collection)

(*left*) A pioneer, now largely forgotten, Jimmie Webster was one of the first people to use the two-handed style now called "tapping" and was certainly the first to write a book about it, titled *Touch System for Electric and Amplified Spanish Guitar* (1952). (Rhode Island Music Company and Paul Ruppa) (*right*) It is almost impossible to overstate the importance of Gypsies to the history of the guitar. Playing by their own melodic and social rules, they created flamenco and gypsy jazz, two of the most dramatic forms of the instrument's expression. This is the great Django Reinhardt, in a photograph published at the time of his death in 1953 at the age of forty-three. (GVA Archive)

Alis Lesley, barefoot rocker, one of the contenders for the title of the "female Elvis." The photo is from a fan-club card, which misspelled her name.

Alice Lesley

In the sixties, the guitar was taken up by the white middle class, both by acoustic folkies and by teenage electric rockers picking up Ventures and Beatles tunes. This is Paul Ruppa playing the Ventures' "Walk, Don't Run" for campers at Camp Thunderbird in Bemidji, Minnesota, in 1965. This class shift also meant a change in the identity and aspirations of the guitarist: for most of the century a guitarist had been a kind of skilled artisan; now he (or she) could aspire to being an artist. In individual terms, it meant that the bespectacled kid, in danger of being a nerd, was cool. (Paul Ruppa)

The guitar at the dawn of the twenty-first century. Dominic Frasca sits with his guitar in his lap, surrounded by the tools of his trade. (Glyn Emmerson)

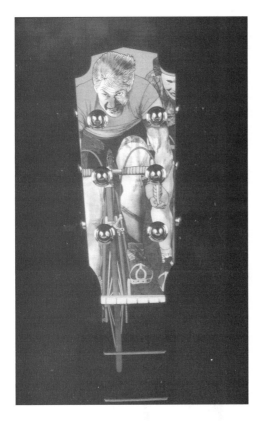

Canadian inlayer William "Grit" Laskin uses his excellent guitars as opportunities for stunning inlay art that goes well beyond decoration into stories, exercises in multiple perspectives, comments on his own art, and jokes at his own expense. This one, Pursuit, is one of his most recent designs, inspired by the Tour de France and the animated film *The Triplets of Belleville*. (William Laskin)

Whoever invented the phrase "if it ain't broke, don't fix it" was not a luthier. At the beginning of the twenty-first century the harp-guitar is enjoying a renaissance. This is Fred Carlson and his Oracle harp-sympitar, which has not only extra bass strings but sitarlike sympathetic strings. The headgear is optional. (Fred Carlson)

Still slightly ahead in the race for Most Strings Mounted on a Musical Instrument Still Called a Guitar is Linda Manzer, with the Pikasso, an exercise in musical cubism originally made for Pat Metheny. (Linda Manzer)

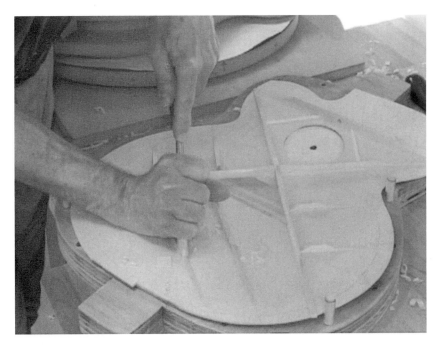

Scalloping the braces. It's not just a question of understanding the acoustics of wood; one slip of the chisel and Rick Davis would have to start making a whole new top. (Bill Kinzie)

Checking the tap tone. With every shaving taken off the braces, the top "opens up," becoming more resonant, sounding less percussive and more musical. (Bill Kinzie)

The finished Running Dog Concert Jumbo #030303. The author (left) is pretending to find a flaw that will justify knocking a few hundred off the price. The builder (right) is having none of it. (William DiLillo)

Women have always played guitar, and in many individual communities or families the best guitarist has often been a woman.

What changed around the end of the nineteenth century was that music became a business and a trade. There were professional musicians in America before 1900, but the businesses of music publishing, recording, radio, and contractual live performance either didn't exist or were in their infancy, and a lot less money was at stake. The most common music profession was teaching, and an unknown percentage, quite possibly a majority, of guitar teachers were women.

As the American media developed, the number of openings for professional or semiprofessional musicians grew rapidly, especially in radio, and we start hearing of substantial numbers of women guitarists emerging especially in the radio barn-dance programs. My theory is that this was in significant part because these girls and young women grew up in rural or small-town blue-collar households where *it was expected that women would work*. Not that they would be musicians, necessarily, but music was a skill as prized on the farm as it was in the parlor, and a musician, female or male, might hope to earn more than a farmhand. (Conversely, because the barn dance shows pretended to be taking place at dances and hoedowns, it wasn't stretching verisimilitude or expectations to include women among the musicians.) Moreover, by the late thirties a girl growing up listening to the Coon Creek Girls or the Girls of the Golden West might realize that she, too, had her opportunities.

After World War II things seem to have changed. Perhaps it was the influence of the strong back-to-the-kitchen propaganda that tried to steer women who had worked during the war to go back to being homemakers, but it seems to me that the emerging women performers were more likely to be singers than instrumentalists. A woman could work as long as she didn't seem to be compromising her femininity. The girl groups of the fifties and sixties especially were packaged to look as if they were off to the senior prom; my suspicion is that allowing them to play their own instruments would have made them look too much like working people. Interestingly, young middle-class women during the sixties would find an easy entree into folk music, which looked more like a vocation than a job. The real resistance would come a decade later when they tried to break into rock, which by then had become a boys' club.

At this early date in rock and roll, though, there may still have been conservatism within the music industry itself, but there was clearly nothing of the kind among fans. A female rockabilly singer/guitarist had the advantage of novelty, and as long as she was good she could potentially become a great favorite.

Alis Lesley was known as "the female Elvis" and a "Five-Foot-Two Stick of Musical Dynamite." On stage, she kicked off her shoes and played in bare feet; photographs of her from the time show a fireball, someone bursting with the newly released energy of rock and roll. She toured Australia with Eddie Cochran, Gene Vincent, and Little Richard, played with Johnny Cash and Marty Robbins at the Grand Ole Opry, but gave up touring in 1959 to care for her mother, who was bedridden with arthritis. She subsequently became a missionary, then a teacher working on Indian reservations. Rockabilly fan clubs (especially in Europe) still keep her name going, though, as they do with another name lost to the American public at large: Janis Martin.

Janis Martin was also called "the female Elvis Presley"—something of a mystery, as the Elvis name was taken very seriously and used only under license. She came into music from a country background, playing the WDVA Barn Dance in Danville, Virginia, at the age of eleven on the same show that launched the careers of the famous Louvin Brothers, Charlie and Ira, and at thirteen Janis was invited to become a regular member of the Old Dominion Barndance in Richmond, Virginia, the third largest in the nation. At fifteen she wrote and recorded "Drugstore Rock and Roll," which sold some 750,000 copies. She began to appear nationally live and on TV and was voted Most Promising Female Artist of 1956, but then things became awkward for her promoters.

"I had eloped with a paratrooper on January 7, 1956," she later told one of the many rockabilly fanzines that thrive in the United States and Europe, "and I didn't even tell my mother and father until he was safely shipped overseas in Germany. Daddy tried to have it anulled, 'cause I was fifteen years old. There was little rumbles about

Jerry Lee Lewis back in those days. We couldn't smoke a cigarette in public, I couldn't do anything. My mother was a typical show business mother so she said, 'Don't you dare let anyone know you're married.' RCA wasn't even aware I was married. Fourteen months later I went to a USO tour with Jim Reeves. My husband got a thirty-day leave and went on the road with me which the end result was my son. Naturally, when my husband joined the tour, the tour manager immediately called RCA and they didn't know a thing about it. When I came back . . . it was suggested very strongly, I will not call names, that I have an abortion. I was about three and a half months pregnant. I was shocked and indignant. I guess I had always been more mature than most people my age because I had been in the business professionally from age eleven. No way would I do that. That kind of burst the publicity thing they had goin' about the fresh-faced girl from Virginia."

Rock and roll has been portrayed as a genre created by radio, and radio certainly allowed black music or black-influenced music to reach mixed audiences. But musicians earned little from radio performances, and with royalties being siphoned off in some instances by the very deejays who were spinning the singles, the only way for a rock and roll guitarist to make money was by the time-honored tradition of going on the road.

Touring has always been less glamorous than it might seem. "People think it's exciting," said Paul Yandell, who worked for twenty-five years with Chet Atkins, "but you just think about getting back home. The best time you have is that two hours you spend on stage. That's where all the fun is. It's not the coming and going—that wears your butt out. But it is better than hauling gravel."

In the nineteenth century, musicians often traveled by river; in the early twentieth century rail became a possibility, many musicians bumming rides or playing for their passage. In general, though, the guitarist traveled by road.

Black musicians, often the poorest of the poor, generally traveled on foot. This was a hard, lonely road, even a fatal one, as one of the most famous blues guitarists of his day, Blind Lemon Jefferson, is said to have frozen to death (or died of a heart attack) walking through a snowstorm after a gig in 1929.

Walking the roads was a hard kind of education, something utterly different from touring by car and plane and staying in a series of hotel rooms. This in turn informed the music, especially the blues.

Josh White, for example, left his home in Greenville, South Carolina, at the age of eight to work as "lead boy" for John Henry Arnold, a blind street-corner guitarist and singer of religious songs. White's jobs, in addition to leading Arnold, were to play the tambourine, go around the crowd with the tin cup, and divide up the day's earnings among the blind singer-guitarists who often moved and played together. Arnold made White skim an extra portion of the day's take, and if his own share was less than he thought it should be he would fly into a rage and beat White. (Arnold, though a mediocre singer and guitarist, could make spectacular sums of money—White said up to $500 a week—and apparently had several bank accounts and even owned two racehorses.) But the treatment the boy received at the hands of his blind master was nothing compared to the treatment White saw African-Americans receiving at the hands of southern lynch mobs. One night near Waycross, Georgia, Arnold and White fell asleep in a field by the road, only to be woken after dark by a crowd of adults and children milling around a bonfire across the street. "Then I saw this—there were two figures," White recalled in Elijah Wald's *Josh White: Society Blues.* "They were stripped other than their shirts. Like on tiptoe. I don't think I could see them dangling, but what I could see and what I can't get out of my eyes: I saw kids, ten, twelve years old, girls and boys my age, mothers, fathers, aunts, adults. The kids had pokers and they'd get them red hot and jab them into the bodies' testicles . . . it was a hell of a thing to see."

This is not a sob story. These are the realities of live music. We hear so much of our music from recordings that we half-forget that recorded music is little more than a postcard of live music. Live music is a human encounter, with all the opportunities for human intensity, drama, conflict, and suffering. And from the musician's point of view, you only really learn about music, and about your instrument and its capabilities, by playing it live, to an audience that will be on your side only if you convince them to be on your side.

Equally, from the learner's point of view, you can learn only so much from recordings, or the radio, or nowadays instructional videos and the Internet. Even today, the front row of any guitar show has its share of finger-watchers, sitting in that half-leaning-forward position, frowning slightly, their eyes—our eyes—flicking back and forth between what the left and right hands are doing.

Being on the road also has its effects on the relationship between the musician and the guitar. It has been said that so many songs have been written about home because musicians spend so much time miles from home, hungry, tired, cold, broke, and alone. By the same token, being on the road makes the heart grow fonder toward the guitar. In the domestic accounts of music in the nineteenth century, the guitar was the familiar object knocking about the house. On the road, the guitar became companion and friend. The phrase "easy rider" is said to have several meanings in black slang of the early twentieth century. It could mean a woman, especially a girlfriend, loose woman, or prostitute. But it was also sometimes used to mean one's guitar, the silent partner, the uncomplaining fellow traveler.

Even for those with a car, road travel was almost unimaginably hard seventy-five years ago. For one gig, Jimmie Rodgers climbed into a car with three other musicians and headed through torrential rain for Hattiesburg, eighty miles away. There were no paved roads in Mississippi at the time, and they had to get out time and again to push the car out of mudholes. "Finally," writes Nolan Porterfield in *Jimmie Rodgers: The Life and Times of America's Blue Yodeler,* "having mired it up to the axles, they gave up and spent the night in the car, fitfully trying to sleep sitting up. The next morning a farmer and his mules pulled them several miles through the mud, and they got to Hattiesburg with barely enough time to clean away the muck and dress for the opening performance that evening."

By mid-century America's roads had improved a little, but the honky-tonks that sprang up along them were primitive and rough. When Hank Williams formed a new band around 1945 he took them all into a pawn shop in Montgomery, Alabama, and bought them all blackjacks, saying, "Boys, if y'all gonna play with me, by God you're gonna need these."

Another Hank Williams story, from around 1947, told by his steel guitarist: "We was playing a dance at a juke joint, and there was a poppin' sound and someone come up and said there was a fella out there shootin' with a gun. Directly, he come in. He was wearin' overalls—no shirt— and he had a big ol'loaded pistol and one of them bullets hit a heater and ricocheted 'round the room. Man, you talk about huntin' a table. Lum run into the girls' toilet—Hank had to go and get him out. Another place down near Fort Deposit they had chicken wire out front of the bandstand so if they started throwing bottles they wouldn't hit the band."

No road trip was as bad, though, as the "Winter Dance Party," more or less the last-gasp tour of the American fifties rock and roll era, which began in January 1959.

The headliner was Buddy Holly, who didn't want to do the tour. He had no choice, though; his assets had been seized by his manager in New Mexico, whom Buddy was suing. He had no money. His wife was pregnant.

The rest of the bill was a thrown-together assortment of musicians, mostly younger than Holly: Ritchie Valens ("La Bamba"), the Big Bopper ("Chantilly Lace"), Dion and the Belmonts ("I Wonder Why," "A Teenager in Love"), Frankie Sardo, Tommy Allsup, Carl Bunch, road manager Rod Lucier, and a young Waylon Jennings, who had been drafted to play bass for Holly. "I was probably the world's worst rock 'n' roll bass player," Jennings later admitted. "I was playin' country bass behind a rock 'n' roll singer."

This touches on a crucial point. What Buddy Holly's audiences saw on that tour was very different from what they heard on the two-minutes-and-change of his records. By early 1959 the record companies were already toning down and sweetening up anything that sounded too much like rock and roll. When Buddy Holly recorded "I Guess It Doesn't Matter Any More" and "Raining in My Heart" they became schmaltzy pop songs with cute pizzicato strings, but he certainly didn't tour with a string section. The audiences who came to see him live got something closer to rock and roll, a whole lot more guitar. Again, the orchestra could make a living at home; the guitar was forced out onto the road, whatever that meant. And in the case of the "Winter Dance Party" it meant the worst road trip any group of American musicians ever took.

The tour party met in Chicago and set out for the Million Dollar Ballroom in Milwaukee on January 23 in what Dion DiMucci later called "a converted school bus."

"It snowed on us from the time we left Chicago," Tommy Allsup said. The bus was so cramped that "some of them climbed into the luggage racks," author Ellis Amburn writes, "where they stretched out and began to snore. Others sat and watched their breath turn to bluish vapor. The bus's heater was woefully inadequate." By the end of the journey Carl Bunch, the drummer, could hardly walk.

They checked into their Milwaukee hotel and took a cab to the ballroom. The cab was so cold Allsup had difficulty breathing.

After Milwaukee they had to backtrack fifty miles to Kenosha. Gale-force winds blew off Lake Michigan. Bunch wore several pairs of socks and hoped his feet wouldn't get any worse.

When they finished the gig in Kenosha in the early hours of Sunday, January 25, they had to get to Mankato, Minnesota, 350 miles to the northwest, by the same evening.

On January 26 they had to play at Eau Claire, Wisconsin, surviving on pretzels, sardines, cheese, and potato chips, "mostly snacks that could be extracted by coin or brute force from bus-stop candy machines." By the time they reached Eau Claire, the temperature was twenty-five below zero. A few of the musicians discovered they'd lost some of their stage clothes and were left with one set for the rest of the tour.

Then it was off to Montevideo, Minnesota, 250 miles away, to play the Fiesta Ballroom on January 27. These hopelessly optimistic Midwest pioneer-town names, these absurdly cheerful dance hall names.

On January 28 they played the Prom Ballroom, St. Paul, Minnesota, then Davenport, Iowa. Bunch could no longer cordinate his feet to play his drum kit. When they left in the middle of the night for Fort Dodge, Iowa, two hundred miles away, the bus heater broke down. By noon they had got only as far as Tipton, forty miles from Davenport, and were forced to stop for repairs. Some of the musicians began talking about hiring a plane, but most weren't making enough to afford their share of the cost.

They made it to Fort Dodge, played the Laramar Ballroom, and left for Duluth, Minnesota, 350 miles north. No economy of planning, the itinerary winding and zigzagging as if to cover the least possible ground in the greatest possible mileage. In Duluth at the Armory, on January 31, one of those in the audience was a boy named Bobby Zimmerman.

After more repairs, the bus set off on the 330-mile trip to Appleton, Wisconsin, but near Ashland, the heater died again. Two hundred miles short of Appleton, where U.S. 51 runs through the North Woods, at 1:30 A.M. on February 1, the engine finally broke down completely: the piston had gone clear through the engine block. The temperature was somewhere between twenty-five and forty below zero.

Bunch was wearing six pairs of socks—all he had with him. At first the musicians burned newspapers in the aisle to try and stay warm. When they ran out of newspapers they stood in the road hoping to wave down a truck. The truck swerved around them, but at least it stopped down the road in Hurley to tell the sheriff's department about the bus. Jeeps were sent out to rescue the musicians and bring them back to the Club Carnival Cafe in Hurley, but the club management refused to serve the bus driver, who was black. The musicians had to take his food to him at the local garage, where the bus had been towed.

Carl Bunch was taken to hospital, where he was diagnosed with frostbite in both feet.

The musicians called the tour management, who were not sympathetic; the Appleton matinee later that day was canceled, but the show that night in Green Bay was not. At 11:30 A.M. the musicians boarded a train, reached Green Bay, and played their evening show, with

Valens, Holly, and Sardo filling in on drums. The Big Bopper played despite having flu.

The following day was supposed to be what any musician would have wanted: a day off. At the last minute, though, GAC was offered a booking at the Surf Ballroom in Clear Lake, Iowa, 350 miles southwest of Green Bay. They took it, and the day off vanished—in fact, the tour party would have to leave Green Bay as soon as the show ended, without even taking a shower.

The bus broke down all the way across Wisconsin and northeastern Iowa until they finally abandoned it and arrived in Clear Lake in a rented school bus.

The next gig was on February 3, the following day, at the Armory in Moorhead, Minnesota, nearly 500 miles away. The thought of another long bus trip was unbearable. Holly made his mind up. He would charter a small plane in nearby Mason City and fly to Fargo, North Dakota, the nearest airport to Moorhead. He told the other musicians he'd take their dirty clothes and have them cleaned and ready for them by the time they arrived on the bus.

The plane would hold a pilot and three passengers. The passenger list kept changing, in part because all of the musicians would have dearly loved to fly, but none of them could really afford it. In the end the passenger list consisted of Buddy Holly, the Big Bopper, who was feeling so sick he wanted to get to a doctor, and Ritchie Valens, who was also starting to feel ill. Valens was afraid of airplanes, he told a friend before he left Los Angeles, but he was getting used to them, and maybe on tour he might even fly.

"What would you do if you crash?" asked the friend.

"I'll land on my guitar," he said.

He tossed Tommy Allsup for the last spot on the plane, and won.

The show finished just before midnight. It had already started to snow.

# Scalloping the Braces

June 17: Cottonwood seeds blow across the valley. The grader has scraped half of Stage Road and the standard foot-high ridge of turned dirt runs up the crown of the road. The greenery on both sides is now so dense I drive right past Rick's house, not seeing it, and have to turn round.

"I've got a small present for you," he says, grinning slyly. He gives me a poster he's brought back from the annual A.S.I.A. symposium he's been running (workshops, instruments for show and for sale, performances, conversation into the small hours). The header, in one top corner, just says "Gibson. Pure." The picture is of a vertical white Gibson Flying V, and next to it the photo of a woman from sternum down, wearing nothing but white hot pants and white high heels, her legs apart at the same angle as the fork of the Flying V. Nobody ever accused Gibson of having highbrow taste.

On the workbench, the glued-and-rosetted top now has a series of braces, made of spruce, glued to its underside. They look like blunt sticks, extending slightly beyond the rim of the top.

The whole question of bracing is a mystery glued inside an enigma. Every luthier makes his braces slightly differently; every luthier is convinced he or she's doing it right. Now that I think back, the first thing Rick did when he took hold of the Fylde was take his mirror-on-a-stick, extend it into the sound hole, and examine the bracing. At the recent A.S.I.A. symposium Al Carruth brought in a pair of guitars, otherwise as identical as he could make them, one of which had the usual X bracing, while the other had double-X bracing, that is, an extra, smaller X of wood below the bridge. Double-X was tried by Gibson for a while with poor results and has been widely dismissed by luthiers, but in this classic blind test, many who played the guitars preferred the one with the double-X. When asked what it was they preferred about the sound of that guitar, though, people gave entirely contradictory answers. Some said it had a sharper sound, some a mellower sound; some said more attack, some said better decay. After examining the results closely, Al discovered that both were right: the double-X had more treble *and* bass. "Pretty cool," he said, but then he went on to show why his life will never be dull: "Now we've got to figure out why."

I've been following this issue because on the 13th Fret, the online discussion site for acoustic guitar makers and players, someone has posted photos of guitars-in-progress, their innards clearly visible, and some of the bracing looks more like the spoked wheels of an MG than the delicate but fairly simple web of struts Rick uses. I ask him about this and, snorting somewhat intemperately, he opens a magazine with photos of another luthier's work. He points out the braces that seem to make sense to him, even if they differ from his own, and those that make no sense at all and seem to have been stuck on at random, or for show, or just because there was a vacant bit of wood available.

This is clearly a delicate issue. I decide to see it all as a science still evolving, and change the subject. Talk me through the bracing in my guitar, I ask, and he replies more or less as follows.

"Every guitar needs slightly different bracing. It's the wood equivalent of graphic equalization." The central feature is a pair of braces crossing like an X below the sound hole, with others running off the arms of the X at right angles. This is known, not surprisingly, as X-bracing. It evolved from a design that emerged during the mid-nineteenth century, a design that in practice turned out to provide much greater strength and support for the top—which in turn enabled it to withstand the extra tension in steel strings. C. F. Martin may or may not have been the first to use X-bracing (he did not take out the patent), but he certainly popularized it.

Beyond the X, things start to diverge rapidly. My concert jumbo, for example, has two "fingers" of bracing running up and out from the X, as opposed to one that he uses on his smaller-body guitars. These fingers aren't just for strength. They also act as transducers; that is, they take the sound input from the bridge and spread it throughout the whole top. Researchers into guitar sound dynamics have taken powder, sprinkled it on the top, played a note, and seen how the vibrations affect the powder. It's fascinating: just from the oval patterns that emerge, you can see where the invisible braces have conducted the sound into the top.

In addition, there's also the upper face brace, which runs across the top above the sound hole to resist the pressure exerted by the fingerboard ("The neck is trying to bend and push the fingerboard down into the top"), which is not only thicker than the other braces but will be the only brace not to be scalloped. Finally, there's the bridge plate, glued underneath the bridge to prevent the tension in the strings from ripping the bridge clean off the top.

The bracing on the inside of the back is simpler than on the top, but still cleverer than it looks. It's called ladder bracing, as it consists of nothing but a series of four braces running from side to side, and for centuries, until the development of fan bracing (in classical guitars) and X-bracing (in steel-string guitars), all guitars had little or nothing but ladder bracing on both top and back. But these simple crosswise struts are cut and glued in such a way that they create a slight pinch, pulling the back into a slight arch to allow it to expand if the humidity is high. Very cunning.

To make the braces, Rick started with a plank of spruce. "Spruce has the highest stiffness-to-weight ratio of any wood I know of." He then cut quarter-inch-wide slices for the braces, strong but light, and a thicker one for the upper face brace.

"How thick is that brace?" I ask, dutifully taking notes.

"Can't remember. It's either nine-sixteenths or five-eighths," he says. "Let me check in the log of another concert jumbo"—he pauses for effect—"that hasn't fallen apart."

Today is all about scalloping the braces, that is, carving them down from straight sticks to skeletal fingers. In places they need to be dense and stiff, like knuckles, and in other places light and flexible, and the skill comes in knowing which needs to be where.

"When the braces are glued on they're monstrous," he says, talking down at the wood that is peeling back over the blade of his chisel. "Really clunky. Then I hack 'em down. Then I do the tapping thing again. Then I start bringing down the nonstructural braces, these two little guys down here. Then that very simple wood will start to get more complex. You'll hear a harmonic series starting to develop, then all sorts of other things on top."

Why do the braces taper away toward the edges of the top, like miniature suspension bridges? "We're making a vibrating plate, and in order to let it vibrate, the braces have to be reduced in stiffness at the edges. If you think of the whole thing as a speaker cone bouncing up and down—I think it does a lot more than just bounce up and down, but that's one of the main ways it moves—then by reducing the height of the braces, you reduce the stiffness."

He's not only taking height off each brace, he's also shaving down its width, working with a chisel that with one slip could easily go straight through a brace and the top, and we would be back to chapter one.

Yet perhaps for that very reason, this is his favorite part of guitar making. He carves two or three cuts, progressively deeper, into one of the fingers, turns the top around and carves back the other way, flicks out the shavings, puts down the chisel, picks up the top, holds it by a shoulder, puts it to his ear, and taps it with his thumb. *Thunk.* Like a timpanist tuning his drum, or perhaps more like someone making a steel drum, to develop all these different resonances instead of one even tension. Then another finger. Now the tap is fractionally livelier.

Then he shaves at the sides of the brace, to reduce the mass of the wood without reducing its height, and now a second pitch appears.

"Archtop builders will lay a top down and gently scratch it with their fingernails," he says, demonstrating. "They'll say, 'Ah. Yes. That's good. Yes.' It's cool. I have no idea what it means, but I like it."

Now there's no doubt: we've got at least two pitches an octave apart, and others creeping in too. The top is, in his phrasing, opening up. Loath to make the final shaving of the X-braces with his chisel, he goes to work with a left-handed finger plane, a beautiful little wood-and-brass instrument that looks like a piece of Victorian drug paraphernalia and cost so much he hid the bill from Joni.

With each set of cuts the tap tone opens up a little more. First it sounds as though it were echoing down a tunnel rather than a tube. Then more bass and more sustain kick in. Then something happens in the mid-range, and it starts to sound like one coherent voicing instead of a small choir of altos and baritones. One final set of chiseling, and the *thumm* becomes fatter, more rounded. Mango-shaped, perhaps.

This is, in essence, the difference between a production guitar and a handmade guitar. A production guitar has bracing that may be preshaped, and even if it is scalloped it may be scalloped to a general template of shape rather than being tuned like this to the acoustics of the top—it would simply take way too long. For the customer, the difference may be as slight as a *thump* rather than a *thumm;* for the maker, it's the difference between work and creation.

The braces now look more skeletal than ever.

"All good guitars are underbuilt and will not last terribly long," he says. "A couple hundred years is definitely the outside for a steel-string guitar, and probably less. If you build them so they are proportionally as strong as a violin, which will last hundreds and hundreds of years, they'll be too stiff to produce the sounds that we associate with the guitar."

This horrifies me. The instrument built to die.

He thinks about my reaction. "I would say it's sort of the racer of the instruments. It's built extremely light and fragile and you're going to use it for a certain amount of time and get the maximum performance out of it, and then it's going to fall to pieces and you're going to say, 'Well, that's how it goes.'" This from a guy who worked on racing engines. He jokes about putting big numbers on the sides of his guitars, like racing cars, and covering them with advertising decals, but I'm still a little shaken. Thinking of greyhounds, and racing fast, getting injured, being put to sleep.

A little more scraping, so that the tips of the scalloped fingers vanish into the top, and it's done. He hands me a pencil and invites me to write something. He always signs and dates his guitars, but he's never had the customer on hand to do the same.

"Write something," Rick says again, smiling, but I can't. I've never had anyone custom-make anything for me more complicated or expensive than a chicken sandwich, and I still can't really believe this is happening. Six months of labor, and such skilled and delicate labor at that—I can't take possession of it that casually. I stare at the underside of the top, with its now finished bracing, and after a long while I sign between two of the fingers, though to do so seems to imply I deserve some of the credit. Rick shrugs, then signs and dates it in a different space. I take the pencil back and write "Thanks!" above my signature. He takes the pencil and writes, "You're welcome."

Nobody will ever see this exchange. It will stay hidden between the ribs of the guitar as long as the instrument lasts.

# The Guitar Just
# Grabbed Me

The thing to bear in mind about the British Invasion is that it began in 1950 and crossed the Atlantic from west to east. Oh, and that it was started by the House Un-American Activities Committee.

"I came to England on September 8, 1955," Ramblin' Jack Elliott says, leaning on a leather couch in northern California at the home of the amazing slide-guitar player (not the cowboy singer) Roy Rogers. He looks at the ceiling and consults his encyclopedic memory for the story of the time when he played the "Muleskinner Blues" for Princess Margaret.

"It was at the home of—I think it was a count, from Italy, and his wife was English. I met them at a party. Princess Margaret wasn't there, but there were all these other dignitaries, lords and ladies. I was hired to play for a hundred lords and ladies who were having a party. [The folksinger] Rory McEwan was supposed to play the gig, but he preferred to go out of town, and he said, 'Jack, how would you like to play for some lords and ladies?' I said, 'That sounds like fun. I've never met any lords and ladies before. Sure, I'll take the gig.' 'Great,' he said. 'They'll pay you, and I'll tell them that you're going to be there instead of me.'

"The lords-and-ladies concert went well, and they asked me, how would I like to meet Princess Margaret and sing for a small group of people? I said sure, I'd love it.

"We met Princess Margaret at the top of the stairs. We shook hands. I bowed and my wife curtseyed. 'Pleased to meet you, ma'am' is what you say under those circumstances. 'Pleased to meet you, ma'am.' She was very relaxed and friendly. She said she was happy to meet a cowboy from America. Big smile on her face.

"I was singing a rather off-color song. Somebody told me that the princess got a big kick out of off-color ditties. It wasn't really foul, but it was bad enough that she liked it. It was called 'Hoorah, hoorah! My mother's going to be shot.'"

He picks up a guitar and sings the song with great relish in a strong western accent, as if he were announcing the good news in a nineteenth-century saloon. The song has several droll verses, each one celebrating the fact that a member of the singer's family is about to be done to death in some dramatic fashion, which serves them right for being mean to him when he was but a tot.

"I learned it from Tom Paley. Tom Paley was one of the best guitar players in the world. He could frail a guitar—you know, like the banjo players frail, with the backs of their fingers? He wore steel picks—backwards over his fingernails—because he didn't up-pick. He frailed the guitar. With a snap. Individual notes and chords. He's the only person I've ever seen do that."

Ramblin' Jack wasn't the first American folk guitarist, black or white, to tour the UK, but his story perfectly catches the cultural changes that were in the air in Britain in the mid-fifties, and the reasons why American folk music became so popular so quickly.

It was a time when the British educated middle classes—and Princess Margaret was famous, or notorious, for behaving more like a commoner than a royal—were just starting to be sick and tired of being stuffy. *The Goon Show* was already blasting the stuffiness out of BBC radio, the Royal Court Theatre was just starting to stage kitchen-sink dramas by Angry Young Men, the empire was well lost, and there was no longer any need to be top dogs, always on one's best table manners.

It was high time for the British to let their hair down, to start being a nation of ordinary people. And who better to show them the kind of spark that an ordinary person might claim than blues players and cowboys from the land of the free?

The American influx started in 1950 when the radical folklorist Alan Lomax fled the United States because of harrassment by the House Un-American Activities Committee and moved to England. Undaunted by the fact that he was in a new country with very different musical and cultural traditions, he carried on championing American folk music, black and white, in partnership with the British Isles folksinger Ewan MacColl, who had met and would marry Pete Seeger's sister Peggy. They produced a radio series for the BBC called *Ballads and Blues* that proved to be immensely popular, introducing Britons to the music of Josh White, Big Bill Broonzy, Jean Ritchie, and Ma Rainey, among others.

Parenthetically, it's worth pointing out that this is just the first of many instances in which the funding structure of British radio and television played a vital part in the evolution of music. Lomax's series would not have been broadcast nationally, commercial-free, in the United States. Likewise, every week from the mid-sixties almost to the present day a deejay named John Peel introduced out-of-the-mainstream music to a national audience on BBC radio. Everyone who is anyone, from Frank Zappa through the Sex Pistols to fin-de-siecle world music players, first aired on John Peel. U.S. audiences have always remained strangers to their own music because of the local and commercial nature of radio and television.

This fascination with what we would now call "roots" music led to one of the most important musical crazes of the fifties in Britain, a strange transatlantic hybrid of jug-band music and American fifties rock and roll: skiffle.

Skiffle involved playing American folk songs at a tempo driven by wild enthusiasm using instruments that called for a minimum of skill and investment. Although the word "skiffle" was first used to describe "rent" parties and their music in the twenties, British skiffle was invented more or less single-handedly by Tony Donegan, a guitarist who so admired the great blues/jazz guitarist Lonnie Johnson, who toured the UK in 1952, that he changed his own name to Lonnie Donegan. Donegan's 1954 recording of Leadbelly's "The Rock Island Line" spent twenty-two weeks on the UK charts and even cracked the U.S. Top 20, something unheard of for a British musician. (He subsequently toured the United States with Chuck Berry, Bill Haley, and the Harlem Globetrotters.) Between 1956 and 1962 Donegan had no fewer than seventeen UK Top 10 singles. BBC radio launched *Saturday Skiffle Club*, which drew a weekly audience of two and a half million. At its most basic, skiffle featured a washboard or a tea chest for a drum kit, a washtub bass, and a three-chord guitar. The guitar was reinventing itself yet again, starting from scratch.

Which it had to, because one of the great ironies of the British Invasion was that it was a guitar-based musical movement that came from a land with virtually no guitar tradition at all. This was an asset, though; everything that happened with the guitar over the next few years had the fervor of discovery about it, and this novelty and excitement created an accelerated rate of progress. In ten years Britain went from skiffle to John Renbourn, Eric Clapton, Jimmy Page, Peter Green.

While skiffle was all the rage, Chris Barber, a New Orleans-style jazz trombonist turned skiffle and blues enthusiast, and Alexis Korner, a French-born Anglo-Greek R&B guitarist, arranged a series of tours starting in 1954 that soon brought Big Bill Broonzy, Brownie McGhee, Muddy Waters, Sister Rosetta Tharpe, Memphis Slim, and other American roots musicians to the UK.

The blues musicians in particular were astounded to find they were better known in Britain (and in some cases on mainland Europe too) than in the United States, and much better appreciated.

"When the boat landed in Southampton," Brownie McGhee said later, "I didn't know what to expect. I'm getting off the boat and the bands was playin', the music was ravin' and the cameras were flashin' and I was ducking my head saying, 'Excuse me, sorry, what do you want?' And they said, 'You.' 'What do you want me for?' I thought I was in the way. They kept taking pictures of me. I said, 'Nobody knows

me here, who'd want pictures of me?' And when Chris Barber got to
me he says, 'Brownie, this is all for you.' I says, 'What for?' He says,
'They're welcoming you here to the shore.' . . . I'd never been out of
the country, and I just couldn't believe it could happen. I'd never been
appreciated in America and nobody thought anything of the blues,
which is American—the blues is America, America is the blues, and I
*am* the blues—so I didn't think I should go anywhere else till America
was understanding it. But when I got there it was altogether a different thing in '58."

At the same time Ewan MacColl, in his own peculiar way (he in-
sisted on absolute authenticity in traditional music, yet he had
changed his own name from William Miller to sound more ethnic) was
almost single-handedly starting the British folk revival, which in the
early days in particular opened its arms to visiting American guitarists
and banjo players. The Hendrix hit "Hey Joe" was written by an
American and a Scot in a coffee bar in Edinburgh in 1956. In the early
sixties Bob Dylan and Paul Simon, both unknown and neither much
admired, would play the British folk clubs and learn songs and arrangements from pioneering British guitarists such as Davy Graham and
Martin Carthy.

The generation of British guitarists who were already adults in the
fifties would turn out to be far less influential in the long run than the
kids growing up, hearing this musical frenzy all around them. Jack
Elliott had no idea what he and his compatriots were starting.

"I went to visit a ship called the *Arethusa*—she used to be a training
ship—down where she was anchored in the Medway. Rochester. I
believe [my wife and I] stayed overnight at a bed-and-breakfast place,
and caught a train back to London. As we were standing on the station platform waiting for the train, I looked across the track and on
the opposite [platform] there were some children aged about—I don't
know—eleven or twelve, thirteen, fourteen years old, waiting to go to
school one or two stops down the line. We're just waiting for a train,
nobody's doing anything but standing around, so I thought I'd entertain 'em a little bit. I got my guitar out of the case and played 'em
some cowboy songs. Across the void. And they clapped, and our train

came, and I quickly bundled up my guitar, waved good-bye to the kids, and we went our way and they went their way.

"One of those children turned out to be Mick Jagger. Little did I know, but I had inspired him to go out and buy a guitar."

It was a time infectious with discovery, a time of self-teaching under ridiculous handicaps, a time of small conspiracies of teenage guitarists.

Kids who would later be Beatles, Stones, and Whos went to see Bill Haley, Buddy Holly, Chuck Berry. Haley was the first to tour; when he was booked into an all-seating hall, the audience tore up seats so they could dance. Brian Jones, later of the Rolling Stones, got a job in a record store just to be able to hear the latest blues releases when they arrived from the United States. He was so excited when he first heard Elmore James ("I discovered Elmore James, and the earth seemed to shudder on its axis") he went out and bought a Harmony Stratatone, with a single pickup, and used a converted tape recorder as an amp. Eric Clapton, who during the day was working laying floors, soaked up Freddie King, Buddy Guy, B. B. King, and T-Bone Walker. At the age of thirteen Dave Gilmour, later of Pink Floyd, inherited a cheap Spanish guitar from a neighbor and learned from a book and record set by Pete Seeger.

"When I was growing up," Jimmy Page said, "there was one other guitarist in my school. He showed me the first chords that I learned, and I went on from there. I taught myself the guitar from listening to records. . . . The early rock of the fifties. Elvis. I was gobbling it all up. Johnny Burnett Rock 'n' Roll Trio. Gene Vincent. Bit by bit—the blues—Muddy Waters, Elmore James. Robert Johnson."

Import restrictions made American guitars hard to come by, and the arrival of a new genuine American guitar was almost as good as the arrival of a genuine American guitarist.

The Who made their own guitars, which were butt-ugly but worked reasonably well for a short time. Unfortunately the glue they used wasn't strong enough and the necks had a tendency to fold up onstage, leaving the player holding what the band described as "a floppy harp."

Hank Marvin and the Shadows, backing Cliff Richard and also becoming famous for Ventures-style guitar instrumentals, played guitars with names that have been deservedly lost to history: an acoustic Hofner Congress, a Guyatone LG50, a Besson Star semiacoustic bass, a Grimshaw Short Scale Deluxe. Marvin played through a no-name amplifier he often described as being about the size of a cornflake box, and sounding like one.

When Cliff Richard offered to buy Marvin a better guitar, the band knew that Ricky Nelson's guitarist used a Fender, and they'd seen Fenders on the sleeves of Buddy Holly LPs, so they sent off to the United States for a Fender catalog, and then a Fender Stratocaster, direct from the Fender factory. When the guitar finally arrived in March of 1959, Marvin said, "It was like seeing something from another planet."

The case alone left them speechless.

"No one had ever seen anything like it," said Bruce Welch, the Shadows' rhythm guitarist. "It had that beautiful birdseye maple neck, the parts were all gold-plated and of course it was that gorgeous pink colour. But first of all, there was the tweed case—the tweed case with all that velvet inside—and when we opened it, it just took our breath away."

From the beginning of the fifties, then, the guitar flowed across the Atlantic from West to East. When did the tide turn? At what point did it travel back to America, reimagined and transformed? Your finger's on the buzzer. You're about to say "*Ed Sullivan Show,* February 1964!" Wrong, I'm afraid. The first assault by the forces of the British Invasion had nothing to do with the Beatles, or anyone else from Liverpool. It was the work of a young guitarist called Vic Flick.

One Monday in June of 1962, Vic Flick invented the most famous guitar phrase in the history of the instrument, a phrase that would be heard in every country in the world, over and over again for at least four decades, a phrase that single-handedly would give the guitar a new adventurous, dynamic image, sophisticated yet sexy, macho as all get out. It was . . . well, I'll tell you the story.

Including Vic, there were perhaps only five session guitarists in Britain at the time, but the number would shortly increase by two, both of whom would ultimately leave studio work to try and seek their fortune on their own. One was John McLaughlin, who would pursue one of the most original and unpredictable careers of any guitarist. The other was the very young Jimmy Page, who was struggling a little at this point because he couldn't read music. This would normally be a fatal shortcoming for a session player, but producers could see at once that he was capable of interesting bluesy bits and pieces on the guitar that nobody else could play or, frankly, could understand, so Page was quite busy.

Vic Flick became a session guitarist because, unlike most guitarists, he could read music. His father played piano in a band, his brother played bass, and a friend played sax. One day a neighbor brought over an old Gibson that Vic grabbed and started learning. To be heard over the other instruments he went to an army surplus store and bought an old tank commander's throat microphone, which he taped to the machine head, amplified through a radio, and he became, after a fashion, an electric guitarist.

Within a couple of years Vic went into TV show studio orchestras, playing whatever was put in front of him in whatever style was needed, backing many of the early British rockers whose names are now remembered only by the faithful (Cliff Richard, Adam Faith, Shirley Bassey, and many more). When not in the studio he played for John Barry, a trumpet player and bandleader of the John Barry Seven, a sort of Anglo R&B band with Flick on lead guitar playing a slightly grungier version of the Ventures style that was the trademark of Hank Marvin of the Shadows.

Barry was also starting to compose and arrange film scores. One day he got a phone call from an unknown pair of film producers, who had commissioned a score for their upcoming movie but discovered that it wasn't all it might have been. Could Barry rewrite and rerecord the whole thing in two weeks?

Barry threw the Seven into the studio, with no time for anything more than one take per sequence. The main headache was the opening tune, the title-sequence theme that would set the tone and the mood for the whole movie. The theme the film company was contractually obliged to use was slow, and . . . um . . . lame. Barry, the horn guy, punched up the horn parts. Flick listened and said, "Let's take it down to the low E string. Make it more dynamic."

Vic Flick got out his guitar. The instrument had another of those names remembered only by the faithful: it was a Clifford Essex Paragon, an f-hole jazz-style guitar, loosely speaking a knockoff of the Gibsons of the mid-fifties, all but unavailable in England. It had a DeArmond pickup (also a venerable relic) and he played it through a DeArmond volume pedal into a Vox amp. The amp had an output of fifteen watts. The little extension speakers I plug into my laptop have more power.

The take began: brasses and a few strings that Barry had hired by the day. Flick came in around the fifth measure, playing Duane Eddy–style, down on the bass strings, a simple riff. They ran through the track, stopped, Barry said okay, and they moved on. Flick says he can't remember what else happened that day ("I did so many sessions I didn't know what was happening. At the end of the day you come out as if you're coming back from Mars") but there was probably another session in the afternoon, when he might have done a jingle or something equally unglamorous. He got paid a standard session rate for the film score: probably seven pounds ten shillings, maybe twenty-five dollars at the time. He forgot the film score almost at once. Neither he nor John Barry went to the premiere.

The film was *Dr. No*. The guitar phrase Vic Flick came up with was the James Bond theme. He had played the riff that was heard around the world, the most famous guitar fragment ever, still macho, still sexy, echoing to this day.

George Martin famously said that what appealed to him about the Beatles, at first sight, was not their musicianship, which was pretty shaky, but their humor. What got the Beatles into America was not their humor, not their songwriting, not even the fact that they were creating the kind of madness in England and Europe that Elvis had caused in the States, but their use of the guitar.

The man who made the decision to release the Beatles was Capitol Records' artists and repertoire producer Dave Dexter Jr., a jazz producer, interestingly, and former *DownBeat* journalist. Even though the Beatles' UK label, EMI, owned Capitol, Dexter didn't like "Love Me Do"—whose harmonica opening was unusual and rootsy in England but perhaps too black for America—and passed on it. He passed on "Please Please Me," which kicked off with a vocal-group harmony attack. He passed on "From Me to You," another vocal-group song. He passed on "She Loves You," which opens with a drum assault. (All were picked up by minor labels and sold very few copies.)

He agreed to listen to "I Want to Hold Your Hand" only under protest, and said later, "The first four bars of the song, that guitar just grabbed me. A five-year-old kid, an eighty-year-old man would have picked that record."

The Beatles opened the transatlantic floodgates. Manfred Mann hit number one with "Do Wah Diddy Diddy," the Zombies made number two with "She's Not There," and more than a dozen others, remembered and forgotten, came too: the Dave Clark Five, Gerry and the Pacemakers, Billy J Kramer and the Dakotas, the Searchers, the Kinks, the Animals, the Rolling Stones, Freddie and the Dreamers, Herman's Hermits, and Wayne Fontana and the Mindbenders.

Perhaps the most important contribution of the British Invasion was in helping America connect with its own past and its alienated present. The small steps that the folk movement was taking to rehabilitate black musicians suddenly seemed ridiculously tentative. When an interviewer asked the Beatles what they were looking forward to visiting in America, they answered "Chuck Berry and Bo Diddley." And when the interviewer stupidly said, "Where's that?" Lennon's indignation flattened the guy. "Don't you even know your own music?"

The liberation was not just of race but also of class. The rockabilly musicians of the fifties had the wrong accent and the wrong clothes, and their guitars arrived with decades of antirural prejudice. The Beatles could play the same songs (in some instances even with nearly the same accents) but they had the massive advantage of coming in from outside the American class-and-region matrix. Their hair, their clothes, their humor, their slang, their Liverpudlianism—the total package obliterated any stigma of the songs' origins, and of course from a teenager's point of view any song that is six years old is already an unknown country. The guitar group was now an English phenomenon, even if most of the guitars the lads were playing were American instruments making a kind of triumphant homecoming, and it was perfectly okay for middle-class white American kids to bug their parents to buy 'em one.

Along the same lines, the British Invasion gave the guitar *range*. In America the guitar was still confined to certain genres and regions, but the Brits, less confined by tradition, took the guitar everywhere. The Beatles alone, thanks to being so musically omnivorous while basically remaining a vocal group with guitars and a very good bass player, gave it dozens of different voices. Spanish nylon-string on "Michelle." Indian sitar flavor. The feedback at the beginning of "I Feel Fine," soon to be a rock cliché. Echoes of Chuck Berry, Buddy Holly, Eddie Cochran, bossa nova, surf sound—but they took those echoes and tied them to such utterly different subjects that never again would they seem so narrow and isolated. By taking a Beach Boys sound and using it for "Back in the USSR," they made the Beach Boys suddenly seem part of a much larger and less shallow ocean.

Even the wimpy and slightly wet bands like Herman's Hermits and Brian Poole and the Tremolos had their part to play: a dopey song like "Mrs. Brown, You've Got a Lovely Daughter" would have been as unthinkable in the United States as "Lucy in the Sky with Diamonds." It was not so much an invasion as a liberation. The guitar was now open for business—any guitar, for any business, in any arena. It was a palette of a hundred sounds instead of a dozen, and guitarists all over America couldn't wait to try them all out.

# Mummified

I'm forced to miss another step in the building process, the one I most wanted to see: the closing of the box.

It wouldn't be just like the mechanic slamming the hood, wiping his hands, I thought. There must be a more organic sense, as if the skin, the final and largest organ, were being pulled over the interior body, taking all of those potential elements of the sound and making them active, turning the shaped pieces of wood into if not a finished guitar, then at least an exquisitely tuned guitar-shaped drum.

As a distant second best, Rick describes the process from his admittedly less romantic point of view.

The first element is the lining, which is rather like quarter-round that has been kerfed, or deeply nicked at regular intervals, so it looks like the crest of skin running up an iguana's back. Kerfing makes it easier to bend, though it does give the corners of the guitar a slightly crocodilian appearance. Rick glues lining to the sides where they will join the top and back, increasing the gluing surface by a factor of a hundred, probably, he says.

He places the sides on the top and on the back, in sequence, cuts the ends of the braces to length, and cuts little pockets into the linings to cup the ends of the braces, and perhaps also to help transmit the vibrations running down the braces into the outer reaches of the top. He does this for all the back braces and the three significant top braces. Then he glues the whole thing together.

Then comes one of the trickiest and most infuriating parts of the whole process: gluing the binding. The binding, remember, is the strip of wood that finishes off the join between sides and top, or sides and back, making the whole thing look squared-off, attractive, professional. Luthiers being luthiers, this is rarely one long whippy length of binding; it may be two or even three, as they add other thin slices (in my case, the blue-dyed maple) so the end result will look even more squared-off, attractive, and professional. So the luthier is wrestling with all these thin, whippy strips like a one-armed wallpaper hanger, trying to get them all in place, aligned, and glued down, into a tight joint in three dimensions that to make matters worse keeps bending back and forth as the sides move out and in and out and in again. (The cutaway at this point must start looking like a really, really bad idea.)

This is the kind of problem for which luthiers love inventing jigs—in other words, ad hoc devices that turn a day's work into an hour's. The invention for gluing the binding is the most amateurish-looking of them all. It involves wrapping the body in strips of cloth or sacking, inch by painful inch, to hold the latest section of binding in place, until the whole instrument looks mummified.

"The whole process is much easier if you use plastic binding," Rick says, but I recognize this as heresy, and ignore it.

# Something Is Happening

While the British Invasion was brewing, the electric guitar survived the collapse of American rock and roll by the most astonishing of tactics: playing instrumentals.

The main rockabilly survivor was Duane Eddy, whose twangy low-string sound, with extra tremolo added, and run by engineer/producer Lee Hazlewood through an echo chamber, became one of the defining guitar sounds of the fifties, joining Chuck Berry's riffs on the first American teenage guitar soundtrack. The Eddy/Hazlewood sound was enormously influential and successful. Eddy had fifteen Top Forty hits between 1958 and 1962 and is thought to have sold a hundred million records in his lifetime.

His daring initiative in experimenting with guitar instrumentals—a genre with virtually no precedent in the United States—was picked up by other bands, and for a few years the guitar leaped into the spotlight with a series of instrumentals that started out as novelties and rapidly became something more substantial.

Perhaps the first of the instrumental bands was the Fireballs, out of Raton, New Mexico, in 1959. On their heels came the String-A-Longs, a band produced by Norman Petty, Buddy Holly's onetime producer, out of Clovis, New Mexico. They had an unexpected instrumental hit called "Wheels," a simple tune, picked crisply with the strings damped with the heel of the right hand; it appeared in late 1960 and peaked at number three in the United States and number eleven in the UK.

In the same year the Ventures, from the Pacific Northwest, expanded and advanced the guitar instrumental, taking it away from its 2/4 rockabilly roots by changing to 4/4 rock time and adding a greater variety of chords. "Walk, Don't Run," released in 1960 (and financed by the mother of one of the band members), became a number two U.S. hit.

It was a sign of the intensity of feeling inspired by the rockabilly bands and their offspring that a degree of guitar brand awareness arose, something that, as I'll discuss in a later chapter, had been conspicuously missing in the field of guitars.

"Gretsches and Gibsons were the guitars of choice by the early rockabilly and western bands," Dick Stewart, a surf/rockabilly guitarist, producer, and historian told me. "It was The Ventures that really put the Strat, Jazzmaster, and Jaguar on the map with the early '60s garage bands. The whole look of Fender in general was so novel that it really put all the other guitars in the back seat from 1959 to 1964. During that time, garage bands were considered nerds if any brands other than Fender were used. It had to be 100% Fender (lead, rhythm, bass) with no mixing of other brands, and the band was even more cool if all were sunburst in color."

The other sound to grow from rockabilly and become a rage was surf rock—not the Beach Boys, who were essentially a vocal group with thin, retro guitar fills heavily indebted to Chuck Berry, but the heavy-reverb, double-picked sound of the Chantays, the Surfaris, and above all Dick Dale. Leo Fender invited Dale, the self-styled "King of the Surf Guitar," to act as a kind of extreme product tester for Fender's amps and speakers, and Dale reportedly blew up forty-nine, claiming that he wanted to re-create the sound of Gene Krupa, described on Dale's Web site as "the famous jazz drummer that created the sounds of the native dancers in the jungles along with the roar of mother nature's creatures and the roar of the ocean."

Surf music had such a distinctive (if rather narrow) sound that it has remained identified with surfing and hot-rod cars, especially on the West Coast, ever since. Dick Dale's classic "Miserlou," which he adapted from a belly-dancing piece his Lebanese uncle played on oudh, turned up in the movie *Pulp Fiction*. It's a sign of some strange kind of lingering power that when the vast corporate conglomerate Clear Channel Communications issued a list of 150 songs to be pulled from the air after the attack of September 11, 2001, one of them was Jan and Dean's "Dead Man's Curve."

While the electric guitar was making inroads from the West, the acoustic guitar was growing in the East. The folk movement had finally acquired both momentum and seriousness of purpose.

One difference between rock and roll and the folk movement was that rock and roll had promoters and folk music had evangelists. In late 1957 the Old Town School of Folk Music opened in Chicago and within two months more than 150 students were taking weekly guitar and banjo classes, learning folk dancing, and taking part in family sing-alongs. Over the next few years Pete Seeger, Mahalia Jackson, Big Bill Broonzy, Josh White, Doc Watson, the Reverend Gary Davis, Dave Van Ronk, Jose Feliciano, and a host of other performers, remembered and forgotten, performed at the school, and Roger McGuinn of the Byrds, John Prine, and the late Steve Goodman and Bob Gibson all studied there.

In some important respects, folk music was about reuniting the divide between North and South, and the Old Town School was well aware of that divide, organizing field trips to take part in music festivals like the one in Mountain View, Arkansas, where "Kids, five and six years old, played fiddle, guitar and banjo. Likewise, their parents, grandparents, aunts and uncles were all playing traditional and old-timey music. Bluegrass was forbidden. . . . Fabulous jamming in the little town square. Dancing in the back of the town jail. Enormous do-it-yourself breakfasts at the Pony Peak Ranch. Quilts for sale hanging in one front yard after another. And music everywhere from dawn to dusk."

A series of musicologists and enthusiasts searched the South to find musicians heard first on old recordings—Clarence Ashley and Doc Watson, Roscoe Holcomb, Almeida Riddle, Lightnin' Hopkins, Mississippi John Hurt, Fred McDowell, Son House, and many others, black and white—and bring them to the Northeast to perform. Guitar skills fixed for years, even decades, like insects in amber, were released into the greater community, into the air.

And in that community a second generation of guitarists was listening, watching fingers, asking questions: Dave Van Ronk, John Fahey, Mike Bloomfield, the young Bonnie Raitt. "I was the weird little white girl playing Robert Johnson songs. They got a big kick out of the fact that a woman was playing slide guitar in the first place, let alone an eighteen-year-old round-faced redhead!" At the age of twenty she was hired by Buddy Guy and Junior Wells as part of their act when they opened for the Rolling Stones, and she has spent a lifetime studying the slide guitar like a monk might study the works of the Buddha, gaining the wisdom and the courage to play fewer and fewer notes.

At the same time, the guitar was taking on a public, political identity in the turbulent times that had already begun with voter registration and civil rights activities in the South and the Free Speech Movement at Berkeley, as it would in the anti–Vietnam War movement and, interestingly, among servicemen serving in Vietnam, whose songs and music are even now barely being archived and studied.

"Wherever I go in the world and I look for forces that are struggling against injustice," said the musician and activist Harry Belafonte, "I always seem to find somebody with a guitar and a voice and they're always singing to something that inspires the community, no matter how ravaged that community may be."

Time and again the television showed a march, or a speech, or a rally, and somewhere in the middle of that mass of people would be someone with a guitar. This became a crucial symbol of small voices calling or singing out in defiance. The very smallness of the acoustic guitar, and its thin, hollow vulnerability, stood for courage and a message in the face of ignorance and oppression. It was the guitar's finest hour.

Sadly, as soon as the guitar displayed its ability to speak for and to Americans en masse, it became vulnerable to exploitation in a way that seems all too reminiscent of singing cowboys and cheap stenciled guitars. In late 1960 Joan Baez's first album, a resinging of traditional songs and ballads, hit the Billboard chart and stayed there for 140 weeks, earning well over a million dollars. In 1963 Peter, Paul and Mary's version of "Blowin' in the Wind" reached number two on the pop charts and sold more than a million copies. Certain parties began to sit up and take notice: there might be money to be made in this folk fad, as long as the political and social element could be toned down. The result was the sudden and brief popularity of the word "hootenanny."

It was never clear exactly what "hootenanny" meant, but it neatly combined the rustic old-time feel of such words as "hoedown" with just enough novelty to appeal to young folkies. (The word "shindig" would soon be used for very similar reasons, and also as the name of a TV show.) As such, it became shorthand for "pipeline-to-vast-untapped-reserves-of-money," as enterprises from every corner of the culture tried to cash in on the folk boom. More than two hundred albums of "folk music" were released in the United States in 1963 alone, including *Jazz Meets the Folk Song, Soul Meeting Saturday Night Hootenanny Style, Kiddie Hootenanny,* and *Hot Rod Hootenanny.* ABC's show *Hootenanny,* already mentioned for its craven support of blacklisting, reached an estimated eleven million viewers weekly. At least two dozen magazines about folk music were being published. The word even turned up in the title of a movie: *Hootenanny Hoot* (1963) starred Judy Henske and Johnny Cash, of all people, in a story about undergraduate folksingers who liked to play guitars on the beach. WCPO in Cincinnati went "100% Hootenanny"—all folk, all the time. Parkway Ford, a car dealership in New Jersey, had a "hootenanny sale," with local

folksingers sitting on the hoods of the cars in the lot. It was Davy
Crockett hats all over again.

Yet in one respect the era was already showing the first signs of
ending: when Joan Baez and Bob Dylan, already stars, stayed in California they didn't play in the coffeehouses along Cannery Row because, Dylan said, he had promised Albert Grossman, his manager, he
would never play in a coffeehouse again.

All this was changed by the British Invasion, whose East-West phase
broke over America in a mass media event that, in effect, helped to
create the very idea of mass media events.

The Beatles' first appearance on the *Ed Sullivan Show* was watched
by an estimated 73,700,000 viewers, the largest audience in television
history to date, but even that wasn't the start of it all. The major
magazines such as *Life, Look, The Saturday Evening Post, Time,* and
*Newsweek* reported on the Beatles even before the *Sullivan* appearance,
in some cases even before they reached the United States. Walter
Cronkite had scooped Ed Sullivan by including a clip of a live European Beatles performance on the *CBS Evening News* and Jack Paar had
done likewise on prime time NBC. The guitar was also all over radio,
jukeboxes, and movie theaters. On March 28, 1964, the Beatles had
ten singles on the Billboard Hot 100. On August 1, *A Hard Day's Night*
opened simultaneously in five hundred sold-out theaters in the United
States.

Dennis Koster, the renowned flamenco and classical guitarist, was
thirteen when the Beatles hit. "It created something of a mania and a
frenzy, a mass insanity" he told me. "All the kids used to go to sleep
with transistor radios under their pillows, and they would spin the dial
to the three AM rock stations. That song was so popular you'd want to
listen to it over and over again, so you'd put it on the first rock station,
you'd listen to it. As soon as it was over you'd spin to the next station,
and inevitably they were playing it, and as soon as that was over you'd
spin to the third station and they'd be playing it, and then by that time
the first station was ready to play it again."

This set Bob Dylan thinking.

In the history of the guitar, at best an amoral instrument, Bob Dylan was, I think, a mixed blessing. When he arrived in the Greenwich Village folk scene in 1961, there was almost no such thing as a singer/songwriter/guitarist. How could anyone, least of all a kid, write a song of the folk? The folk movement had developed as a revival movement, not a creative one, despite the fact that its saint, Woody Guthrie (now wasting away in hospital with a degenerative disease) wrote songs of social protest all the time. Dylan's après-Woody protest songs galvanized songwriting, especially for the guitar, and Phil Ochs, Tom Paxton, and hundreds of others followed his lead.

Yet with startling suddenness Dylan abandoned his social agenda and began to write cryptic songs of almost hallucinatory vividness with a personal rather than social thrust. This was seen as something of a betrayal, but also as a liberation. Dylan broadened the emotional palette of the popular song to the point where, for the singer/songwriter/guitarist, anything was fair game. As Nanci Griffith has written, "He's great at writing bitter songs. And that, fundamentally, is what I realized when I first heard Dylan—that you can express anything in songs."

In doing so, Dylan also created the beginnings of a new repertoire and vocabulary for college-educated guitarists. Five years previously, college kids were listening to the poppy acoustic folk of the Kingston Trio. Dylan was writing material that was caustic, superior, and contemporary. A new class was emerging, the intelligent and aware young middle class, and Dylan was the first person to write its curriculum. Dylan gave them a voice, or a series of voices, that no student body in America had had. In doing so he helped redefine the acoustic guitar as a modern instrument, as a thinking person's instrument, and as a middle-class instrument. He also, in *Nashville Skyline*, drew white middle-class attention to country music, flying in the face of decades of prejudice and inviting a reconnection between two divergent streams of guitar history.

Most important, perhaps, he did this with only entry-level guitar skills. Great guitarists don't tend to cause guitar booms, because it takes years to be able to play like them. All over America (and elsewhere) people who had never played guitar started singing Dylan songs.

This era came to an end on July 25, 1965, at the Newport Folk Festival. Newport had presented the best of both the "rediscovered" white and black folk musicians and their young admirer/counterparts since it first had been staged in 1959. Dylan was the biggest attraction on the bill in '65, the spearhead of folk music, but when he appeared at the festival he played "Maggie's Farm," "Like a Rolling Stone," and "It Takes a Lot to Laugh, It Takes a Train to Cry" backed by the Paul Butterfield Blues Band. That is, he went electric.

Accounts of audience reactions vary. Some booed, though it's not clear if they were booing Dylan's abandonment of acoustic folk music or the fact that the amplification was so poor and the band so untogether that the performance was a disaster. Albert Grossman, Dylan's manager and folk music's most financially successful entrepreneur, and Alan Lomax, master of ceremonies on the day, got into such a heated argument they began rolling on the ground, fighting. The gentle Pete Seeger (who stresses that "Maggie's Farm" is a great song) told me, "I went to the soundman and said, 'Fix the sound; nobody can understand the words.' He hollered back, 'No, this is the way they want it.' I hollered back, 'Dammit, if I had an axe I'd cut the cable.'" In either event, the cable remained uncut, and the invitation went out to America to turn folk into folk rock.

Dylan was certainly not the first musician to go electric in the United States in the wake of the British Invasion. The electric guitar seemed to promise the popularity of the Beatles, the broad-spectrum cool. All over the country kids were forming garage bands; the early Byrds were Beatles clones, down to the twelve-string Rickenbacker, the hair, the stage pose, the capes. But Dylan gave the imprimatur to folk rock, and in doing so he inevitably siphoned energy, money, and enrollment away from the folk movement. Folk rock has been credited with making pop music intelligent, but it could equally be said to have robbed folk music of some of its punch and clarity. With the exception of Clarence White's bluegrass-style innovations, folk rock tended to be instrumentally unambitious, and as Pete Seeger said, you couldn't hear the words, which tended to sink into the mix of electric rhythms and vocal harmonies.

Another point: American folk rock became a quintessential guitar medium, for better or worse. While British folk rock tended to include traditional instruments such as fiddle, accordion, tin whistle, Northumbrian pipes, and even hurdy-gurdy, in the United States "folk rock" meant Rock Lite, and one of its unfortunate effects was to grant the guitar a sweeping victory over more traditional folk instruments. Acoustic folk music also turned out to be far more durable in the UK than in the United States, perhaps because of the extensive network of folk clubs that had sprung up during the fifties and early sixties, many of them connected to pubs, while in the United States coffeehouses were declining. (The fate of an entire branch of music may have rested on the drinking age, and the fact that there's more money to be made selling beer than selling coffee.) By the early 1970s the diversity of American music was actually diminishing. The guitar had defeated all comers, and the world was the poorer for it.

Dylan also affected the folk movement in one more important way: he took away some of its heart, its well-intentioned, open-armed, collaborative Pete Seegerness. From the late sixties onward, folk music would be reinterpreted to center on the personal lyrics of the privileged. The political agenda was left to secondary players such as Country Joe McDonald. Over the next two decades the revival element would shear off and focus on bluegrass or old-time music or blues, and the social concern would increasingly consist of persuading rockers to play high-profile benefits. Interest in the guitar as an instrument of performance drifted toward Celtic, new age, and world music.

The rise of women's music, spearheaded by Joni Mitchell, provided so many strong singer/guitarist/songwriters that, like a new celestial star cluster, they created their own gravity. A woman performer who might once have been regarded as a folksinger might now be called a feminist musician, like Holly Near, or new country, like Iris DeMent or Lucinda Williams, or as a phenomenon in her own right, like Ani

DiFranco. In any case, she might find it harder and harder to get airplay or recording contracts because the conclusion the music business came to as a result of this fragmentation was that folk music no longer sold.

Even that wasn't the most disheartening blow, because folkies had always operated by marginal and creative financing. The hardest thing was that by the early eighties it no longer seemed as if you could save the world simply by picking up an acoustic guitar. With the ascendancy of Reagan, the religious right, and rabid antienvironmentalism as personified by James Watt, it was clear that the Age of Aquarius had been replaced by the Age of Babbitt. Idealists became entrepreneurs, and the educated college-age middle class were applying to business schools and getting their own credit cards. Solo singer/songwriters began to seem not only powerless but foolish. The acoustic guitar in the raised fist faded into an image on a poster in the attic, and for the first time in decades sales began to decline.

# Inlay

As I'm on my way up Stage Road a trio of hikers, crossing the road on the Long Trail, wave me down. "There are three baby bears on the road up ahead." Sure enough, what I've taken for a Newfoundland frolicking on the edge of the road is a black bear cub; as I drive very slowly toward it, it gallops into the woods, running as if its paws are still too big, followed by its two siblings.

In Rick's little shop, the neck is lying on the workbench, gleaming, sanded, and polished and ready for lacquering. You have to lacquer the neck and body separately before fitting them together, Rick explains, because if you spray the combined unit with lacquer you'll never get the two pieces apart when you want to carry out repairs.

Zoe was right: you don't consciously see the thin strips of blue veneer on each side of the ebony spine—they just add warmth to the ebony, making it seem faintly blue-black. The faceplate, now glued onto the front of the headstock, is breathtaking but surprisingly light, a golden brown rather than a rich red. Even though the lacquer supposedly contains anti-UV agents, the cherry will darken and redden, Rick said—quite dramatically over the next month, then steadily over the longer term.

He has another guitar in progress, intended for Healdsburg. I notice that the fingerboard is not very black—it seems slightly dusty in color, halfway to charcoal—and I wonder if it is actually some kind of dark rosewood, as that's the only other wood hard enough to be commonly used for a fingerboard. No, it's ebony, he says, just a lightish piece. Ebony varies. "Most companies dye their ebony fingerboards," he said with a touch of disgust. "And they use some pretty strange shit. Like this." He picks up a container of black leather dye. "I use the best ebony I can get, and if the client doesn't like it . . ."

But I'm here to look at the inlay on my guitar.

Considering that the entire conception and design of this guitar started with the inlays, you'd think that this would be the one area where everything goes smoothly. It isn't. It's the one aspect of the guitar about which I will end up feeling distinctly lukewarm, though this probably says as much about my mixed feelings about inlay as about anything else. Rick's, too, probably.

I told Rick, "Well, you know about the inlay. Maple leaves. Perfect. Go for it."

Next thing I know we have maple leaves falling down toward the sound hole, twisting this way and that, not in a straight line down the middle of the fingerboard but slightly windblown to one side or the other. Fine. But at the octave, two snowflakes. And above the octave, little diamonds.

These aren't maple leaves, I say, unnecessarily.

Maple leaves won't fit, he points out. The frets get narrower, after all. Inwardly, I grumble: why couldn't he have pointed this out before? When I think about it, though, it makes perfect sense. The snowflakes at the twelfth fret turn the neck from autumn to winter, and the diamonds at the thirteenth, fifteenth, and eighteenth now look like ice crystals. A classic statement about Vermont, combining beauty and pessimism.

I also said something, those many months ago, like "So let's do a maple leaf on the headstock." I guess I should have made it clearer, but what I had in mind, having spent so many months salivating over luthier Web sites, is a large maple leaf, a stunning maple leaf, maybe two inches across by three inches high, made of countless slivers of iridescent abalone—or maple, for that matter. I didn't mind. I just wanted it to be unforgettable. I even told him I didn't like his signature Running Dog retriever image, a silhouette of Alta chasing after the Whiffle ball, on the headstock and he agreed to forgo it in the name of my maple leaf.

What he's come up with is two small leaves, one high up on the headstock where the maker's signature or logo might go, one roughly halfway down to the nut. They look inconsequential; the second looks almost like an afterthought. I challenge him in my timid way; he provides unexpected resistance and points out that to change it now will involve making a whole new headstock. All too aware of how little I'm paying him and how much work he's putting in, I give in with a poor show of graciousness.

What has happened is that I've been dragged into the rising tide of guitar inlay, a series of changes as radical and potentially controversial as anything else happening in the guitar world. Inlay has become more common, more elaborate, more ambitious, more colorful, more broadly available. It's not just a question of degrees of ornamentation, though. Inlay is also changing the very nature of the guitar—well, some guitars, at least—from being a functioning, attractive musical instrument to a work of art. It's also changing the relationship between the owner and the guitar to the point where the guitar can now be something unique to the owner, a totem that adds degrees of meaning to the already intimate connection between player and plaything.

The earliest surviving guitars are florid with inlay, a harlequinade of decoration. (This may, in fact, be why they survived while plainer instruments perished, one exception being a guitar by Antonio Stradivari, which is as elegantly simple as a violin.) Vines and fleurs-de-lis crawl from headstock to rosette, or along the slim panels that make up the back. Discs of mother-of-pearl rim the top and sound hole, and elaborate foliage curls up around bridges like a horticultural mustache. One French guitar took tortoiseshell decoration to such an extreme that the entire back of the instrument was a single tortoise's shell, with ceramic head, feet, and tail added. Another turned the fingerboard into a miniature replica of the Colonne Vendome in Paris, built to commemorate the victories of Napoleon, with Bonaparte himself standing on the headstock.

By the late nineteenth century inlay work on American guitars had settled into a set of conventions, especially floral and geometric forms. Archtop jazz guitars in the 1930s developed an art deco look. The only other innovation took place in country music, where Jimmie Rodgers had his name inlaid up the fingerboard of his guitar, beginning a tradition that country musicians have followed ever since. Not banjos. Not fiddles. The country singer and his guitar were buddies. They were one.

Two changes took place in the sixties, one fairly transient and superficial, and one that took place in the heart of commercial guitar making. The first was that guitarists began painting, sticking, attaching, or inlaying all kinds of symbols, icons, and bric-a-brac to their guitars in a kind of "instrument tattoo."

The second was that Martin Guitars, which as yet had no custom shop or inlay specialists, asked two musician/luthier/inlayers, Mike Longworth and Dave Nichols, to develop a custom shop. Martin became increasingly successful with replicas of its own smaller-bodied guitars from the late nineteenth and early twentieth centuries, complete with turn-of-the-century inlay patterns. Martin sent Nichols fingerboards, pick guards, bridges, headstocks, and other essential components, and he inlaid them and shipped them back. He was a cottage industry, and Victorian vine inlay became not only a common sight on guitars once more but also a marketing strategy by which Martin reminded the public of its pedigree among American guitar companies.

The inlay revolution moved up several gears in the nineties thanks to a series of high-priced commissions and a new way of producing and selling inlay, which had previously come in small chips but was now laminated into plates of workable abalone in a wider range of colors and materials. As a result, when Harvey Leach created a guitar as a memorial for the September 11 attacks on the World Trade Center and the Pentagon, the Statue of Liberty alone was composed of more than a hundred pieces of malachite, jade, varasite, and other green reconstituted stones. The flames were of orange spiny oyster, the fireman's helmet was black mother-of-pearl and sterling silver, and the American eagle was mother-of-pearl, coral, yellow corian, ebony, and turquoise. An ultra-thin wafer of mother-of-pearl, translucent only from certain angles, was overlaid in places to create the almost holographic effect of mist and cloud.

Meanwhile, computer numerically controlled (CNC) inlay machines were designed to cut large quantities of inlay in extremely fine detail—a Celtic knot, for example, whose line is no thicker than a thread. For the first time, a major guitar company could add delicate and attractive inlay to a mass-produced guitar at low unit cost—and charge substantially more for the guitar because of it.

It was the Canadian luthier/inlayer William "Grit" Laskin, though, who transformed the entire meaning of inlay, turning the guitar headstock and fingerboard into wooden canvases for works of inlay art that not only had special meaning for him or the guitar's owner, but were often ironic narratives or self-reflexive commentary on inlay itself.

The first thing that Laskin did was to broaden the range of the inlayer's palette without sacrificing subtlety of color or shading. What was once a cartoonish form became, in his hands, capable of remarkable life and dimensionality. A gymnast's leotard in red-stained bird's-eye maple is so right a match for the shell of her arms, legs, and back that we can virtually feel the garment's texture. He also allowed himself to incoporate his quirky and complex sense of humor, and also to play with perspective in the fashion of M. C. Escher, and his sheer dexterity was stunning. One inlay shows a scroll of music unspooling from a crack in the earth—it's a faithful rendering of Chopin's "Nocturne in E-flat Major." Question: how to engrave the lines of the staff, which need to be perfectly parallel? He tried to invent some sort of tool that could cut the five lines at once but in the end he cut the equal-spaced lines one at a time, freehand.

Laskin's guitars raise tricky questions, though, about the nature of the guitar. What happens when the guitar becomes an objet d'art rather than an instrument? Harvey Leach's September 11 guitar was made as a present for his brother, who doesn't even play guitar. Some of the best work by Dave Nichols and Larry Robinson has gone straight into museum cases without ever being played—flattering, certainly, but not very musical. The more astonishing (and valuable) the inlay, it seems, the less likely the guitar is to be played. This gives new meaning to Laskin's view of the guitar body as a canvas, or as a window. Is a guitar a guitar if it is never played?

This changes the playing field. Nowadays it's hard to be satisfied with a guitar if it isn't also a work of art, yet the art itself can diminish the guitar by clashing with it, or making its natural symmetrical dignity seem unimportant or even dowdy. The traditional vine inlays of the seventeenth to nineteenth centuries may have been conventional and unimaginative but at least they contributed to the overall conception of a guitar that was both aurally and visually harmonious. Ironically, few guitars are as stunning as Laskin's own uninlaid classical and flamenco guitars, which display the grace of the guitar's form at its very best.

All this talk of playable art and million-dollar inlays makes me think of a slightly different piece of guitar decoration, a kind of folk inlay maybe, which may have started with Ernest Tubb. After a performance, as the audience applauded, Tubb would flip his guitar over and show the crowd the back, where he had painted the word THANKS.

# Satisfaction

In the early sixties the guitar finally became an exciting instrument, not just because of what one instrument might do in the hands of one player in one club but because of what a variety of guitars were doing in a variety of hands all over the country.

In classical music, where the phrase "classical guitar" was still not regularly used, and the number of top players was still very limited, Segovia realized that it was no good being good; he had to groom a generation of successors to carry on his work.

As a teacher Segovia was demanding to the point of tyranny: he had standards to create and maintain, and he didn't care if there were corpses along the way. In 1964 Christopher Parkening, in his mid-teens, was chosen to be in Segovia's first United States master class, at the University of California at Berkeley. "All of the nine performers were sitting in a semi-circle on the stage and there were about 2,000 auditors in the concert hall," Parkening told me.

I got immediately nervous. You never knew when you were going to play. Segovia would look through those thick Coke-bottle glasses of his and suddenly point to you and say,

"Parkening," and you'd have a mild cardiac arrest! You reached
into your guitar case to pick out your guitar to come up and
play for him and you're realizing, you're playing the guitar for
*Andres Segovia.*

If Segovia liked your playing he was very gracious. He was
really an old-school gentleman. He loved to tell funny stories.
But if he didn't like your playing, especially in the earlier days,
he let you know, and could be very, very hard with the performer. One performer, a Spanish student, made the terrible
mistake of playing his own transcription of the famous Bach
*Chaconne* for Segovia, and Segovia had done a transcription of
that monumental work that was absolutely a masterpiece.
Beautiful fingerings and exquisite transcription, and this young
man foolishly had the nerve to play his own terrible transcription of this great piece. You could see an explosion was coming.
It's a twelve-minute-long piece, and you could see Segovia's
knee and leg start to fidget, building and building and building,
and finally he stamped his foot on the floor and the guitarist
stopped and he pointed to the door and he said "Leave town!"
That was it.

He was very hard with me. I—foolishly, and not knowing
the difference—the third day of the month-long masterclass
played the same piece, the Bach *Chaconne.* And my former
teachers had completely re-fingered the piece to make it
simpler to play, cross-stringing many notes, taking all of the
musicality of the piece. I had no clue that I was destroying
this masterpiece.

Cross-stringing, which is standard practice by, say, electric guitarists, simply means playing a scale or a run by moving from one string
to another rather than by moving up or down one string. It makes playing fast scales much easier, and on an electric it's perfectly justifiable.
On a classical guitar, though, each string has a different timbre, and a
guitarist with a good ear will take that into account.

So here I start the piece, in front of Andres Segovia, his wife sitting next to him, the other eight performing students, the two thousand in the auditorium, and I get about a third of the way into the piece and the next thing I heard was his foot come *crashing* down on the stage floor. I stopped playing and I looked up and his hands were over his head and he was livid. He said, "Why have you changed the fingerings?" His wife was kind of holding him back, and I'm melting on stage. Here's my idol and he's *furious* with me. And I said, "I didn't change the fingerings. My teacher changed the fingerings." He said, "Who is your teacher?" I told him. He said, "Change it back tomorrow!"

So I went back to my dorm room and I spent all night long re-learning the famous Bach *Chaconne*. I played it for him next day with his fingerings—it was like learning a new piece—and after that he was very gracious with me. I studied with him when he came to Los Angeles, and he invited me to Spain to study with him, and in fact to judge an international guitar competition with him. We became friends over the years. Every time he came to LA we would have lunch or dinner together, and I'm very grateful for that friendship.

Segovia could never have won such admiration simply by being a tyrant and a bully. Apart from his charm and kindness to those he liked, he also had a rare, even poetic gift for putting the guitar's qualities into words. When one interviewer discovered that Segovia was still playing over a hundred concerts a year all over the world, the guitarist replied, "I feel under my feet the roundness of the earth."

There's a beguiling blend of modesty and arrogance here: he is using poetry to maintain the image of the genius. He did it again when he trotted out the old saying that the guitar is an orchestra, but then added a beautiful little cadenza, perhaps one of his own: ". . . an orchestra that came to us from some smaller and more delicate planet." These Segovia aphorisms, still widely circulated among classical guitarists, were part of his teachings. If you are not a poet, he was saying, why play the guitar?

One of the corpses Segovia seemed only too happy to step over as he gave the classical guitar its due eminence was that of the flamenco guitar. When Segovia died in 1987, his obituary in the *New York Times* listed his life's goals. The first was "to redeem [the] guitar from . . . flamenco."

Given that the world's most influential guitarist spent his entire life damning flamenco, and given that it flourished in the small and belea- guered Gypsy subculture in Spain, and especially given that for gen- erations Gypsies refused to teach their guitar techniques to outsiders, it's amazing flamenco guitar took root in the United States at all. Must have something to do with the fact that it's the world's most exciting acoustic guitar music.

The collection of songs and dances that make up flamenco as we know it today explained Dennis Koster, one of the country's top fla- menco guitarists and the author of a three-volume flamenco method book, is only about 150 years old but the origins of the music go back to Moorish—that is, Arabic—southern Spain before 1492, when Moors, Jews, Gypsies, Christians, and other cultures created something of an artistic golden age. When Ferdinand and Isabella conquered Granada and subsequently the Inquisition was installed, all three cultures— Jews, Gypsies, Arabs—were considered heretics and were persecuted. The music of persecution, a kind of Spanish blues, became what we now know as flamenco, and its genius is that it combined Hebraic/ Arabic modal scales and melodies with North African rhythms, Span- ish folk dances, and European harmonies. (Arabic music tends not to use harmony in the sense that Europeans understand the term.) As a result of this fusion, Koster believes, "flamenco strikes a deep genetic chord in everyone."

For most of its existence flamenco was primarily a dance form, with singing. Given that the dances often took place out of doors and the musicians were playing small instruments, the guitars weren't expected to do much more than provide a dramatic, percussive accompaniment echoing the dancers' movements and steps.

The flamenco guitar grew up as the poor cousin of the classical, made of cypress, the only wood native to Spain that would work for guitars. The classical players got the good instruments, made of the imported woods such as rosewood, with the expensive German metal tuners instead of the cheap wooden friction pegs that make the flamenco guitar a very difficult instrument to tune.

It had fewer struts inside, tap plates on both sides of the sound hole, and a low action to provide more slap and percussive sound to the playing, at the expense of sustain. Anyone who's playing fast, or strumming fast, doesn't want much sustain: one note will hang around too long and muddy the next.

Guitarists seldom played solos—in fact, flamenco was a perfect Gypsy form in that it was an ensemble activity, a performance by the extended family, with the dancers as the featured performers. Even when dance troupes began touring internationally, in the 1930s and '40s, they were essentially family groups, traveling islands of Gypsy culture.

The man to change this was Ramon Montoya. He was a friend of the great Spanish classical guitarist Miguel Llobet, who in turn was a pupil of Tarrega, the inventor of modern classical guitar technique and composer of much of its early repertoire. Montoya didn't read music, but he watched Llobet carefully, took in his voicings and fingerings, and began to expand flamenco in every direction. Flamenco, like much folk guitar, had previously been limited to first position and had used primarily just the thumb and index finger of the right hand, but he used the whole fingerboard. He applied the full classical sophistication to the right hand, adding arpeggios and tremolos; and he began to compose like a classical guitarist, introducing new voicings, new keys, more complex structures, sophisticated counterpoint. When the Spanish Civil War broke out Montoya was smuggled out of Spain and played sold-out concerts in Biarritz and Paris, where the notoriously contemptuous French critics found themselves having to drag out and dust off long-disused superlatives. He became an antifascist symbol of freedom. War had also made him a solitary refugee; lacking his family and a dance company to accompany him, he had every reason to be the first flamenco soloist.

Meanwhile, the world was starting to know about flamenco as a dance form. By the early thirties American dance companies were starting to include their interpretation of flamenco in performances, and soon afterward the first flamenco companies, in all their turblent Gypsy-family self-contained chaos, crossed the Atlantic. It's not clear who came over first, but the most successful was Carmen Amaya.

During the Spanish civil war, Carmen Amaya, who had been dancing since the age of four in the taverns and music halls of Barcelona and had become famous in Madrid and Paris, crossed the Atlantic and fascinated audiences from Argentina and Brazil to Cuba, Mexico, and the United States. The *New York Times* called her a "Spitfire-Gypsy" who "exploded on the entertainment world last winter like an incendiary bomb." She made films in Hollywood, appeared on Broadway, and danced for Roosevelt and Churchill, accompanied by her musical director, the great guitar virtuoso Agustin Castellon Campos, known as Sabicas.

"Sabicas was, in my opinion, the greatest guitarist who ever lived," said Dennis Koster. "I don't think anyone, even the great classical guitarists, played the instrument better than he did. His touch, his tone, his phrasing were so perfect he absolutely made the instrument come to life. He played with a tremendous sound that could fill up any concert hall."

That Sabicas grew up poor goes without saying. At the age of five, the story goes, he fell in love with the guitar and wished he could have lessons from the local maestro, but there was no money, so Sabicas sat under the window while wealthier students had their lessons, then ran home and played the lessons by ear, from memory.

After leaving Spain Sabicas moved to Mexico City, then spent the last thirty years of his life living in New York City. Flamenco had left home. In the early sixties Sabicas was joined by his cousin Mario Escudero, from whom Koster took lessons. Escudero was a god, as respected as Sabicas. As a boy he had learned flamenco directly from Ramon Montoya himself.

"When my teacher told me I would be studying with him, I almost fainted," Koster said. "I idolized him completely and utterly."

Escudero didn't speak English yet, the fifteen-year-old Koster didn't speak Spanish; they learned in the Gypsy manner, "guitarra a guitarra." Escudero, like many Gypsies, was a tough teacher: he didn't write out any of the music he showed Koster, and refused to tape it, so Koster had to memorize everything on the spot, and play it over and over in his mind on the train ride home so as not to forget it. Not surprisingly, what he played back to Escudero was often a parroted version, and when this happened Escudero laughed at the boy for playing like a machine. He even called his wife over so she could laugh too. Koster calls this "a Gypsy lesson in musical interpretation."

By the mid-sixties New York had become a center for flamenco. "There were flamenco studios and flamenco cafes all up and down Fourteenth Street, and there were some very fine Spanish dance teachers. There was always work. There was a lot of interest in those years." In 1965, at the age of fifteen, Koster got his first professional job, playing in a flamenco cafe for five dollars and dinner. He was also hired to play guitar in a dance studio.

The sixties were the beginning of a (sadly, brief) golden age for flamenco in the United States. Sabicas, Mario Escudero, and other flamenco guitarists played in venues large and small. Jose Greco, an Italian-American who grew up as Costanzo Greco in Brooklyn, founded his own dance company. Carlos Montoya, Ramon's nephew, had also moved to New York, having had the distinction of becoming an American citizen even though, when asked if he liked the American form of government, he misunderstood the question and said, "No."

It must have come as quite a shock for the musical producers of New York to deal with Gypsies. "In business deals," Koster said, "everything had to be in cash. Sabicas's entire estate, I'm told, was in jewels. He didn't believe in paper: as soon as he got paid he would buy diamonds." Koster became close with both men. Sabicas refused to give formal guitar lessons, saying that since he never had a teacher, he had no idea how one should teach. But Koster learned that when the atmosphere was right, Sabicas would spontaneously pick up a guitar and show him something, like a parenthesis of fingers, the conversation leaping from words to music. Koster found that he learned the most on the evenings when Sabicas would come over to his apartment to watch fights on TV.

A new current was mixing into jazz guitar, thanks to the always re-freshing influence of Brazil. The newcomer was Djalma de Andrade, known as Bola Sete. (Bola Sete means "seven ball," the only black ball on the table, as he was surrounded by white guys.) Like Laurindo Almeida, he played a nylon-string guitar fingerstyle, quietly but with enormous dynamic range and emotion, combining narrative and tran-sitional phrasing with those great unexpected Brazilian chords.

He rode in on the bossa nova craze, which started out in Brazil as a guitar-rich music but tended to be played on horns in the United States simply because not many guitarists were capable of playing Brazilian-style. It's fascinating to listen to him in duet with the pia-nist Vince Guaraldi, composer of the *Peanuts* themes. Sete's playing is lyrical and full of surprises; alongside him, Guaraldi sounds unimagi-native and monochromatic. Sete's unamplified guitar sounds like a man actually playing an instrument of wood and air. Like Charlie Christian's bebop lines, this Brazilian material sank deep into the book of jazz guitar, and players are still drilling down into its depths, draw-ing up new and unexpected sustenance.

Between 1950 and 1960 the Spanish-surname population of Los Ange-les County doubled as a result of an influx from Mexico, Latin America in general, and Puerto Rico, though many Puerto Ricans made the shorter journey to New York. Latino music grew steadily in and around the Latino communities, in many forms. Cuban music was always popu-lar, as was Caribbean or tropical music in general. Mambo, Tex-Mex, cha cha cha, polka—a broad nightclub gamut with the guitar as an es-sential ingredient. Mariachi began in specific restaurants but grew to include touring bands. Here's an account of live music in the early six-ties at the El Monte Legion Stadium, in El Monte, California.

A typical weekend dance at the Legion would pack in crowds that were 90 percent Chicano, 10 percent Anglo. The dancers sported khaki pants with a Sir Guy shirt and a charcoal gray suit coat, one button roll, and spit-shined French-toed shoes. The girls had stacked hair and wore white shoes called "bunnies," black tight short skirts, and feathered earrings.

Of all the dances, the Corrido was the wildest, sort of an early form of slam dancing. Two or three lines would form, people arm-in-arm, with each line consisting of 150 to 250 people. With the band blasting away at a breakneck rocking tempo, the lines took four steps forward and four steps back, eventually slamming into each other (but making sure that no one got hurt). . . .

An evening at the Legion always ended with tight, slow dancing, called scrunching, usually to ballads by locals like "Handsome" Mel Williams or Vernon Green and the Medallions. After the dance, it was out to the parking lot for the grand finale. Where's the party? *Quien tiene pisto? Mota?* Who's got the booze? Weed? Rumors would fly all night as to which gangs were going to throw *chingasos*—come to blows. The Jesters Car Club from Boyle Heights, which dominated the Eastside, would parade around the parking lot in their lavender, maroon, or gray primered cars, wearing T-Timer shades (blue or green colored glass in square wire frames). In what was an inviolable ritual every weekend, the police would eventually break everything up and we'd caravan back to the Foster's Freeze at Whittier and Mott or to Johnny's at Whittier and Ditman.

The British Invasion had its most widespread guitar effects among white kids. Motown, one of the distinctive sounds of the sixties, was almost entirely unaffected by it. For the Motown guitarists, in fact, Detroit might as well still have been in the fifties. And Motown deeply affected the development of black popular music over the following decades.

Berry Gordy, the boxer turned songwriter/entrepreneur who would
turn Motown Records into the largest and most successful black-
owned business in the United States, had a background in jazz and
had briefly owned a jazz record store. His sense of the guitar's place in
pop music was largely a jazz conception: the guitar was part of the
rhythm section and should know its place. For more than a decade,
from the late fifties to the early seventies, Gordy's guitarists created a
compelling and influential jazz/funk rhythm sound for Motown, but
in return they received no credit, no respect, and not much in the way
of money.

At the height of the Motown era the guitar section had three players: Robert White, Joe Messina, and Eddie Willis. Willis was more
bluesy, White and Messina more jazzy, and the three combined remarkably well. Sometimes they'd find their own lines (the documentary *Standing in the Shadows of Motown* includes a great shot of White
playing the famous opening guitar riff to "My Girl"; he plays every note
with the side of his thumbnail), and sometimes the writers would sing
the lines they wanted. The guitarists often didn't hear the melody or
even know who the singer would be. "We just put down our tracks,
and moved on to the next song," Messina said with a remarkable lack
of bitterness. "I always thought we weren't featured enough. No one
really got a chance to stretch out. I always expected to play more when
I got there, but there wasn't much happening solo-wise."

Even though each of them was perfectly capable of playing as a featured soloist (as Messina did on Soupy Sales's *Night Show*), guitar was
never more than a texture, on a par with the backup chorus or the
vibes. Bass (the brilliant James Jamerson) was far more prominent—
a feature that would carry over into funk. Even when Jimi Hendrix
introduced a far more effects-based concept of blues-funk and
Motown added another guitarist (Dennis Coffey) to play wah-wah
guitar on "Cloud Nine," it was another texture rather than a lead
instrument.

Whatever the song's success, Gordy paid them a flat rate—at first
below union scale, then at scale. Overtime pay was a joke, and the
rhythm section rarely if ever received musician credits. Under the cir-

cumstances, it's hardly surprising that the guitarists saw the entire Motown enterprise as pretty much just a day job.

"We played pop music during the day," Messina said, "but at night, we'd go blow it out jamming in the clubs. We never listened to pop radio. We'd have a number one hit and not even know it! 'So what?' we'd say. As soon as we left the studio we put our jazz programs on."

Martha Reeves, complimenting Robert White, gave him the same faint praise jazz guitarists had been getting since the thirties when they were the almost inaudible beat of the big band orchestra. Nobody, she said, was "steadier."

If I had to sum up the excitement the guitar inspired in the mid-sixties, I'd play the first five seconds of "Satisfaction." Not just because it's a great song, or that the defiant raspberry created by the fuzztone is the perfect raised finger of rock and roll, but because it's a sign that the electric guitar had finally discovered that it was not just a new instrument but an infinite number of new instruments, and that from now on a guitarist would create not only in terms of music but in terms of sound.

Ever since the electric guitar had been invented, it had been struggling to find a voice. As anyone knows who first plugs an electric guitar into an amp, clean and without effects, the undeveloped voice of the electric guitar is thin, metallic, and dry, and all it does is to make your mistakes all the more apparent. Ever since the early forties engineers and guitarists had been making sporadic attempts to coerce the thing into sounding more interesting.

An early example happened by accident to Paul Burlison, of the Rock 'n' Roll Trio. When Elvis came along, he said, "We just did anything we could to sound a little different. If something sounded good, we just used it. And it was a little wild in those days. I'd lie on my back and play guitar, get down on my knees."

In 1956 he dropped his amp. "It happened as an accident. We were playing in Philadelphia, and I was walking down the hallway to the stage, and the strap on my amplifier broke. When that happened, the amplifier fell to the floor. I picked it up, put it under my arm, and carried it out to the stage. And I plugged it in, not knowing what had happened to it. There was no time to check it out. The announcer introduced us and the curtain opened, and we started playing."

The guitar produced a sound he describes as "fuzzy." The band looked at one another, shrugged, and kept playing. After the show Burlison found that one of the tubes had become displaced and was acting as a dimmer switch, delaying the sound and creating a fuzz tone. He shoved the tube back into place and it worked fine. Later, in the studio, he remembered the tone, opened up his amp—it turned out that the Fender Deluxe was the only amp that would make this particular glitch—and played with the tube until he got the fuzz he wanted.

"I liked it, but I didn't know it was going to create a big stir until engineers started calling me, asking what I was doing on this thing? A lot of people had taken razor blades and sliced their speakers and stuff like that, trying to get that sound."

A similar creative accident happened when Ike Turner and his band the Kings of Rhythm drove to Sun Studios from Mississippi to record "Rocket 88," often thought of as the first rock and roll record. One of the amps fell out of the car and its speaker cone was ruptured. Sam Phillips stuffed a wad of paper into the ruptured diaphragm and recorded anyway, the distortion only adding to the rock 'n' roll punch.

If it wasn't slashed speakers (the guitarist Link Wray stabbed his speaker cone with a pencil), it was the first experiments in reverb, tremolo, echo. Across America, studio engineers started tinkering around with, rearranging, and mistreating any piece of equipment that might carry a signal. The guitar was developing a distinctive and unique voice, unmistakable, unforgettable. It was beginning to find its mythology and its idiom, and for at least the time being that idiom was characteristically American.

The first consistent and intentional signal distortion (after the efforts of Les Paul, which seemed to come and go like a meteor shower, leaving little apparent effect) was probably the use of echo that, combined with the use of the tremolo arm or "whammy bar," defined the rockabilly and surf sounds of the fifties and early sixties. The sixties, though, broke the box open: fuzztone, the "sitarmatic" bridge, preamps for overdriving amplifiers, the Vibratone, the CryBaby Wah-Wah and the Uni-Vibe phase shifter, heard on Hendrix's "The Wind Cries Mary" and "Are You Experienced?" (Syd Barrett was experimenting with wah-wah in London at the same time as Hendrix; the difference was that Hendrix had the better chance of remembering next day what he had just created.) And these would blossom into phase shifters, analog delays, octave dividers—anything to make that thin metal sound interesting.

"It was a time," said Aaron Newman, former vice president of the Guild electronics division and one of the founders of Musitronics, "when everyone used effects." The names of the effects boxes alone alone capture the kaleidoscopic excitement of the times: the Orange Squeezer, Red Ranger, Purple Peaker, Blue Clipper, Yellow Humper, and Green Ringer. You plugged your guitar jack in the little box that sat on the floor and when you wanted to activate it you stomped on the depresser switch on top. Easy as that.

Guitar gear has become such a cliché that it's hard now to understand the excitement of running the output of your guitar through an old record player or radio just to see what sound came out. Nowadays the whole caboodle can be bought in a single effects box that gives the naked signal the sound of a wide variety of effects (flanger, chorus, rotary, compressor, delay, and so on) played through an equal variety of amps (British blues, Tweed, tube, and other heyday hardware).

This experimenting with sound, by the way, was paralleled by experiments in body shape. The Gibson Flying V, shaped roughly like an arrow, and the Explorer, shaped roughly like a lightning bolt, were unappreciated when they came out in 1957 and 1958, respectively, but in 1958 Bo Diddley began playing a rectangular Gretsch and in 1962 Vox issued a pentagonal guitar and, the following year, a teardrop-shaped body made famous by Brian Jones. By 1970 double necks and eccentric body shapes were as much a part of the scene as paisley shirts and surreal Roger Dean album covers.

To try and understand the seduction of gear, I lug my little amp down to my friend Bill's studio, where he plugs in one of these universal effects boxes and lends me an electric guitar.

Bear in mind two things: I've never owned an electric guitar, and this particular instrument is an old bottom-of-the-line single-pickup Danelectro, which looks as though it has been cut out of a tabletop in an industrial accident involving an escaped table saw. Its plastic tuners are the color of tobacco-stained fingers and it is missing the high E string. Bill has a soft spot for the Danny, calling it "an old tug boat that played on a bunch of records from early fusion in the seventies to punk/new wave in the eighties, not to mention the jingles and industrial music it reluctantly agreed to create," but either way, if an effects box can make this machine sound good, it can make anything sound good.

The box makes the Danelectro sound amazing. On the Fuzzbox setting, the amp hisses and growls even before I play a note. A chord is too much for it, an explosion on every frequency imaginable. A single note has that explosive rudeness of "Satisfaction." The Rotary setting makes it sound a little like an electric organ, and I play "Summertime" over and over until one of the studio techs comes in and gives me a look. The Swell setting is like playing a chord with the volume knob turned way down, then turning it up—the opposite of decay. Delay turns out to be a dying echo . . . echo . . . echo . . . echo that encourages the playing of fugue counterpoint, singing to one's own echo like the flutist Paul Horn recording in the Taj Mahal. Chorus makes it sound as if I've hired several other dudes to play quietly and obediently behind me. And the Flanger setting (so called because the sound was supposed to be like an effect created in the days of reel-to-reel by holding on to the flange of the reel) makes it sound as if the chord is being chewed over thoughtfully by a large genie accustomed to telling long, implausible stories.

This is the real magnetism of the electric guitar plus effects: the effects box makes the guitar sound not louder but fuller, more present. Everything I play sounds more interesting, more *plural*; each effect is another instrument, and the guitar is no longer condemned to being the solitary instrument, the starvation box. I can imagine playing solo for hours and never feeling insubstantial, or alone. And this has nothing to do with volume. I never have the volume higher than 2, and when playing through the fuzzbox even 1 is higher than I want.

If I had this box when I was seventeen, I'd have turned into the classic obsessed pale teenage guitarist. I'd never have seen the light of day.

Mind you, this experiment isn't an analogy to the experiences of the sixties and seventies. This effects box is all retro: instead of introducing new horizons it recalls familiar ones, and I find myself playing songs that go with the sounds—clichés, in other words. Back in the late sixties, these were all new sounds and the electric guitar was all about discovery. The ever-expanding world of gizmos gave the guitar an open-endedness that no other instrument could offer. Starting with the very basics, a guitarist could make his own instrument system, and his own sound. It was no longer the instrument and the repertoire that represented the horizons of possibility but electronic science itself. How much more exciting could an instrument be?

Bill is lending me the ugly-as-sin Danelectro to play at a four-hour wedding gig that if played on an acoustic would leave my nails shredded and my left-hand fingertips bleeding.

"I'll buy you a new set of strings," I offer in return.

"Or even just a top E," he shrugs.

# INTERLUDE:
# REDUCING RICK
# TO JELLY

Rick makes a request. My guitar will be ready just before he has to leave for Healdsburg. Will I allow him to ship it out there and display it at his booth as an example of his work, a sales tool? I stare at him. Of course. Why not? It doesn't seem like my guitar, it seems like his. I may have given some specs, but everything worthwhile—the skill, the taste—is clearly his.

When I tell Barbara this, she points out how remarkable it is that I have a relationship with my guitar's maker. "I have a Haynes flute, but I've never met Mr. Haynes," she says. "You don't have a relationship with Fylde."

It's true. There's something perfectly continuous, or contiguous, about this. Even if I weren't supplying my meager and stumbling minimum of specs, it would still be a special instrument to me, simply for having watched it come together.

That's part of the miracle. Rick's making the music too, by making the thing that makes the music.

The other part of the miracle is the fact that this Japanese lantern, this little wooden lung, is going to enable an invisible transformation in the air itself that will have the capacity to move people. It's as if Rick and I are frittering around the edges of this inexplicable wonder, just enabling it to exist in the world of matter. A box of air.

Rick's e-mail response:

OK, I've just had two glasses of wine (and I'm a cheap date, so that's about as much as I can handle and still drive or type). So take this in that context.

I'm not musically talented. That's fact, not self-deprecation. Lack of exposure as a child, bad neuronal connections, too much cereal and not enough Scotch: whatever. As much as I appreciate and value music, I can't really participate directly. So what's left for me? Critic (I'm constitutionally unwilling to judge those who do what I can't), promoter/presenter (tried it—fun but not satisfying), builder. The last works.

I'm kind of the stage crew for guitarists. That is, I can help make them look good by giving them a working instrument, a backdrop to their art. It isn't without intrinsic value (like a good stage set has a value of its own) but it becomes complete only when it's used.

That's why I push the "craft not art" and "guitar maker not luthier" distinctions. As a builder of musical instruments, I'm an aide to art, not an artist.

So in your writing and musing, don't overlook the privileged position I have assumed: handmaiden (well, let's not get into gender issues here) to the arts. It's meaningful and valuable to me that I can participate in the creation of good music, even at one remove. The real reason I give discounts to the professionals whom I admire is not that they can sell guitars for me (for the most part, they don't), but that their compliment of choosing one of my instruments reduces me to jelly.

# Guitar Rock
# Takes Over

Looking back forty years, it sometimes seems as if America strode through the sixties with guitar in hand. Not true. Mainstream America began to accept the guitar only in the seventies.

In the sixties the guitar was still a minority instrument, even if the guitar's minorities now included educated white middle-class college kids. Many parents were still forbidding their teenagers to buy one, or protesting about the vulgar din. The seventies, anti-eulogized by Garry Trudeau in *Doonesbury* as "the worst of times," and "a kidney stone of a decade," was in fact the decade when the sixties finally spread out across the broad, flat map of America, and the guitar was part of that spread.

This gradual shift is wonderfully illustrated in Bruce Macleod's book *Club Date Musicians*. A club date, he explains, is any formal social gathering for celebrating a ritual event: "weddings, bar mitzvahs, debutante balls, anniversary parties, retirement parties, holiday dinner-dances, or charity balls."

In other words, these are the gigs where as a musician you have to play for pretty much everyone. You may have a Latin-tinged repertoire for an elderly Jewish audience, you may have special numbers or sets for Italian or Irish gatherings, but you certainly can't rely on everyone or even a significant portion of the audience to be young and hip, or even just hip, or even paying much attention. All in all, you're following the white stripe down the middle of the road. By the time the guitar became accepted for club dates or casuals, it had become accepted, period.

Most club date bands did not use a guitarist, even a jazz-style guitarist from the big-band era. In the forties and fifties the line-up would consist of horns, perhaps an upright bass, percussion of some sort, and either a keyboard player or an accordion player.

Guitar music edged very slowly into club dates because these were adult affairs, and adults by and large detested rock 'n' roll. Even when the Beatles began making guitar music more popular, many club date bands simply didn't know how to play modern music.

"At first," said a club band guitarist called Bruce Bergman, looking back from the mid-seventies to an unspecified time possibly as little as a decade earlier, "the club date orchestras were simply unable to play any rock. Then, to meet the demand, they developed a few rock tunes. However, musicians schooled in show tunes and standards, no matter how good they may be, cannot play music which approaches authentic rock, particularly without a guitar sound. If you've ever heard piano, drums and trumpet try to copy the Rolling Stones you'll know what I mean."

The shoe was on the other foot: no longer was a guitar trying to sound like a horn but a horn was trying to play like a guitar.

"Most non-rock players have not grown up with rock music and therefore neither understand it, know anything about it, or like it. Not only don't they play it, but they have no knowledge of the requests. All this being the case, club date offices sought out a musician to meet the trend—the rock guitar specialist."

For most bands, the rocker was a specialist guitar player who sat in for rock numbers, like the dark, Latin-looking guy in the ruffled shirt with the maracas or timbales hired for gigs when the booker specified a Latin band.

For the sixties guitarist, a club date must have been as much a curse as a blessing. He became the token hip guy, responsible for singing anything even vaguely contemporary, even if it had nothing to do with rock or the guitar. Macleod cites some chilling examples: "The Look of Love" (1967), "Raindrops Keep Fallin' On My Head" (1969), "We've Only Just Begun" (1970), "Tie a Yellow Ribbon 'Round the Old Oak Tree" (1972), and "The Way We Were" (1973). These are, of course, exactly the kind of song the guitarist took up guitar to avoid in the first place.

Macleod has a keen sense of the economics that accompanied this whittling away, pointing out that if the money stayed the same, the guitarist had to replace another band member. A six-piece band would consist of drums, keyboard, possibly bass, and three horns—sax, trumpet, trombone, but with a guitarist someone had to go, and the first casualty would be the trombone. A five-piece band with sax and trumpet would replace the trumpet player. A four-piece band would replace the sax player. Hardly surprising, then, that lifetime journeyman musicians resented the guitarist.

Pity the poor accordion player, by the way: in the days before electric organs and portable electronic keyboards, club date bands often had an accordion player because the house piano was usually so wretched. As guitars and electric keyboards took over, the accordion died—interestingly, not so much because of the sound of the instrument, which in many ways is much more versatile and expressive than that of a cheap electric organ, according to one bandleader, but simply because they looked wrong. Old, that is.

By the late seventies, everything had changed. Even the most conservative client expected a rock 'n' roll number or two, and without an electric guitar, a band looked terminally square.

One bandleader told Macleod: "If you come in and do a wedding or bar mitzvah now—when I say wedding, I mean any kind of ethnic group: Italian, Irish, WASP, Jewish, anything—and do it without rock and roll, you've got a disaster. Because you didn't include half of what everybody wants to hear. And I'm including the sixty-year-old grandmothers too, because the whole thing has become a standard part of the scene. Now *that* has come about in the last six or seven years."

Parenthetically, it's worth noting that Macleod's subtitle is "Playing the New York Party Circuit," and although he's really writing about much of the Northeast, this is very much a regional perspective. In the Southwest, for example, a good all-purpose gig band would be able to play country, rock, Western swing, rancheras, and polkas for different occasions. As such, the guitar was possibly more common.

By the time Macleod completed his second round of interviews in 1989, there was a new hierarchy in musical instruments. From the bottom up: accordion, violin, congas, timbales, trombone, trumpet, sax (with clarinet and flute double), acoustic piano, electric bass, drums, synthesizer, and at number one finally after all these years, the guitar —specifically the electric guitar.

Mind you, just in case you're starting to get the idea that club dates are now a guitarist's paradise, I should pass on one last anecdote from Macleod, who points out that it's a bad mistake to play too well, especially at the wrong time. He tells the story of a guitarist who started to play "Over the Rainbow," slowly, as dinner was being served—but he played it too well, and several couples left the tables and started dancing.

When the caterer saw what was happening, he ran over to the guitarist and gave him a piece of his mind. The guitarist stopped at once, and played something as arhythmical as possible, and to the caterer's relief people stopped dancing and sat down to eat, the music safely relegated to a background twitter.

For the guitar to have been kneaded so deeply and so effectively into the multigrain, doughy mass of American culture, something unusual and potent must have been happening in the world of music. To be sure, the guitar had been growing steadily in popularity since the heyday of the singing cowboys of the silver screen. In 1940, 190,000 new guitars were sold, more than any other instrument; the piano came second, with 136,332. Between 1940 and 1959 guitar sales doubled. By 1964 they had doubled again, and by 1970 they had doubled yet again, to more than two and a half million, more than all other instruments combined.

Perhaps most interestingly, sales of acoustic guitars, which of course had a head start over electrics, were just beginning to lose some of their acceleration. The real growth, starting in the sixties and gathering momentum for the rest of the century, was in electrics. In 2003, for the first time, sales of new electric guitars in the United States would catch up with and pass sales of new acoustics.

This historic shift was the result of the colorful, creative, self-indulgent, brilliant, irresponsible, frequently stoned and sometimes deafening era now conveniently abbreviated in radio parlance to the phrase "classic rock."

The point was this: the electric guitar was that rare beast, a new musical instrument. It might have been in existence for some four decades, but it had developed within very specific musical limits. The Grand Ole Opry, for example, at first refused to have anything to do with electric guitars. Jazz players restricted themselves to certain sounds. The amplification equipment imposed all kinds of restraints. With the Beatles explosion of the early-to-mid sixties the electric guitar became the weapon of choice among young guitarists, but nobody knew what its full capabilities might be. Meanwhile, the youth revolution meant that for the first time these young musicians were free to behave like guitarists and refuse to be told what they could and couldn't do. The world of music was theirs—but what exactly would they do with it?

British bands of roughly 1969 to 1972 were especially ambitious. This was a time when it seemed as if rock music could become the new classical music, though it wasn't clear exactly how. King Crimson experimented with concept albums and a wide variety of guitar and synthesizer sounds. Emerson, Lake and Palmer adapted Bernstein's "America," Bach's "Toccata," Copland's "Rodeo," and Mussorgsky's "Pictures at an Exhibition." The Who composed the rock operas *Tommy* (1969) and *Quadrophenia* (1974). Deep Purple recorded with the Royal Philharmonic Orchestra. (This breadth of vision rapidly narrowed, though more recently shred guitarists have attempted the big musical picture. Katherine "The Great Kat" Thomas, for example, a Juilliard-trained violinist, has adapted works by Vivaldi, Beethoven, Liszt, and Wagner for shred guitar and classical orchestra.)

Other bands decided that instead of taking over the classical music concert hall, they'd take over the theater: David Bowie, Iggy Pop, Kiss, Alice Cooper—a line of evolution that began with androgynous facial makeup and led to Phish flying a giant hot dog over the audience or building massive sculptures on air force bases and then setting fire to them. Much of this was fun but largely silly. One particular avenue, though—one of the earliest—led to one of the great iconic guitar acts of its time. It had something to do with theater, something to do with art, and something to do with adolescent rude boys going berserk.

Art school, almost entirely irrelevant to American musicians of the sixties, was central to the British Invasion bands. Pete Townshend went to art school. So did Ray Davies of the Kinks, John Lennon, Keith Richards, Eric Clapton, Jack Bruce, Ginger Baker, Syd Barrett, and probably several thousand other would-be musicians. They went to art school because it meant they could get a government student grant without having to work as hard as the students trying to get into university. They then took up music because it seemed to require even less work than art school.

Going to art school meant more than just hanging out in what might euphemistically be called a creative environment with others of similar interests, or lack of them. At one of a notorious lunchtime series of avant-garde "lectures" Townshend saw the jazz bassist Malcolm Cecil enact an early piece of performance art by sawing through a double bass. In his own way, Townshend took this arty iconoclastic statement and made it louder, more public, and generally unforgettable.

"Pete had a thing in the act where he used to put his fingers on a chord and smash the guitar into the speaker cabinet so that it would resound in a crash," the Who bassist John Entwistle explained. "He had another thing where he used to put the guitar above his head and spin around and then spin back again. We were doing a gig at the Railway, which had a high stage made out of beer crates and a rather low ceiling. The guitar that Pete was using was a Rickenbacker, which had been considerably weakened by him hitting it into the amplifier for so long. He forgot it was a low ceiling and put his guitar above his head, and the neck fell off. He got into a bit of a temper and smashed it to smithereens with a mike stand. He had a guitar spare, a 12-string Rickenbacker. He picked that up and carried on as if he'd meant to do it."

The following week, when Townshend didn't repeat the guitar-breaking bit, Keith Moon wrecked his drum kit instead.

At the same time, two other facts of life were weighing on Townshend: one, the fact that the amplifiers of the time were terminally wimpy; and two, the fact that ever since Daltrey had been forced to give up guitar because working in a sheet-metal factory had ruined his fingers, Townshend had to play both lead and rhythm. This meant that he was busily inventing techniques that would later become the basis for power-trio playing, but by his own account he was terribly intimidated by the other emerging electric guitarists, such as Clapton and later Hendrix (for whom London was a second home), who were free to play lead guitar alone and be simply astounding. Seeing himself as unable to compete on sheer skill, Townshend said, "I tried to make playing the guitar look lethal." Townshend was creating a central tenet of the rock guitarist: that he is a killer, and that his guitar is his weapon.

As early as 1964, Daltrey has said, the Who were well aware of the importance of image (another feature of British bands that their American counterparts lacked was the hip/sleazy publicist), and they also had the important insight that live music represents a form of psychological warfare. "We hit on the idea of having the biggest cabinets you've ever seen in your life," Daltrey said, "yet inside we'd have this little 12-inch speaker in the bottom."

They also invented, more or less by accident, the Marshall Stack—the pile of speaker cabinets, the literal manifestation of the wall of sound and a central feature of guitar-based rock. Jim Marshall, ironically, was outraged at this irresponsible use of his speakers. A rep pointed at one speaker sitting on top of another and protested that the sheer volume might make the top speaker vibrate and fall off. "Pete sneered, 'So what?' and knocked it over."

Seeing Townshend smashing his guitar and speakers had the effect of making him, and by extension any skinny, spider-fingered guitarist, seem powerful, possessed of insane energy and strength. Paradoxically, the act also transformed the image of the guitar: instead of being a delicate box it became an ax. Soon the activity moved offstage with the smashing of hotel rooms. The guitar-based rock band became incandescent and irresistible with energy, a battery of loose cannons.

Even so, it wasn't Townshend who took this transfiguration of the lead guitarist to its most vivid and expressive form. It was Hendrix, who, upstaging Townshend badly, set fire to his guitar. In doing so, he not only provided more evidence of the latent incandescence, the electricity of the music, but combined it with a kind of ritual sacrifice. The music was no longer music, it was the more organized manifestation of the explosive act of playing guitar. It was the goal of every concertgoer to see a guitarist so transported by passion, his fingers so fast, the solo so high and loud, that the climax would be spontaneous combustion.

To my knowledge this happened only once, and even then only in retrospect. I'm thinking, of course, of Hendrix playing his version of "The Star-Spangled Banner," an act of musical flag burning, with the lights flashing off the body of his Strat, with every extraneous riff, every departure from the melody leaping off the anthem like a flame.

Some of this experimenting was interesting, some was technically skillful, some lyrically interesting, much of it unbearable. Some of it was also lethal: the seventies were the years of electrocutions.

I don't suppose anyone will ever know the name of the first guitarist to be electrocuted. A 1933 Volu-Tone amp, according to Michael Wright in *Vintage Guitar*, "went about picking up the instrument's vibrations using a unique, not to mention potentially deadly, method. The pickup, which mounted to your favorite steel-stringed instrument, had to be charged up with a short blast of high voltage current provided by a special jack mounted to the amp's chassis. . . . Considering the amp was not equipped with a fuse and the casing of the plug was metal, it's hard to imagine that a) Volu-Tone was allowed to even sell these, and; b) the company stayed in business from the summer of 1933 into at least the late '30s without being shut down due to a wrongful death (or at the very least, a serious personal injury) lawsuit."

The earliest reference I've found to actual electrocution dates back to the early fifties and appears in a brief Web bio of the accordion player and inventor Charlie Watkins, whose PA amplifiers were all the rage at the big outdoor UK pop festivals of the late sixties and early seventies.

"He made a first batch of twenty amplifiers in 1952," wrote Tim Fletcher and Steve Russell in their online bio of Watkins, "but that enterprise was near-disastrous as he had to recall them upon hearing of a guitarist being electrocuted by a similar AC/DC unit."

The most famous near-electrocution was Bob Weir's experience at Woodstock, where it rained so much it's surprising everybody didn't get electrocuted. "Every time I touched my instrument," Weir said, "I got a shock. The stage was wet, and the electricity was coming through me. I was conducting! Touching the guitar and the microphone was nearly fatal. There was a great big blue spark about the size of a baseball, and I got lifted off my feet and sent back eight or ten feet to my amplifier."

Leslie Harvey of the Scottish band Stone the Crows was electrocuted on stage in a Swansea, Wales, club on May 3, 1972, but not by a guitar. The culprit was a microphone that wasn't grounded (in contrast to the unfortunate Les Harvey, who was). The mike had been plugged into what presumably was an improperly wired amplifier providing an energized connection to the mike cable shielding, and Harvey was killed.

The seventies were a dangerous time for electric guitarists, in fact. John Rostill of the Shadows was electrocuted in 1973 while playing his bass in his basement studio, and Keith Relf, formerly of the Yardbirds, reportedly died while plugging in his electric guitar in 1976. In the same year Kiss guitarist Ace Frehley was nearly electrocuted during a concert in Florida when he touched a short-circuited light, but after being carried offstage he returned ten minutes later to finish the show. Not very impressive, frankly, but that's hardly his fault: by using 220–240 volts, the UK has a built-in advantage in the electrocution business.

The past half decade seems to have seen a revival in onstage electrocution. In 2002 the Calling's guitarist, Aaron Kamins, took a serious enough shock in Bangkok to make it onto MTV Asia News. The Anglo-Irish band Jetplane Landing nearly lost Cahir O'Doherty in Ireland, electrocuted during a sound check and rushed to a hospital. Craig Macintosh of the Scottish band Dogs Die in Hot Cars nearly followed in the Stone the Crows tradition.

The trouble is, all these stories start sounding alike after a while. Electricity seems to be losing its power to shock. As a result, electrocution stories seem to have ripened into a decadent or rococo phase: some of the most modern stories sound like outtakes from *This Is Spinal Tap*. Here's the saga of Calphalon Spear's guitarist Il Duce, taken from the band's online tour diary.

We were playing at a barn dance in Greensboro, North Carolina, and Dick forgot to ground the PA system. It just so happened that Il Duce was standing in the middle of a puddle of cow piss when he put his lips to the mike to sing backups while his other hand was on the guitar, dampening the strings. Well, suddenly he falls to the ground and just starts shaking his left leg. I've seen him do this kind of stuff before, over dramatizing something, being that he's always stressed out and stuff, but we all realized, almost too late, that he was getting electrocuted. We didn't realize it until his Gene Autry belt buckle let out a spark and his pants caught on fire. Abbey rushed to the rescue, grabbing the guitar and unplugging it, and then rolling Il Duce and his flaming pants in the cow piss to put the fire out. It's a good thing he's into cowboys and shops for cheap pants at thrift stores, because if he was wearing a pair of classic Levi's like the rest of us, we might not have noticed in time to save him.

In the end it's just a hazard of the trade: golfers, farmers, and rangers get struck by lightning, guitarists get electrocuted on stage. Keith Richards observed nonchalantly, "I've been electrocuted so many times now, it's quite a buzz, actually." Well, that would account for the hair.

Speaking of hair: in 1970 the band Earth changed its name to Black Sabbath. It was the year zero in the history of heavy metal.

I have a certain affection-at-a-distance for heavy metal, and I speak as one who went to a White Lion/Twisted Sister show and felt the sheer weight of sound pressing my contact lenses against my eyeballs.

Heavy metal deserves its place in history as the first genre to link the guitar with a piece of punctuation—the German umlaut, two dots over a vowel to indicate that the vowel won an Iron Cross at Stalingrad and worships Satan. For all its Nazi gear and iconography, though, metal takes itself—its history, its lyrics, its art, its clothes, and the importance of its music to society at large—very, very seriously. The film *This Is Spinal Tap* wouldn't be funny if metal bands didn't take themselves seriously.

Deena Weinstein's *Heavy Metal: A Cultural Sociology* (a book that takes itself as seriously as its subject does) tracks down the origin of the phrase "heavy metal," crediting the author of Steppenwolf's "Born to Be Wild," who has the suitably warlike name Mars Bonfire. "I used the phrase 'heavy metal thunder' . . . to help capture the experience of driving a car or motorcycle on the desert highway of California. . . . Afterwards I realized that I had been aware of the term 'heavy metals' from high school science. It is a part of Mendeleyev's Periodic Table of Elements." Another first: no other genre, as far as I know, was inspired by the periodic table of elements.

Weinstein stratifies heavy metal into five eras: the era of eruption (1969–1972), the era of crystallization (1973–1975), the golden age (1976–1979), the surge of growth era (1979–1983), which also included the New Wave of British Heavy Metal (NWOBHM), and the crystallization-into-fragments-and-subgenres era (post-1983). No word, though, on the relative popularity of the umlaut. Is it on the rise? The decline? Is it in danger of being replaced by the circumflex?

She also discusses Metal Lite, which encompasses Def Leppard, Van Halen, Poison, Bon Jovi, and Ratt and seems to overlap with Big Hair Metal; as well as Speed/Thrash Metal, which was influenced by NWOBHM groups such as Venom, Diamond Head, and Iron Maiden and also by the punk revolution.

Weinstein goes on to make the astute observation that "the heavy metal code always includes a singer" along with the lead guitarist, and the two are inseparable.

"The two are dual foci, like the twin foci of an ellipse, around which the music is described. . . . Like political parties in a two-party democratic system, guitar and voice must compete and cooperate, getting neither too close to nor too far away from each other."

Examples of dual foci in long hair and tight trousers include the founders of the two-party heavy metal system, Robert Plant and Jimmy Page of Led Zep, plus Phil Mogg and Michael Schenker of UFO, Ritchie Blackmore plus any number of singers in Rainbow, and Rob Halford of Judas Priest plus the dual lead guitarists K. K. Downing and Glenn Tipton—Judas Priest apparently consisting of a triple-focus ellipse, which no doubt is a mystical symbol in the darkest depths of Mordor.

As for what the guitarist actually plays, Weinstein points out that "heavy metal guitar technique requires great manual dexterity, familiarity with a wide range of electronic gadgetry, such as wah-wah pedals and fuzz boxes, and the ability to treat sounds not merely as notes of discrete duration and pitch, but as tones that can be bent into each other."

The difference between metal and punk is that while punk doesn't give a toss about skill, heavy metal guitarists take their skills very seriously indeed. (There are other differences, such as punk's grievous lack of umlauts, but we'll let that pass.) Metal guitarists popularized one-string solos with pull-offs and a modified tapping technique—very advanced stuff—in order to be able to play so fast that the individual notes blur into a scream, a metal twin of the vocalist's scream.

As always, though, the most advanced skill in metal is its exponents' ability to explain what they do, which when it comes to the analysis of guitar playing is so feverishly intellectual that the terminology becomes an art form in itself. Here, for example, is Jimmy Brown, writing in the metal-reinforced magazine *Guitar World* on the track "Dogs," from Pink Floyd's album *Animals,* which for some reason metal fans like to claim as one of their own.

> As always, Gilmour's note choice and phrasing are impeccable. He begins this solo with a tastefully articulated upper-register lick, beginning on the ninth of the underlying Em9 chord, F♯, and uses the notes from the E Dorian mode (E F♯ G A B C♯ D) to construct a descending melodic line. In the fourth bar, as the chord changes to Fmaj7sus2/C, he builds an ascending phrase using notes from the C Lydian mode (C D E F♯ G A B), a scale that doesn't exactly "agree" with this chord theoretically (because of the F♯ note) but nevertheless seems to work in this context. The bass sounds a low C note beneath this chord, and in all likelihood Gilmour heard this note as being the root and intuitively gravitated toward a C Lydian sound.

I sent this analysis to Rick, thinking that his musical education might be a little light in the area of heavy metal, and he replied, "That stuff about changing modes? They're called *mistakes.*"

To be serious for a moment: heavy metal is, in a sense, the quintessential electric guitar genre. Heavy metal is what happens if the guitar takes over its owner by offering him all its seductive attractions—volume, power, the ability to ignore everything else and do nothing but play faster and faster. For a long time, in fact, I never associated the phrase "heavy metal" with motorbikes or medieval steel weaponry or any of the trappings of the genre. I assumed it referred to the guitar, the heavy, metal instrument that had, in the Pink Floyd phrase, put its wires in the player's brain. Demanding to be the center of attention, the icon. Demanding to be turned up to 11.

The last two guitar waves, which provided a welcome countercurrent to the mostly guitarless tides of disco and techno, were reggae and punk. Reggae gave a new set of rhythms to the guitar, but its most remarkable achievement may have been spiritual. As author Charles Schaar Murray has pointed out, in taking a religion (Rastafarianism) that was a minority creed even among the inhabitants of one of the smallest and poorest nations of the Western hemisphere and making it a worldwide musical phenomenon, Bob Marley might be one of the most influential guitarists of all time.

Punk was greeted with exactly the same cries of appalled horror that greeted rock and roll and then heavy metal. The bad behavior! The hair! The clothes! The brutal guitar noise! All three genres have turned out to be remarkably durable, though, which suggests an axiom: the greater the outcry when a new music style emerges, the more likely it is to catch on. (This was also true of rap, though in rap's case, for once, the guitar didn't get blamed.)

Punk was another British Invasion that began in the opposite direction. In December 1973 an ex-marine named Hilly Kristal opened a bar in the Bowery. "When I first opened it as Hilly's on the Bowery, I ran it for a while as a derelict bar, and bums would be lining up at eight in the morning, when I opened the doors. They would come in and fall on their faces even before they had their first drink." From these refreshingly unpretentious beginnings evolved the music bar soon to be renamed CBGB–OMFUG, an acronym for Country, Bluegrass, Blues and Other Music for Uplifting Gourmandizers, or CBGB's for short. The early bands were a mixture of art-rock bands such as Television and the Talking Heads, art-punk-poets such as Patti Smith, Richard Hell—author of the punk anthem "Blank Generation"—and the Ramones, who had no interest in art and just wanted to make some serious noise. The Ramones evolved the guitar-driven, high-speed amphetamine sets that came to characterize punk: seventeen minutes for eight songs such as "Now I Wanna Sniff Some Glue."

They also collectively began to model punk fashion, loosely based on the leather-jacket Elvis/Eddie Cochran/Marlon Brando look of the fifties. When they went to England in 1976, following the release there of their first album, they started a fire.

"I heard the Ramones' first record and I thought that it was fucking brilliant," said Billy Idol, who subsequenty formed the punk band Generation X. "We got that first record and every song was under two minutes and it was like a revolution."

Punk added some interesting dimensions to the guitar. It wasn't the first appearance of power chords (the Kinks were playing power chords in 1964) but in their eagerness to sound jarring, punk guitarists spat on the tradition I-IV-V triad of chords and went from, say, E major to B flat major, as hard and fast as possible. Solos, like hair, were deliberately messy; often the whole band's sound clashed badly. In a sense punk was an experiment in modernism, helping to jar guitar music out of the blues-flavored rock that was fast becoming a predictable standard.

The accessories of punk, though, always threatened to capsize the music. By June 1977 both Bonwit Teller and Saks, hot off the mark, were selling gold safety pins for up to a hunded dollars, and Bloomingdale's was selling Zandra Rhodes ripped outfits for as much as a thousand dollars.

By the mid-eighties punk seemed to have become a cliché. Not only had the clothes gone mainstream but even the guitar companies were trying to cash in by bringing out punk-looking electrics: duct-tape-gray guitars, guitars with graffiti custom-painted on them.

Yet there was something elemental about punk that refused to be ignored. The electric guitar could emit the primal scream of adolescence, and that would always be useful. Over the next twenty years punk shrank down to that very specific population, where it cross-pollinated with heavy metal and other unlikely forms to produce a healthy genetic diversity. At a punk show recently (in deepest Appalachia: fans and musicians regularly drove hundreds of miles to shows) three young teenage musicians ran down the roster for me. This band was Christian metal. This was folk punk, or maybe thrash. The next one was Christian punk. Sometimes they had ska bands. Several were eco-punk—a strong pro-environment message was a common thread. One girl who played banjo was thinking of starting up an all-girl punk band. That was the great thing about punk, she said. Anyone can do it.

Which leads to the last point I want to make, about punk music and what it tells us about the nature of the guitar.

Around the time Dylan went electric at Newport, the guitar changed its identity as a tool of social protest. It went from being a quiet, hollow, light, vulnerable instrument, embodying the small but brave voice of the oppressed, to something tougher and louder that would make its point by shouting down the opposition. The oppressed as oppressor, in fact. A bit of a bully.

The irony here is that the electric guitar is, in its own way, just as vulnerable and fragile as the acoustic. I had never fully realized this until punk, which pushed "tough" and "loud" to an extreme, showed me.

I was living in England during the punk craze, teaching at a college for sixteen- to eighteen-year-olds, and almost at once half a dozen student bands sprang up, sporting studded collars and wristbands, ripped clothing, their hair blackened and spiked with shoe polish. One of the bands was fronted by a guy who, frankly, scared me and most of the faculty: tall, muscular, and rude, he'd added to his natural punk attributes by shaving his head and freezing his face into a permanent intimidating unblinking stare. His name was something ordinary like Derek, but he took on a nom de punk that I've forgotten. I'll call him Rat Boy.

For a no-bullshit movement, punk had a curiously strong sense of manifesto. The whole point of punk was to react against the genteel middle-class smugness of the folk music, the swollen excesses of seventies pop megastardom, (read: Rod Stewart and Elton John) and subsequently the naked greed of the Thatcher conservatives. Punk's purpose, we were told time and again, was to produce an egalitarian form of music that was so much of the people that the musicians were no better than the audience—no more skillful, no more deserving of being put on a pedestal, or on a stage. This made for some very, very basic music, but that was the price you paid for hearing truth from those who otherwise went unheard. Punk was constantly emerging from the rude swamp of social chaos, especially at Queen Mary's College, Basingstoke.

One evening a month, the students took over the auditorium and put on a live music event they called Madhouse. A couple of teachers had to make sure they didn't electrocute themselves or set fire to the building, and one time it was my turn. Rat Boy's band was setting up when I got there early. He gave me his usual fuck-you stare and set his guitar, which of course by punk union rules he could barely play, on the stage. After a while people started to turn up and mill around. The first band went on, thrashed about, screamed, went off to the requisite round of boos, hisses. No spitting, as I recall—they weren't that good. Then the next, and the next, and after a while I took to patrolling the outside of the building where the noise was no more than painful. I was somewhere out by the flower beds when Rat Boy and one of his musical associates burst out of the door, looked around, saw me, and came running over. I braced myself. To my amazement, Rat Boy was almost in tears.

"They ruined my fucking guitar!" he whined. "They ruined my fucking guitar!"

He was almost incoherent with outrage and grief. The others weren't much help, either, mumbling, "They fucked him over," or "They fucked it up," or "They fucking fucked his guitar up" until I followed them inside and got the full story.

It turned out that Rat Boy's band had played last, the pole position in the evening's lineup, and as usual he had charged onto the stage, grabbed the mike, and started telling the audience to fuck off. The audience, of course, anticipated this and started yelling at him to fuck off even before he could yell at them. A few started spitting, and maybe he spat back, or maybe it was the other way around, but in any case someone had decided that Rat Boy's band was good enough to deserve an upping of the ante of rudeness and threw a raw egg at him. It missed Rat Boy, but hit his guitar, still in its stand on stage, right on the pickups. Being occupied in his introductory remarks, it was some time before Rat Boy turned around to get his guitar to play the first song (I use the word loosely) and by then the egg had started to congeal in among the electrics.

"Look at it!" he bleated, holding it out to me. "It's ruined!"

Rat Boy's unfortunate guitar had closed the logical circle. The punk manifesto had always maintained that punk's job was to puncture the bogus posturing of the would-be star, and now Rat Boy himself had been punctured.

And that was pretty much it for the evening, which everyone agreed was not only the best Madhouse ever but the epitome of what punk was really all about.

# INTERLUDE:

## AT THE ISBIN CONCERT

Rick and I go to see Sharon Isbin, one of the country's leading classical guitarists and someone who has pioneered the instrument in two important respects—by getting concert series and orchestra leaders to accept it as a legitimate classical instrument and by commissioning new pieces by contemporary composers for classical guitar.

She plays a couple of these contemporary pieces, which leave me unmoved: they don't sound like pieces that have sprung out of the guitar; they sound as if they have been written for the guitar by someone who usually writes for other instruments—which, in fact, they were. Then she plays one of the warhorses of the Spanish classical guitar, the Asturias by Albeniz, as transcribed by Segovia, and the piece seems to be utterly at home in its idiom, to have grown up in the same village as the guitar, to have hung out smoking cheap cigarettes on the same corner. More specifically, as she plays one single note and lets it swell out in that rich, fat-stringed classical guitar sound, I have the sharp and distinct sense that this is one of those Iberian pieces that were composed (or in this case transcribed) by someone who knew exactly what the performer and the instrument were capable of at their best, and knew intuitively how to capitalize on those strengths. Equally, it's being played on a guitar that has been built by someone who has the same deep understanding of idiom and skill. Maker, composer, transcriber, player—all seem like childhood friends who grew up kicking a soccer ball on the streets of São Paulo, who without even being able to articulate it have inherited and taken in by osmosis the accumulated wisdom of their surroundings.

A classical guitar is a remarkable instrument. Like other instruments of the orchestra, it has the graceful, austere beauty of pure function: its looks are defined by its sound. Light and deceptively simple, a classical guitar is driven by the demands of the repertoire, which insist that every fret of every string can be used and counted on to produce resonance, power, and quality of sound and (in most cases) to do so without amplification using strings that are far less bright and loud than steel. Like the performer, a classical maker, knowing the extreme demands on the instrument, is skirting the edge of what is physically workable.

A classical guitar has far more shades of color than a steel-string, and classical technique teaches a far greater range of expressive emotion. A classical guitarist may deliberately move his or her right hand over the sound hole, or close to the bridge, to get certain tonal qualities, or play with different parts of the finger- or thumbnail or other parts of the hand altogether. And he or she will be trained to do so because the repertoire will call for that effect; and the repertoire will call for that effect because the composer knows that the player will be able to produce it. And the maker knows that when the composer calls for it and the player executes it, the guitar had better deliver.

The classical guitar strikes me as a glider, a miracle of flight, so delicate it needs to be aware of every invisible air current, while a steel-string, especially a dreadnaught, is an F-15, which will get there by sheer force if necessary.

I run this analogy by the Toronto builder Grit Laskin, who makes superlative classicals, flamenco guitars, and steel-strings, and he says that it's even more true of the difference between a flamenco and a steel-string. A flamenco has to have an even thinner top than a classical, even lighter bracing, an even lighter neck, and a lower saddle and bridge, so that the strings are closer to the frets and fingerboard for the player to achieve the percussive effects. It's the trickiest action to achieve of all guitars.

The Isbin concert leaves me thinking two things. One has to do with the triumvirate of maker, composer, and player. The United States has produced world-class classical players, and world-class classical guitar makers, but no world-class classical guitar composers. Why not?

Laura Oltman, half of the Newman and Oltman guitar duo, Ensemble-in-Residence at the Mannes School of Music in New York, offered several suggestions. "There are a lot of composers writing almost exclusively for the guitar, and there are a lot of composers writing for everything else and not the guitar," she said. "What we don't have are composers who write well in general and include guitar in the music they write"—in the way that Bach wrote for a wide variety of instruments and ensembles, including lute music. Exceptions, such as Leo Brouwer, who was a brilliant guitarist, and Benjamin Britten, who didn't play guitar but worked closely with Julian Bream, are few.

Modern students of composition, she went on, aren't required to learn the first thing about the guitar and its idioms. "They are required to learn a little bit about all the instruments of the orchestra," which does not typically include the guitar, "and anyone who goes to college to get a music degree is required to learn the piano, however marginally." In the world of classical composition, then, the guitar is still an outsider.

This creates a number of problems. The guitar fingerboard is much smaller than the piano keyboard, but the guitarist has to span it with only one hand. A composer may create a wonderful piece that is devilishly hard to finger, given that a middle C is only one key on the piano, but can be played in four different locations on the guitar fingerboard—each of which, moreover, has a slightly different timbre. "This aspect of the guitar makes all kind of things both possible and impossible," Oltman said, "and the only way to know the difference is to play the guitar pretty well."

Take a straightforward example, she said: power chords. A power chord is a perfect example of guitar playing at its most familiar and idiomatic. The guitarist holds a specific fingering that clutches all six strings (or, in an even more simplified version, just the bass strings) and then slides that hand-position up or down the neck, producing not only strong major chords but a nice glissando or slide from one chord to the next. "Of course, all these chords are possible in other fingerings, but the sound of the power chord is sliding on the basses." A classic lick that totally depends on this sound is the beginning of "Smoke on the Water." It's so familiar, in fact, that as in much of classic rock, you may know the lick even if you have no idea what the song is called.

"Villa-Lobos exploits this same sound all the time in his guitar music. Listen to almost anything he wrote and you will hear a section of parallel harmonies that is played by sliding the same chord fingering around the fingerboard."

The danger, though, is that the guitarist-composer will write lick-based music—like most popular guitar music—and be held back by the very idiom he or she wants to expand.

The other thought that strikes me after the Isbin concert is that a good classical player develops a far more acute ear for color and timbre than a steel-string player, and we steel-string guitarists haven't yet come to terms with what a steel-string guitar is really good at, or capable of at its best. In very rare instances a very good guitarist will play a very good steel-string guitar with such an ear for the individual sounds that you can hear an individual note take shape, like a flame, but this hardly ever happens. Most of us play it as if it were a Schroeder's toy piano in *Peanuts* or a musical tambourine, or when the bluegrass guys play it, a tin fiddle.

When I first heard Michael Hedges playing a standard six-string Martin using tapping techniques, which produce all kinds of slurs and snaps and percussive timbres, it was like opening a cupboard and finding it stocked with groceries left by an unknown guest. If these sounds were possible, what else about this instrument hadn't yet been discovered? Fascinated with bright colors and decoration, played but hardly explored, a steel-string seems still in its adolescence.

# Applying the Finish

On a fine, sunny day in late July, Rick and I drive up around the northwestern corner of the Green Mountains to Cambridge, where a small, anonymous modern factory building next to the rail bed of the old Burlington and Lamoille Railroad has become home to Rigel Mandolins.

This is the thing about the lacquer finish used on guitars: it's toxic. When Rick built his workshop he added a largish closet beyond the workroom to use as a spray booth, where he would hang his finished guitar bodies and necks (separately) and spray them with nitrocellulose lacquer, but it's a messy, expensive, and unhealthy business, and in the end, like four or five other local guitar makers, he started taking his guitars to Pete Langdell at Rigel to be finished. Rick's former spray booth is now a wood-storage room, and Pete does a good job for a price Rick couldn't match.

On the way up, as the suburban fringes of Chittenden County give way to farmland, then to damn poor farmland, then to attractive outcrops of ledge punctuated by rough pasture, we talk finish.

The purpose of finish is to protect the wood. Unfinished, the wood registers every knock and blemish, and is also horribly vulnerable to changes in moisture, waxing and waning with every breath of humidity. Yet here, as in every other aspect of instrument making, there's no certainty and a dozen conflicts of opinion.

Finishing is ludicrously labor intensive. My guitar, I'm told, has received three coats of lacquer initially, then was cured for two days and level-sanded. Three more coats of lacquer were then applied, followed by two more days of curing. After that, the instrument was level-sanded again and buffed out. Sanding and buffing both remove some of the finish, so the result is that I am buying a guitar with the equivalent of about four coats of lacquer with a total thickness of about .005 of an inch. This inefficiency makes finishing one of the areas currently under intensive experimentation. Taylor, which for a sizable guitar company tries a lot of new ideas, finishes by spray under UV light, the guitar turning like a chicken in a rotisserie. Rick guesses that the Fylde has twenty to forty hours of labor in the finish alone. A Taylor has under two hours.

Pete Langdell turns out to be a cheery guy preceded by a comfortable belly. We meet in a metal box of a room by a bulletin board on which are pinned work orders for different finishes: tobacco, seafoam green, chocolate. Tobacco is the most commonly requested finish, Pete says, that dark brown that might also be molasses, the background to a million sunburst cowboy guitars and mandolins. I ask both Rick and Pete about the origin of the sunburst. Pete has heard two theories: one, that Gibson invented it as a way to mimic the aged look of Italian violins; the other, that they invented it so that the darker color and the lacquer itself would cover up imperfections caused when they scraped the bindings.

The conversation turns to the science of finish, and Pete and Rick go round and around the familiar questions like dogs sniffing a tree. Does finish really enhance the sound? And, if so, why don't all makers finish their guitars both outside and inside, as the classical makers do? Ah, but they use only a very thin coat inside to allow the wood to breathe and age. Do they do so for good acoustic reasons or simply because this is what violin makers do? Well, violins are so delicate and light that they need more finish or they may crack—and it's possible,

Pete says, that a harder finish helps the treble ranges. So much so, that some finishers put gemstones in their varnish. They grind up quartz and other superhard rock in a mortar and pestle and add the resulting fine particles to their varnish in order to give a very thin finish that is exceptionally hard wearing. "They all have their secret recipes."

"The violin guys are completely nuts about finish," Rick agrees affably.

One reason why they're nuts about finish is that the recipe for making the varnish that all the golden age Italians used has been lost. The logic goes like this: since those old violins sound so good, and since we can copy everything else they did except the finish, the finish must be the secret. A logical fallacy, and a seductive one.

What is the difference between varnish and lacquer? Pete and Rick have difficulty giving me a clear answer, so I write to Al Carruth.

"Traditionally," Carruth writes back, "finishes that change chemically once they are applied, so that they are insoluble once cured, have been called 'varnishes.' Traditional varnishes were normally mixtures of a drying oil (such as linseed or walnut) and some sort of resin that were cooked together until they combined chemically. The resulting tarlike goo was mixed with a solvent, such as turpentine, to brushing consistency. On application the solvent dries out, leaving the sticky mass as a thin film, which then oxidizes and polymerizes hard. Once it is fully cured the varnish film is unaffected by exposure to turpentine."

Lacquer was originally shellac, made from secretions of the lac insect, a relative of the mealy bug native to India and Southeast Asia. "This was dissolved in alcohol and applied to the surface," Carruth continues. "When the alcohol evaporates you are left with a film that can be dissolved again in alcohol. Nitro, and acrylic, lacquers are later synthetics that are dissolved in less common solvents, but they work the same way and so got called by the same name.

"There have always been exceptions: Japanese 'lacquer' is the sap of a sumac shrub: thus japonica. It is a latexlike emulsion. On application to a surface the water evaporates, and the thin film that is left behind reacts to become insoluble, and darn near bullet proof if you build it up enough. Laquerware has been found in flooded tombs that had been floating for hundreds of years, and was totally unscathed. Too bad we can't use that on guitars! One trouble: *Rhus japonica* is closely related to our poison ivy, and some people react to laquerware.

"Modern catalyzed lacquers change chemically to become more inert once they are applied. Epoxies do too (Ovation tops are finished with epoxy). These things are more like varnishes than they are like the old shellac, but they call them 'lacquers' in recognition of their ancestry."

"We use catalyzed lacquer," Pete says. The catalyzing agent makes the chemical reactions happen a lot more quickly, rather like adding the hardener to epoxy resin. As such, it has to be used very quickly. "It has a pot life of twelve hours."

The other advantage is that "it's less toxic because it uses fewer solvents than nitro. The toxic fumes become inert more quickly. It smells horrible. Nitro smells sweet and pleasant, but it does a hell of a lot more harm."

Rick has heard that the chemical reactions in nitrocellulose continue for up to ten years—it takes that long to reach maximum hardness.

Because of these environmental concerns—practically speaking, because of pressure from the EPA and OSHA on the furniture industry—water-based finishes have been developed, but both Pete and Rick pull long faces, saying they're hard to apply and hard to touch up, all in all very finicky ("We could use them, but we wouldn't get anything done," says Pete), and Rick says that they always leave a slightly milky finish instead of a clear one.

Rick adds more about the voodoo of finishes. One researcher found traces of cat urea in a Stradivari finish, and for a while the violin community went crazy—Strad's secret ingredient had been found—but eventually it was decided that this was in fact an anomaly. In other words, in this case a cat had simply peed in the varnish of its own accord, not on command.

Eventually Rick asks Pete, "Well, should we show him his guitar?"

"I guess we can't put it off any longer," Pete sighs.

Rick opens a case—well, he actually opens the wrong case, on purpose, and pretends that someone must have stolen my guitar, and I say har har, and he opens the right case and I am blown away.

The guitar is utterly amazing. Especially without the neck and headstock, it hardly seems to be an instrument; it's more like a painting in wood. The color, shot through with a thousand shades of reddish gold, is riveting; the grain and the chatoyance ripple and shimmer. The finish has given them a third dimension, a depth that seems virtually bottomless. It reminds me of those patterns that, if you adjust your eyes to the right focal length, turn into 3-D designs that recede into infinity. The sides look like stirred honey.

Even Pete Langdell is impressed. "I didn't know cherry could have figure like that," he says.

"No, you can't have the rest of the board," retorts Rick.

Another feature of the finish is that now the wood looks as if it's under glass; the term "showcase" takes on a new and literal meaning. It takes a second to realize that one day I'll actually be playing this thing instead of just admiring it. Might almost have to put a few dings and dents in it deliberately, just to make it feel like a working guitar.

On the way back Rick tells me that the classical makers often french-polish their finished instruments. A french-polished finish looks wonderful but is extremely delicate; the slightest amount of sweat will degrade it, which is why classical players often carry their guitars very strangely, as if they were radioactive, and some lay a piece of silk between their skin and the guitar to protect the finish.

"That's the problem with french polish," Rick says. "It's vulnerable to sweat and alcohol. Steel-string players are inextricably connected to both. They're a lost cause."

# "Vintage" Guitars

In the eighties, the guitar underwent a radical and far-reaching cognitive shift: it became self-conscious. What had previously been just an old guitar became a vintage guitar, and an increasing number of Americans (and Europeans and, even more so, Japanese) became convinced that an old Fender, an old Martin, or even an old Sears Silvertone was worth admiring, buying at great cost, and hanging in a room with a fleet of other guitars or stringed instruments in general. Needless to say, most of these admirers / buyers / hangers were guys, who in general seem far more likely to fetishize guitars than women.

For most of history the phrase "vintage guitar" would have made as little sense as "vintage broom" or "vintage boot." A guitar that had seen its share of the world would simply be called "old." To most Americans, the phrase "vintage guitar" was at least pretentious and almost an oxymoron. Yet in 1986 it was used as the title of a magazine. Likewise, for most of the history of the instrument a guitar—even a good guitar—was rarely seen as a brand-name product. In reading some two thousand references to the guitar in nineteenth- and early-twentieth-century newspapers, books, magazines, diaries, and letters I didn't come across a single writer who identified the maker of the guitar to which he or she was referring. By and large, a guitar was a guitar in the sense that a boot was a boot, even if it was a well-made boot, an expensive boot, or an old faithful boot, it was still a boot rather than, say, a Gucci.

Here's a sign of the times—an advertisement on the Web site of Mandolin Brothers of Staten Island, the best guitar shop in New York and probably the universe:

43-0696 John D'Angelico Excel, blonde, #1746, entered in John's logbook as March 7, 1947, tone bar braced, in excellent condition with a 1950s Gibson style brown leatherette hard shell case. In or around 1950 a Mr. Al Borelli accompanied a young musician named Rudy C. to the storefront at 37 Kenmare Street, whose proprietor was famous for building high grade archtop guitars. I play exactly four chords, Rudy says now, just like I did then, but Al was convinced that I needed a good guitar and this guy, he said, is the best. Rudy continues, John D'Angelico listened to what my professional requirements were and he says "Wait here." He goes into a room behind the main counter and comes out with this gorgeous blonde Excel. He says "The guy who I made this for hasn't paid me. If you want it, it's yours." How much? Rudy C. asks. "This is the Excel, it's $300," says John. Rudy C. happens to have $300, buys the guitar and is delighted to get it. Interestingly, in John's logbook it says that this guitar was made for Ed Sterner, so Ed, if you're still hiking the tranquil trails with the rest of us, if you regret having not paid for the Excel and taking possession in 1950, it's here for you. If, however, Ed is levitating over the halcyon habitat of the post-ambulatory economy, then I hope he is applauding the reappearance of this superb instrument, finally coming to roost on the resale market.

After this conversational opening that establishes the instrument's pedigree, the ad continues with several hundred words about the technical specs that are a guitar nut's wine and cheese: the flamed maple sides and back, the pineapple-and-pediment preferential peghead, the parallel-grained hand-selected spruce top, the DeArmond Rhythm Chief jazz guitar pickup, and so on, finally coming after a great deal more scrolling downscreen to the bottom line.

$20,104 or, at our cash discount price, $19,500.

For a D'Angelico, that's actually pretty cheap. Flipping through the catalog of Elderly Instruments (founded in Michigan in 1972 by Stan Werbin) shows that "vintage" guitars get pricey very quickly. Fifties Gibson electrics command strong prices, notably a 1958 Flying V ($44,500), one of eighty-one made, and a 1957 Flying V prototype ($50,000), which is presumably unique.

Classic rock guitars seem to fetch more than classic jazz guitars. The very first production-model Gibson Byrdland, a jazz guitar, is cheaper at $25,000. Two classic Gibson ES-335s from 1960 are cheaper still at $15,000 and $18,500, respectively, despite being in excellent condition. The archtops and resonator guitars in stock are even cheaper, the top mandolin in the catalog is $8,500, and the most expensive banjo is a mere $6,500. Up to this point the message is clear: these are the Guitars of Your Life, the ones after which the customer salivated when he was seventeen, starting his first high school band, forced to make do with a crappy old junk-shop guitar with no chrome switches or brass volume knobs, nothing to wow his friends.

There's another category of customer, though, and another kind of guitar—and a whole 'nother stratum of price. Elderly has an entire section devoted to Martins. Nobody has benefited more from the new concept of vintageness than Martin. A series of prewar models rise from $13,500 to $78,000, and just when I thought I'd scanned the columns thoroughly and had already gone way beyond the highest price anyone was likely to pay for a guitar never owned by a dead celebrity, I came across this: Martin D-45 (1941), "very rare and desirable . . . one of 91 prewar D-45's made": $135,000.

An old guitar that costs more than my *house*? And all this fetishism of model years and numbers, of the cosmetics of appearance, this sudden fascination with America's least favorite subject—history? How did this happen?

It began with collectors. Plenty of people have collected guitars, but two in particular became collector-sellers, and then dealers: Stan Jay, owner of Mandolin Brothers, and George Gruhn, owner of Gruhn Guitars in Nashville.

George Gruhn, coauthor (with Walter Carter) of *Gruhn's Guide to Vintage Guitars*, is the kind of guy who can and will tell you that the Gibson ES-335TD, introduced in spring 1958, can be identified by its two humbucking pickups, two tone and two volume knobs, one switch, Tune-o-Matic bridge, stop tailpiece, optional Bigsby vibrato, laminated beveled-edge pick guard extending below the bridge, single-bound rosewood fingerboard with dot inlay, and, by the fact that it has a single-bound top and back and a crown peghead inlay, that the neck joins the body at the nineteenth fret and it comes in a sunburst or natural finish, so if you have a model with a cherry finish it must date from late 1959 at the earliest.

He has a Salman Rushdie beard, round glasses, thinning hair. He delivers long sentences, grimacing as if the world is a slightly painful and potentially dangerous place. The word on the street is that, at fifty-eight, by Gruhn standards he is now a mellow and affable guy. We meet on the second floor of his store in Nashville, surrounded by old banjos, old mandolins, old and new guitars, weird old lap steels, lots of cases, some looking like small stuffed crocodiles, and a stand-up cutout of Elvis in a gold suit, promoting Epiphone guitars.

Gruhn didn't start out to be a dealer; he started out as an addict.

"I was going to college at the University of Chicago and my parents were footing the bill. Every month they gave me money up front for room, board, and books. They also had agreed that they would buy me one guitar, and in 1963 I bought my first guitar." One thing led to another. "My fourth guitar, a few months later, was a 1924 Gibson L-5, signed and dated by Lloyd Loar. Cost four hundred dollars at Sid

Sherman Music on Wabash in Chicago. Four hundred dollars was tough for me to come up with—I basically had to eat canned beans for four months—but I was able to put a deposit down and pay it off over time.

"Collecting something is very much an addiction. I started out with a guitar-every-ninety-days habit, and then it became a guitar-a-month habit, then a guitar-every-couple-of-weeks habit, then a guitar a week, and by the time I was living in Nashville, before I had a store, if I hadn't bought, sold, or traded a guitar that day I was going to have withdrawal symptoms."

He searched school bulletin boards, classifieds, and hock shops, of which there were plenty, especially on 63rd and 47th in what he describes as "a solidly black area."

"I set out looking for some pre–World War II Martins or some pre-war Gibson Mastertone banjos and Artist Model Gibson mandolins. I was not interested in electric guitars. I don't play electric. But you go in the hock shops and they've got a 1957 black Fender Stratocaster with gold-plated hardware that looks brand-new, and in 1964 on Sixty-third Street I bought it for seventy-five dollars. It would bring at least thirty-five thousand dollars today. At that point Jimi Hendrix wasn't known, Eric Clapton wasn't yet doing much with Strats. At that point the Stratocaster was simply a model that nobody gave a damn about at all."

The price of a guitar is intimately connected to hero worship. When Mike Bloomfield began to play Fender Telecasters, Gruhn said, "all of a sudden [used] Telecasters went from about seventy-five dollars to about six-fifty or seven hundred fifty dollars." When Bloomfield switched to a '54 Gibson Les Paul Goldtop, "with the P-90 single-coil pickups with white plastic covers and that stud-mounted non-Tune-o-Matic bridge," all of a sudden those guitars went from $75 up to about $750.

"When he was playing the Tele, nobody gave a damn about any Les Paul. In fact, I remember people claiming that Les had been in an auto accident and broken his left arm so severely that he ended up with one arm shorter than the other, and that [Les Paul] guitars were weighted for a player who had one arm shorter than the other. Normal people couldn't comfortably play a Les Paul. And they weighed too much anyway, and they weren't worth a damn. But those people couldn't remember having said a *thing* like that as soon as Bloomfield picked one up and was playing the '54 Goldtop."

By chance, Hank Williams, Jr., found out about Gruhn and began buying his guitars—a relationship that flourished to the point where Williams persuaded Gruhn to move to Nashville, found him an apartment, helped him set up in business in 1970 across from the old Ryman Auditorium, and continued to buy several guitars a week from him.

While Gruhn was getting started in Nashville, Stan Jay, an immensely likable, irrepressibly cheerful guy looking exactly like an elf supervisor in Santa's workshop, was selling instruments out of his apartment on the waterfront in Staten Island.

"You had to walk up a narrow stairway wallpapered in that deep-textured wine red that one generally associates with certain houses in New Orleans. One stepped from the landing into our showroom, that anybody else would call their living room. On the left was the dining room with the 1920s round oak lion's-claw table. About fifty guitars, banjos, and mandolins hung from three walls. On the outside wall they were positioned above a circa 1900 rococo upholstered couch, on which Joni Mitchell fell in love with the 1915 Gibson K-4 mandocello that inspired her to write that legendary song to her friend, about going to Staten Island "to buy myself a mandolin."

If there's the faintest whiff of Rodeo Drive boutique-to-the-stars about these two enterprises in their early days, it's because until the eighties almost nobody but the stars had the money or the desire to spend serious cash on a used guitar. All that changed quite suddenly, thanks to what Gruhn calls his Antibiotic Theory of History.

"The baby boomers grew up with guitars," he began, speaking in sentences that got longer and faster, as if history itself were accelerating, "but the baby boomers were different from any generation from *Australopithecus* to the present in that we grew up from birth onward with antibiotics. No previous generation ever had. Turn-of-the-century life expectancy in the U.S. was about forty-two years, which wasn't much different from what it was in ancient Greece. As a result they had no mid-life crisis and they didn't have hobbies in mid-life."

Thanks to antibiotics, he argued, the baby boomers were healthy and flourishing as they approached forty, so they could afford to spend a little of their accumulating wealth on themselves. I would add that the baby boomers were the first middle-class, educated generation for a century to have grown up surrounded by guitars, which meant that as they rose to positions of influence, for the first time in history America had a sizable group of affluent middle-aged consumers with a fondness for guitars. Some still played; some thought of taking up guitar again now the kids were no longer keeping them up all night; some thought of passing their love of guitars on to their kids. And some (especially as they approached fifty, and as retirement income began to shift away from conventional retirement pensions and more toward the stock market) began to think of buying guitars as investments.

I wonder if another force wasn't coming into play, too. The rise of the vintage guitar seems almost like a response to the Great Synthesizer Scare of the early eighties, when sagging guitar sales were further attacked by the guitar's old enemy, the piano, reborn as the cheap electronic keyboard. The keyboard pointed up one of the guitar's major flaws: it hurts. Anyone thinking of buying a seven-year-old, say, a beginner guitar faces issues of size (all but reduced-size guitars are going to be hard to hold, and hard to play) and discomfort. At the very least the kid's wrist will ache; if the instrument is a steel-string, it'll slice the tender fingertips. And the cheaper the guitar the more true this will be. The synth came not only pain-free but with all manner of interesting sound effects. Both my daughters have been through their synth phases, which were all about making funny noises. That, probably, was what saved the guitar: the sound effects, the very thing that made the synth fun, also made it a passive form of entertainment, and after a while it lost its appeal, unless the kid had made it on to the (distant) next stage and was actually creating music. This is all speculation, but it would certainly make sense that high-end guitar makers would want to stress that though their product might be more expensive than a Casio it had history and quality on its side.

In any event, by the turn of the millennium the guitar was being touted as the collectible of the future, the Stradivarius of the Woodstock generation. In 1990 Jimi Hendrix's Woodstock white 1968 Fender Stratocaster sold at auction for $334,620. (In the same year, a red violin by Antonio Stradivari sold for $1.7 million.) In 1999 Eric Clapton's 1956 sunburst Fender "Brownie" fetched $497,500. In 2003 George Harrison's rosewood Telecaster, which he'd played on the rooftop during the *Let It Be* sessions, sold for some $435,000. Two guitars played by Jerry Garcia sold for $789,500 and $957,500.

Around the same time, two other collectors emerged to accelerate the inflationary cycle. The first was Akira Tsumura, who reportedly played banjo in an Ann Arbor Dixieland band, the Boll Weevils, while a business major at the University of Michigan during the late fifties. During the eighties, back in Japan, he amassed in his house what was probably the world's largest and most valuable collection of stringed instruments, specializing in American banjos and guitars. A few years later, Scott Chinery of Toms River, New Jersey, a collector who bought the Batmobile, also began buying expensive guitars, accumulating about a thousand. (Perhaps it says something about the times, but both men, oddly, made their millions in vitamins and herbal medicines.) The vintage guitar market had never been hotter. People began saying that it was only a matter of time before a guitar changed hands for a million dollars.

Chinery (and to a lesser extent Tsumura) also fueled that guitar-as-art market by commissioning new guitars from the top luthiers and paying the prices he thought they deserved. No single act brought more attention to America's guitar makers than when Chinery, who had always admired a one-of-a-kind archtop guitar made by Jimmy D'Aquisto and finished in an unusual absinthe shade of blue, invited twenty of North America's finest archtop builders (and one from Europe) to make him their own interpretations of the blue archtop. The Blue Guitars, as they became known, ended up displayed at the first ever guitar exhibition at the Smithsonian

Institution. Vintage guitars were fetching all-time high prices, high-end new guitars by the top makers were getting serious respect, and a whole network of interests—guitar magazines, guitar dealers, big and small guitar makers, auction houses—was boosting the value *and importance* of guitars. People began calling the 1990s the Golden Age of guitarmaking.

Then three things went wrong: Tsumura was indicted for misappropriating his company's funds, the stock market crashed, and Scott Chinery suffered a fatal heart attack. Chinery's death was widely mourned, and not just for its effect on the prices of instruments: he was universally described as a good guy.

These events didn't break the guitar market but they exposed its vulnerability. Suddenly less money was floating around, and to make things worse the vintage guitar sellers no longer had the guitar pie to themselves. Now the high-end guitar builders were also trying to play the investment card, and though very few builders have such prestige in their names that their instruments grow in value as they age, they still represented competition. If you have $15,000 to spend, do you buy a vintage Martin or a custom-made Kevin Ryan with one-of-a-kind bespoke inlay design by Larry Robinson?

Not to mention the fact that there were just more decent guitars waiting to be bought.

"If you go back to 1985," Gruhn said, frowning and sounding worried, "guitar production in the USA was not more than a tenth of what it is today. In 1985 Taylor made six hundred and eighty-one guitars. Last year they made about forty thousand. In 1985 Martin was making close to seven thousand guitars. Last year they made over seventy thousand guitars. In '85 Fender didn't even own a factory. Bill Schultz and his group had just bought them, and all they had was a name and Japanese imports. They didn't even have American guitars. Now they have hundreds of thousands of Fender guitars coming in from the U.S., from Japan, from Mexico, from all over the place. And then there's numerous companies that weren't even around in '85, like Collings.

"If you look at the future of the market," Gruhn went on gloomily, "it becomes a sort of scary scenario for me. I figure I'm doing pretty well right now. I'm fifty-eight years old, twenty years from now will put me at seventy-eight years old . . ." He sighed deeply. "I don't know. The younger players of today don't show nearly as much interest in sophisticated collectibles or truly high-end instruments. One wonders how many more years Martin, Gibson, Fender, PRS, you name it, can go on introducing an item that does not become obsolete and will last three hundred years with good care if you build ten to fifteen times as many as you did fifteen years ago and they never go away. How soon is it before you're up to your neck in them? I'm amazed at how many still get cranked out every year and still sell."

Meanwhile, the pawnshops are no longer full of Fenders for sixty bucks.

"In those days," Stan Jay said wistfully, "finding instruments for resale was like fishing in a privately stocked stream. We couldn't pick up the phone without there being an original owner with a prewar or wartime instrument on the other end. This was pre-FAX machine, pre–e-mail, near the beginning of the age of the IBM Selectric typewriter. Cokes and pay phones were still a dime. Life was good. Today that stream has been fished nearly dry. Oh sure, we still find nice vintage pieces every now and then, but we might now have just one example in stock of a particular type when we used to have half a dozen."

This historical self-consciousness has spread, paradoxically, to new guitars. What do you do as a guitar-making company when your new models are competing with your own vintage models for a finite number of purchasing dollars? Martin Guitars, trying to have it both ways, has brought out an apparently endless series of copies of their vintage models and limited editions bearing the names of famous guitarists ancient and modern: Del McCoury, Honky Tonk Angel Kitty Wells, Clarence White, Joan Baez, Veteran's Mondel (with dog tags), Eric Clapton, Judy Collins (plus twelve-string), Lonnie Donegan, Philadelphia Folk Festival, Grand Ole Opry, and many, many more. Gibson even makes vintage strings.

"So-called limited editions," Gruhn said dismissively. "Today Martin, Gibson, Fender, Rickenbacker, Taylor—you name it—they all make limited editions, so-called instant collectibles, which to me is not what I'd want to put my money into. They're very good guitars but they're priced extra high because they're a limited edition, and often enough they have goofy ornamentation, or they're so fancy you wouldn't do anything except put them in a glass case, you wouldn't actually *use* one. Have you seen anyone *use* a PRS Dragon on stage? A Paul Reed Smith Dragon is a great-sounding guitar, but so is their regular standard model. Why would you want to spend twenty thousand dollars-plus for something with a whole bunch of ornamentation that's so fancy you can't even see the position markers? It's just a public statement that you have lots and lots of money."

This coalition of mutual interests has had to face competition from a new threat: eBay.

"I hate eBay with a burning passion," Gruhn said. "One, it obviously is competition, and I don't like that, but that doesn't in and of itself mean that it's bad for the public. But eBay offers things as is, where is, from people who frequently don't know flop about them, and often enough deliberately or unintentionally misrepresent them. eBay is a great way to get screwed. We provide a guarantee of authenticity, and I have seven people full time in repair doing restoration just on the instruments we sell."

Just a few days previously eBay had carried the following listing: "Robert Johnson's National Woodbody guitar. Actual guitar owned and played by famous blues singer Robert Johnson in Mississippi in the 1930's. Has been in possession of well known record producer for last 15 years. Notarised Letter will be provided detailing the acquisition of this valuable instrument in Greenwood, MS in the 1980's."

The asking price: $105,000. The catch: Robert Johnson, as far as anyone knows, never owned a National.

The beginning of the twenty-first century is a confusing time in the history of the guitar, possibly a period of maturity, possibly a period of decadence. For the first time, some serious historical guitar research is being done, but much of it is simply being used as a means of manipulating price. The qualitative terms "important" and "significant" are bandied about as airily as any auctioneer's adjectives.

Celebrities are using a guitar for one show, autographing it, and then raffling or auctioning it off for charity—a worthy aim in one sense but a strange devaluation in instant history. Above all, it's hard to distinguish between admiration and avarice. I salivate over a John Monteleone Electric Flyer, one of the most beautiful guitars ever made, in the Mandolin Brothers online catalog, but if I had $15,000 would I buy it? And if I bought it, would I play it? And if I did, what would I do with my other guitars, now pushed aside? Finally, are really good instruments either important or necessary? Paul McCartney has said, "I never had a really good instrument, but it didn't matter. The whole thing with the Beatles was we never really had great instruments, we never really had great headphones, we never really had great microphones or PAs; we somehow learned to muddle through. In fact, I think it was quite good for us. . . . We always made do with whatever we had."

Luckily, I don't have $15,000, so instead I periodically check out the listings offered by Bernunzio Vintage Instruments of Rochester, New York, with its pawnshop photos and its litany of forgotten names: National Debonaire, Regal, Hollywood Hawaiian, Cathedranola, Weymann (Jimmie Rodgers played a Weymann), and Stapleton. May Bell, featuring the May Bell Recording Master and the May Bell Pinnacle of Perfection. Joseph Bohmann, Harwood, DiSerio, Galiano (Nick Lucas played a Galiano), Ciani, Bacon, Bruno, Fairchild, and Heinrich Fuchs, a guitar looking exactly like the animated teapot in Disney's *Beauty and the Beast*.

And the variety! Guitars in black or red; guitars covered with some kind of crystallite or green ivoroid. Here's a Harmony guitar with a bridge shaped like an airplane to commemorate Lindbergh's flight, as if a guitar were a postage stamp. Here's the Harmony Caribbean Series from the 1950s in beautiful delicate pastels (spring green, copper, Sahara yellow, salmon-and-white) and chromelike Harmometal trim. These are the guitars that America played.

These are guitars that have been used; these are guitars with stories. The weakness of history is that it tends to be written by the winners. These companies on the Bernunzio pages may have been the losers, but they have their lost stories too, which may for all I know be far more interesting . . .

. . . Like the story about the elderly woman who went to Richard Bruné, a master luthier and guitar restorer working in Chicago, and showed him photographs of a baroque guitar. Could he restore it for her, she asked? It had been in her family for a long time and before she died she wanted to be able to play it.

He looked at the photos, raised a mental eyebrow, and asked her more about it. The guitar, she said, had been in her family since the late eighteenth century, when her great-great-grandfather Ferdinand Fabri, who was the postmaster general of Würzburg, was given the guitar by French refugees in the employ of Marie Antoinette, who had fled France when the monarchy fell and wanted to give the guitar to Fabri to thank him for offering them shelter. It was, they said, Marie Antoinette's guitar.

Astonishingly, the elderly lady could prove at least the Würzburg part of the story, for she had the diary of Ferdinand's granddaughter, which faithfully recorded the event.

Nobody in the Fabri family played the guitar, it seemed, so it was hung on a wall and left there. For decades. In July 1850 they tried to sell it through the *Neue Wurzburger Zeiting* (the lady had a copy of the newspaper with the ad in it), but it didn't sell. The family moved to Switzerland, the guitar hung on a different wall, until eventually the present owner moved to the United States. After many years it came to Bruné.

The guitar, Bruné concluded, was made between 1650 and 1690, the earlier date being the more likely one. The restoration required opening up the instrument, and Bruné found that the interior was papered with French legal documents, raising the fascinating possibility that, no matter how valuable the guitar, something in the paper holding it together might be even more valuable. But the documents had been slathered with glue—this was common practice in guitar making at the time—and separating them would be a job in itself, so he just repaired the guitar and replaced the papers.

"Once restored, I found this guitar to be the best-sounding baroque guitar I had ever played," Bruné said, another argument for it being a good enough instrument for royalty. Unfortunately Bruné lost contact with the owner, who by then was not only elderly but unwell. He no longer knows who owns Marie Antoinette's guitar, where it is, or even if it is still in one piece.

"This guitar is living testimony that a well-made guitar is literally a lightbulb that doesn't burn out, as it has had a useful musical life of nearly three hundred and fifty years so far," he said. "I only hope it is being kept in proper humidity-controlled conditions."

# Pickups

To Rick, a pickup is a poor excuse for drilling a hole through the tail of a good guitar, and I feel slightly guilty even asking him to do it, let alone asking his advice on the best pickup to use. Yet hard experience has taught me that if you're a fingerstyle player, playing a cocktail hour without amplification is a good way to break three nails and feel bad about your playing. I may never turn the volume knob above 4, but I really need the option if I'm going to continue this half-professional guitar playing.

He lays out my options, though first he points out, "My first consideration for any pickup is that it require as little modification to the guitar as possible. I used to advocate this to limit the effect on acoustic performance but really it's because whatever you install now will be outdated within six months. As long as the technology changes so rapidly, it is best to use pickups that are readily removable. So, what's out there, AFAIK . . ."

One: magnetic pickups, which are essentially the electric guitar system adapted for use with an acoustic.

"Very little modification to the instrument. Measures string movement, not vibration. Quite feedback resistant. Favored by jazz players, ex-rockers, the deaf."

Two: undersaddle pickups, which Rick says tend to be "dry," "barky," or "quacky."

Three: internal microphones, that is, tiny mikes mounted inside the box. Used alone, an internal mike is a near disaster. It's prone to feedback, hard to locate for good sound, and easily jostled out of position. But it makes some sense if combined with . . .

Four: soundboard transducers, which he describes as "teeny little discs—for the most part—that sense movement of the soundboard, or wherever they're attached." I once had a cheap transducer for the Fylde, a button-sized piece of wood on the end of a wire, which I stuck on the top with removable putty. Worked okay, but unsightly as a wart. The ones he's talking about seem to be smaller, and are mounted internally by his usual dentist's apparatus of light, mirror, tiny metal tools.

He offers product reviews, in which he describes the owner of one company as having "the heart—and head—of a hippie drug dealer." Finally he comes down to one system that consists of three transducers with the option of an internal mike added to get some of the air sound.

"Easy installation: glue your fingers to the bridge plate along with the transducers, then slice off whatever you don't want left inside the guitar. I invariably leave bloody fingerprints on the bridge plate, but that's part of the charm."

He makes three recommendations; I go with the bloody-fingerprint option.

The next step in acoustic guitar technology won't even bother with the pickup, according to Rick Turner, the founder of Renaissance Guitars, as modest, quiet, and articulate a guy as ever mixed sound for a Grateful Dead tour and the man who probably knows more about pickups, acoustic and electric, than anyone alive.

No, the future will be something he describes as "an elaborate three-dimensional equalizer" that contains a digital library of sound profiles for the very, very best acoustic guitars and "superimposes the air and wood resonance of a digitized guitar onto the hand and string envelope response coming out of the guitar you're playing." In short, it makes your guitar sound like a Traugott. Or a McAllister. A $10,000 guitar, to put it crudely.

Note: this is not the same thing as a guitar synthesizer. A guitar synthesizer uses the guitar simply as an input device, and all sorts of things come out the other end. Pat Metheny created a Stevie Wonder–style harmonica solo by playing his guitar through a synthesizer. Joni Mitchell uses a synth to change the tuning of her guitar without touching the strings; the synth simply transposes what pitch a particular string "means."

I'm rather worried about what this means for luthiers, and so I ask Rick. He says that once the novelty wears off, people will turn back to wood and steel, just as they've turned to acoustics and tube amps now that electrics and electronics have become the norms.

I hope he's right.

# Sound Check

To try and gain a token sample of where the guitar stands in the America of 2004 I go down to the New York Guitar Festival's annual Guitar Marathon, but instead of showing something about the direction of the guitar at the beginning of the twenty-first century it takes me back to pickups, and it answers a different question: What is the *sound* of a guitar at the beginning of the twenty-first century?

The Guitar Marathon, held in the 917-seat Kaufmann Concert Hall at the 92nd Street Y, is an all-afternoon-and-after-a-short-intermission-all-evening event that throws every kind of guitarist at the audience until even the most desperate guitar addict leaves feeling as if he's just about had enough for now, and maybe he'll go home and lie down with a cool cloth on his face and listen to some Enya.

The odd thing is that, even though the Guitar Marathon is almost inhumanly long, the sound check is longer. The marathon lasts about seven hours, including brief onstage interviews and song intros. The sound check lasts about ten hours. Ten hours.

Or perhaps I should say "sound checks," because they take place in three chunks: one, mainly for acoustic guitarists, runs from 10 A.M. until nearly 2 P.M. on Saturday; another acoustic sound check runs from

9 A.M. until about 1:30 P.M. on Sunday; and between the two halves of the Marathon, say from 5:30 P.M. until almost 7 P.M., the electric guitarists wheel out all their heavy gear and start plugging in the cables and slapping down the duct tape.

Something very strange is going on here, but it's not apparent at first because everyone's so accustomed to sound checks. First up are Abdoulaye Diabate and Banning Eyre. The two play duets of music from Mali, where the guitar is finding a place in traditional music between the kora (harp) and ngoni (lute). In the 92nd Street Y, though, they plug in. Banning has a cord as long and thick as a garden hose.

Dennis Koster, playing a flamenco guitar, delivers a series of strums like rolling thunder to demonstrate the high-end volume of his program. Flamenco evolved to generate as much attack and volume as possible, and Koster sits regally through the sound check, his leonine head erect, as if he could blow the doors off the hall all by himself, if necessary.

Dominic Frasca, playing minimalist music in the tradition of Philip Glass, has his own ideas of how a guitar should sound, and if a guitar can't actually make those sounds, it will have to change. He plays a ten-string with a normal classical body by Tom Humphrey and a neck like the flight deck of an aircraft carrier. Having spent probably $10,000 on this custom instrument, he has drilled holes through the fingerboard so he can add what might be called "incidental capos"— small clips that can be turned to pin down a given string at a given fret and thereby change its pitch. He also has what looks from a distance like a standard classical guitar, except that he's added two narrow slats, like flattened chopsticks, next to the top end of the fingerboard, running up past the lower rim of the sound hole. At first they look as if they've been glued to the top of the guitar, but they are fixed only at one end, and lie fractionally clear of the soundboard. These are "tappers."

Tapping is a complicated and counterintuitive style, in which the player moves the right hand up toward the neck until it's over the fingerboard and then, in addition to playing notes and chords with the left hand, strikes the strings with the fingers of the right, creating amazing percussive sounds that make you look around not only for the hidden second guitarist but also the hidden conga player. When Dominic plays tapping-style he can play notes with the first two fingers of his left hand up at the high end of the fingerboard while tapping on these slats with his third and fourth fingers. The tappers act like the keys of old Morse code telegraph sets: the finger hits the slat, the slat hits the soundboard, which in turn amplifies the sound. It's essentially a slightly more constructed version of the flamenco technique of rapping on the guitar with a finger, adapted to suit Frasca's style and the pieces he plays. Both of these "prepared" guitars have MIDI pickups, so the foot of the guitar has not one but two jacks, both venting a bundle of cables.

David Starobin, playing a nineteenth-century program by Fernando Sor on a curiously futuristic classical guitar, sits through his sound check patiently, as if being fitted for a suit he doesn't really like but has to wear.

Paul O'Dette is playing a renaissance lute, and it goes without saying that in a hall this size he's going to need some amplification. The lute is a neat, bird-like little instrument—on which O'Dette is an acknowledged master—but for the lute the 92nd Street Y is Shea Stadium, and the sound check equipment list for O'Dette runs as follows:

AKG-535 talk
Schoeps stereo mic left
Schoeps stereo mic right
Schoeps cardioid guitar top
Schoeps cardioid guitar bottom

I have no idea what these mean.

The last guitarist of the day is Vinicius Cantuaria from Brazil. He's also the only electric guitarist of the day, and in a sense he does his own sound check, playing with a knob or two, then sitting there as if wondering what all the fuss was about, taking the opportunity to run through a few sequences with his spidery fingers. Joe Pass said that the electric guitar enabled him to play more quietly. Vinicius plays so quietly that at times the guitar sounds as if it's breathing. He has a Yamaha hollowbody archtop electric with gold hardware like the fixtures in Louis XIV's bathroom. He holds the tremolo arm delicately between his fingertips and gives it an experimental waft back and forth, waiting to be told he can go.

Later, someone asks Vinicius how they handle amplification in Brazil when they play outdoors. Vinicius shrugs in a very French way. "We use more guitarists," he says.

During the Sunday morning sound checks all these strangely shaped pieces start coming together and it becomes clear what a strange set of illusions are being created.

First to sit down among the small thicket of microphones, like desiccated black cacti, is Bob Brozman, the world-traveling slide player. Having suffered through more sound checks than he cares to remember, Brozman is smart enough to introduce the key player in the sound check, a party who has been present all along but unnoticed: Ryan, the sound guy.

Ryan is up on the balcony, far enough back that, like everyone on the lower floor of the auditorium, I can't see him. In my mind he is Invisible Ryan, whose job is to be heard but not seen—to create a product that can be heard but not seen—using a series of devices that for the most part can't be seen either: the mikes are as unobtrusive as possible, the cables carrying the output up to his mixer in the balcony are buried in the fabric of the building, the tall house speakers on each side of the stage are as camouflaged as they can be against the walls and the room's decor. In short, Ryan is an illusionist.

Bob runs his sound check with the almost fanatical precision and focus of one who has had his sound messed up on five continents. He knows the sound he wants, the EQ settings he wants, and he's even brought his own mike, a Neumann KM-150, a type not made anymore. To give Ryan an indication of the range of sound to expect, Bob bangs the top of his National with the heel of his right hand, his forearm, his thumb, his knuckles, zips a pick across the strings above the bridge, and generally carries on—then sets that guitar aside, picks up his

Weissenborn, a slope-shouldered Hawaiian-style guitar, then his charango, a small-bodied ten-stringed instrument originally made from the shell of an armadillo. "Fastest sound check in the East," he says, thanks Ryan, marches briskly off.

Ed Gerhard also takes his sound very, very seriously. He even has his own preamp on a small dolly beside him onstage, though it isn't doing what it should. "I could try reversing the phase on this," he calls up tentatively to Ryan, sounding like Scotty from *Star Trek*. There's a pause, then Ed says sheepishly, "I've got it plugged in the wrong way round."

He and most of the other acoustic guitarists, I begin to notice, treat Ryan with the greatest respect, several asking his name and addressing him by his name. When the marathon itself finally gets under way, four of the guitarists will thank the sound crew, two mentioning Ryan by name.

Ed gets down to playing a few notes and listening, tuning not just the pitch of his guitar but its sound, cracking jokes but staying very focused.

"I'm adding a little bit around two-twenty—not to be too thumpy, just to add some cohoneys," he says. "This song needs buttloads of 'verb . . . Let's get a little more predelay." He asks Ryan if there's sound coming from under the stage. "Sometimes they have subwoofers under the stage and when they kick in it's like getting a deep colonic."

Ed is by far the most scrupulous about his sound, because he is going to depend on it more than any other player. The critic Whitney Balliett wrote that the trouble with guitarists is they play too many notes. Ed has taken this advice to heart: he plays fewer notes than anyone. Each one is played to be heard, to take shape like a colored bubble and float out into the auditorium, just so.

Is this gorgeous, rich sound really the sound of a guitar, though? He's playing a good guitar, but in a sense he's also playing a good mixing board. Rick Davis says later that when he knows that a guitar he's building will always be played amplified, in a sense he makes it *less well*. He aims for a drier and cleaner sound, with less richness and fewer overtones to overload the mike, and then leaves it to the sound guy to fatten it up.

Next Patty Larkin, also an expert in graphic equalization, comes on and sings up and down the range of her voice, picking out dry or raspy spots in the amplified response like an elevator operator checking floor by floor for sticking doors. While she's doing this, Ed Gerhard and Bob Brozman swap sound-check horror stories. Ed says he lives in mortal terror of the church basement sound guy who refers to the mike as "the acoustic." Bob tells the story of one of the big-name rock guys meeting the sound guy before a show, describing the sound he wanted in every possible synonym of "full": "rich," "fat," and so on.

"Got it," the sound guy sez, turns around to his buddy, and calls out, "Crispy!"

Then the classical guitarist Michael Newman starts his sound check, and all the intriguing paradoxes of the situation follow one another out like a series of ascending diminished-seventh chords.

Michael is scheduled to play a set on his own and another set with his wife, Laura Oltman, and as Michael settles in his chair onstage and Laura takes a seat about ten rows back in the auditorium to give him feedback (so to speak) on how he sounds, we get the first signs of discord.

The discord arises because Michael and Laura make it clear right away that they are purists. They want only a *natural* sound. They won't use monitors, and as soon as Laura hears any output coming from the tall house speakers set in the walls on either side of the stage she complains that it sounds canned.

In almost the same breath, though, Michael asks Ryan if he can take down the high end to minimize the sounds of string squeaks and nail clickings. Invisible Ryan, ever affable, says sure. The process of tailoring the sound has begun.

Up among the gods, as they say in opera, Ryan starts playing with the sound output. "That's good!" Laura says suddenly. "It sounds as if nothing is coming out of the speakers at all." As far as I can tell, nothing *is* coming out of the speakers. But by now the seed of doubt has been sown onstage, and Michael is wondering whether, if he and

Laura have no amplification at all and they come on after someone who's been really beefed up, they'll sound fatally weak.

Ryan answers this question in the best way: after a few seconds, the sound of Villa-Lobos comes out of the main hall speakers, and it is warm, rich, yet delicate, neither tinny nor brassy, as politely assertive as a butler's discreet *ahem*. "That's good!" Laura says, and she's right. It is the perfect facsimile of a well-recorded guitar.

From one extreme to another, David Cullen ambles onstage with another classical guitar but the first thing he does is grab a cord and plug it into the jack at the butt-end of the instrument. "It's a Ruck with a pickup," he grins. A Ruck is a classical guitar made by Robert Ruck, one of the top classical luthiers in the country. "Kind of an oxymoron," he adds, grinning, aware of the sacrilege.

He's perfectly okay about amplification and sound carving. "I love it," he chuckles, shrugging. "We can, so we should. People are used to that kind of sound now." He too has his little mixing box, with knobs on the front and cables sprouting from the back. "I'm sending you the D.I. which is split here by the T.C.," he calls up to Invisible Ryan, "and that has some f/x on it."

Last of the morning is Russell Malone, the jazz guitarist, a young man with the dignity of a deacon and a permanent look of mild surprise. Russell, like Vinicius, is playing an electric, so he creates his own sound from the almost infinite palette available to electric players and comes up with a deep orchestral sound, like soft horns. When he plays a cascade of artificial harmonics they sound like lavender rain. His sound has no string buzz, no fingernail scrape, no strum-scratch, no evidence of his finger running over each fret as he slurs, no sound of strings hitting the fingerboard. He makes the least fuss of all and waits out his sound check by singing a love song to the blonde on the radio sound crew.

After Russell everyone is done, at least for the time being. It must be said that none of these players has taken sound checking to an extreme. Nobody is playing the concealed wireless amplifier/transmitter system used by Sharon Isbin. Nobody is playing through a laptop like John McLaughlin. This is sound business as usual.

As soon as the first half of the Guitar Marathon is over, the electric guys charge on stage for their sound checks. They all have to get power up and sound straightened out between the first show, ending late at nearly 5:30, and the second, starting at 7 o'clock. Fourteen people are on the stage at once, three electric guitarists cranking and wailing, two drummers beating assorted implements, others setting levels or standing around looking at the equipment like mechanics watching a car with the hood up and the engine revving. The wooden floor of the stage has disappeared; the place now looks like a twenty-second-century junkyard, or a music store.

Yet there's something authentic about this sight: at least we know what we're getting. The equipment lugged on stage by the electric guys is like the earth-moving equipment at a construction site—it gives a glimpse of just how much effort and artifice is involved. With the acoustic players the same transformation has been taking place, but most of the mechanism was hidden. It's an interesting feature of the electric guitar, when you think about it, that it has never bothered to try to hide its workings. Almost the reverse, in fact; the famous Marshall stack behind the player became an essential furniture, a point of pride, a demonstration of power like the Russian warhead drive-pasts at the May Day parades.

As Steve Kimock plays he constantly adjusts the volume, the tone, the switch positions. The guitar is part of the system. Playing the electric guitar is all about control. An electric guitarist creates his own sound, and the further he moves from the twang of strings, the less what he's playing is a guitar—it's a signal processor with a guitar-style input device.

The progressive guitarist and prankster Henry Kaiser has what John Schaefer, the emcee, describes as "the wreckage of an electric guitar." Raoul Bjorkenheim, Henry's partner in crime, plays several instruments, including an electric viola da gamba exactly the same shape as a wooden swordfish. He also plays an electric guitar "prepared" by having a flat sliver of wire shoved between the strings above the pickup. He plays the strings. He plays the sliver of wire. It sounds like a musical hailstorm heard from inside a shack with a tin roof. At one

point there's a curious *gonging* sound. I assume it's one of the guitarists until I notice that the percussionist is actually playing a gong.

Which brings up the question of the day: What is the sound of a
guitar?

The electric guitar can now make the sound of any other instrument, or the sound of any other sound. Yet that's just part of the co-
nundrum, because even the characteristic attack-and-decay shape of
a guitar note is now obsolete; one trick electric guitarists learned at
least three decades ago was to play a note or chord with the sound knob
on zero and then turn it up, so the attack-and-decay was reversed, and
instead the sound *swelled.* That trick is even on the effects box I played,
so you can get the swell effect without even having to know how to
turn a volume knob.

Even the effects box, though, assumed that one instrument played
one sound at once. How quaint! Lead guitarists often speak of building or constructing a solo; at the Guitar Marathon, David Torn (aka
splattercell) takes this concept and runs with it until he's so far out in
left field he's no longer in the stadium.

He isn't even in real time. Pioneers such as Les Paul in the electric
guitar field and John Martyn in the acoustic field played with systems
that took a note, held it, and then released it or repeated it so the
guitarist essentially accompanied him- or herself. Les Paul did this in
his garage/workshop/studio in New Jersey using tape; nowadays it's
done digitally. Torn plays a phrase on his guitar and stores it in his
onstage computer so he can replay it from his system's memory at will,
adding to it, playing off it, reshaping it, distorting it. It's like self-
sampling or collage-in-progress. It means, in fact, that much of the
time he's producing audible sounds even though he isn't fingering the
guitar. In fact, pottering around on stage examining his system and
playing with the controls, he has the air of an amiable middle-aged
painter working alone in his studio. He just happens to be wearing a
gunmetal-gray guitar thing that looks disturbingly like an Uzi.

His already distant relationship with the conventional guitar is further stretched by the fact that his guitar has a theremin patch, which
is activated just by waving a hand in its general direction. He doesn't

even have to play the strings. The defining features of the guitar one by one are being seen as limitations, to be bent or broken. The configuration of the guitar is useful only in that it is familiar to the musician who has grown up playing it and can produce notes more fluently and expressively by playing strings on a fingerboard than on a keyboard, say, or a keypad.

The guitar evolved as one of the most intimate of instruments. Without technical assistance, it can be heard by perhaps a couple of hundred very quiet people or a dozen rowdy ones, but the size of its ideal audience is one. This is why it's the instrument of introverts and seducers.

As an audience at the start of the twenty-first century we ask the impossible: each of us wants that sensual intimacy, all 917 seated in the Kauffman Concert Hall. For the guitarist, these are the modern realities of playing guitars to an audience large enough to pay for a hotel, a plane ticket, and sneakers for the kids. In addition, we are now an audience that typically hears its music not live but recorded under ideal circumstances that can't possibly be replicated tonight. These are the constraints of playing to people who believe in the possibility of perfect sound.

Ironically, during the Guitar Marathon it's the electric guys who suffer from dodgy sound. As one of the tech crew points out, the more devices you plug together, the more vulnerable they become, and the harder it is to figure out what's not working. Vinicius sits down and finds he has no sound at all; he turns knobs helplessly, his already wounded eyes looking crushed. A couple of acts suffer through a faint constant hum. When David Torn's ensemble takes to the stage the sound-equipment thicket is so complex that his bass player spends several minutes squatting on stage amid tentacular cables and foot pedals trying to fix his silent bass.

The acoustic guitars, in Ryan's expert hands, sound perfect. They sound like CDs.

# Setup

Healdsburg is only days away, which means that Rick, along with every other custom guitar maker in the country, is racing to finish two or three guitars at the same time. What this mostly entails is setup.

"Setup" essentially means "putting the strings on the guitar, and all the thousand headaches that encompasses." No phase of the building is less rewarding and more punishing. At no point do the tolerances need to be more precise, or does Rick have to be less like a woodworker and more like a machinist. Maybe those years working on race-car engines really help at this point.

I'm not exactly banned from his workshop, but he's under such pressure that he can't tell when he'll be working on my guitar in particular—it may be in the middle of the night. So he gives me a swift rundown of what this stage involves.

Strip the masking tape off the fingerboard very carefully so as not to chip the lacquer at the edges. Clean up the edges of the neck where it'll attach to the body, and the body where the fingerboard extension—the seven and a half frets that extend between the shoulders and the sound hole—will lie. Bolt the neck onto the body, using one of those cunning bolts that come with Ikea furniture. Glue down the fingerboard extension. The guitar is now, finally, in one piece.

Ream the holes in the headstock where the tuners will go—this has to be done "rather precisely"—and install tuners. Level the fingerboard.

The fingerboard, which becomes the main focus during setup and will, of course, be the main focus once the guitar is finished and being played, is the first indication of what extraordinary precision is involved in fretted instruments, and in playing music generally. If the action (i.e., the distance between the strings and the fingerboard) is too high, it's not just that they are harder to play. The act of depressing a string stretches it, and the more the stretch, the more it affects the pitch of the note. Conversely, if the action is too low or the fingerboard is not level, the clearance between the string and the fret will be less than the amount that the string vibrates, and the string will buzz against the fret wire. *Every mistake he makes now, even invisible mistakes, will be audible.* The ear is sharper than the eye.

Take a deep breath. Measure and locate the bridge, whose position is crucial to the entire diffusion of sound through the braces, and also to the scale length—the length of the strings, basically. Strip off the finish where the bridge will go, as glue doesn't work well with lacquer. Glue the bridge, using the vacuum plate again. While it's setting, polish the fingerboard. Now it's fret time. But first a brief cadenza on the subject of frets, Galileo, and the pope.

The earliest European guitars had frets made of spare gut strings tied across the fingerboard, like lute frets. This had two advantages: the frets could be adjusted as the guitar responded to heat and humidity; and, being softer than metal frets, they didn't tend to wear through the gut strings, which were expensive.

The spacing of the frets was the cause of a surprising amount of friction, so to speak. Vincenzo Galilei, the father of the famous astronomer, introduced the concept of equal temperament, which in fretted instruments means that the frets are spaced so that the instrument can be played in any key and remain in tune. This might seem uncontroversial, but in fact the Catholic Church refused to allow keyboard instruments to be tuned in equal temperament because equal temperament violates the supposed numerical perfection of the world advocated by Pythagoras and the Greeks, later adopted as dogma by the Church.

Richard Bruné, the outstanding luthier and restorer of antique instruments, makes the impish suggestion that Galileo would never have had such a conflict with the Church over the earth orbiting the sun if the family hadn't already been identified as radicals and trouble-makers thanks to his father's heretical ideas about frets.

Even now frets inspire disputes in guitar-making dogma. It might seem that frets should all be parallel, almost a no-brainer, like the sun going around the earth, but ever since the seventeenth century some luthiers have used a system called "fan fretting" where even this axiom is abandoned, and the fret wires fan out so the bass frets are farther apart and the whole device looks rather like a sundial.

Jeff Traugott, one of the country's top builders, learned about fan fretting from Ralph Novak and now has half a dozen fan-fretted guitars on order. Fan fretting, he explained, arises from the notion that, as any harpist will tell you, bass strings should be longer than treble strings. If you twist the bridge, though, making it diagonal so that the low E string is some two inches longer than the high E, you need to adjust the fretting. Jeff handed me one of his fan-fretted concert guitars and invited me to take a shot.

It was a strange experience. Around the mid-range of the guitar the frets are almost parallel, and they felt familiar; down by the nut, though, I had the weird sensation that someone had broken my wrist and reset it at the wrong angle. The guitar sounded wonderful, and I could feel myself getting used to its oblique geometry; all the same, for the next few days, whenever I played an orthodox guitar I never quite trusted my fingers to find their own way around and kept examining them suspiciously to make sure they were where they were supposed to be. Bruce Sexauer, who also builds some fan-fretted guitars, said, "It's quite transparent as long as you don't think about it."

Fret wire comes in rolls. Rick cuts it to length with metal nippers, bends each to match the radius of curvature of the fingerboard, clips off the end of the tang (the foot of the fret, like the stalk of a mushroom) so it won't hit the binding that runs up each side of the fingerboard, uses a triangular file to chamfer the edges of the fret slot so the fret will go in more easily, then bangs the fret in with a brass hammer. "Then I use wee little tiny files to clean up."

Until the 1920s, he says, luthiers used "bar frets"—frets that were rectangular in cross section, hard to slide a finger over, with no crown, no tang, and therefore prone to moving. Early Martins, lacking truss rods, had necks that tended to curl up because of the force exerted by the strings, so repairers would hammer in thick-tanged frets to act as wedges to drive into the fingerboard, stretching it and driving the neck back down again. Now the fret wire is rounded, it lets your fingers slide over it far more easily, and Rick is actually using a slightly wider fret wire, roughly 0.1 inches instead of 0.08 inches, to make those slides easier still.

Next: drill holes through the bridge and the soundboard for the bridge pins, the toothlike items that pin the head of the string in place. Taper the holes to match the pins, cut relief slots in the leading edge of the pin holes; these tiny grooves are where the strings will lie.

So much for the easy part. Now for the nut and saddle. The nut and saddle are the strips of bone at each end of the string, one up at the head, the other mounted in a slot on the bridge. These are where the strings will be grounded, defined. Precision is critical. At this point, everything that has gone before starts to seem gross and haphazard.

Here we go. Select the bone, thinning it down roughly to size. Cut the saddle bone to length, flatten the bottom, and round the ends so it fits into its slot. That's it for the time being, but we'll come back to the saddle in a minute. Well, an hour or two. Well, an eternity, because the nut, though not quite two inches long, takes forever to make.

It's a more intricate shape than the saddle because the headstock leans back from the neck. The nut has to match this angle of tilt, and it also has to have its ends cut to match the profile of the neck around them, an especially important point because this is where the guitarist's left hand spends most of its time. He glues the shaped nut in place and then cuts the slots for the strings.

This step calls for algebra most luthiers haven't used since tenth grade (and most guitarists, needless to say, never learned at all). The slots can't be cut at equal intervals because the strings are of different thicknesses, so Rick measures a suitable amount in from each side of the fingerboard and cuts slots of the right thicknesses for the top and bottom E strings. So far, so good. Now comes the math. He measures the space between the inner edges of the two E strings, subtracts the total thicknesses of the remaining four strings, divides the result by five (for the five remaining spaces), takes the result and measures that much in from the inside edges of the E strings. That tells him where the outsides edges of the B and A strings should go. Cut slots for B and A. Rinse and repeat.

Of course, even the monosyllabic word "cut" underestimates the difficulty. Anytime anyone cuts something, the cut tends to wander slightly. With the nut and saddle, Rick is working to tolerances of three thousandths to five thousandths of an inch. The slightest wander and he has to rip the nut out and start again.

Rick slaps a set of strings on the guitar. Don't even think of asking me what brand he put on my guitar. His requirements are different from mine. He needs strings that are consistent (or else he won't know whether he's built a bad guitar or just bought a set of crappy strings) and resilient enough to stand up to several dozen sets of poisonous fingers playing the guitar over four days at Healdsburg. Poisonous fingers—that is, ones owned by people with especially acidic sweat—can kill a set of strings in twenty minutes. What do I need? I need to try out a range of strings to see which best suit my tastes and needs. I'll never know whether I've bought the right guitar or not until I've tried it with the right strings.

Strings mark the guitar's passage through time, especially its passage from an agricultural to an industrial world.

For some four centuries, many of the best strings in the world were said to come from a single Italian village, called Salle. The Mari family, famous for La Bella strings, came from Salle, as did the D'Addarios, another of the top names in American strings, not to mention at least two Italian companies.

The tradition of using gut to make strings, according to the La Bella company, goes back to around 1300 A.D. when Salle was already famous as a town of sadlers—that is, saddlemakers. The thread for sewing the saddle leather was made from the intestines of mountain sheep, which, so the story goes, had tougher digestive tracts and produced stronger, stringier gut than domestic sheep.

So far, so good. From this point history starts to sound awfully like myth. I'll let the La Bella Web site take over.

> Tradition at Salle says that at the dawn of the fourteenth century one Erasmo was employed in the chief industry of the town, the making of saddles. As this man was drying some sheep intestines in order to make his thread, some were carried away by the wind, and became lodged in a thorn bush. Erasmo noticed that sweet musical sounds were emitted as the material was vibrated by the wind blowing through the bush. Being an observant man, and an ingenious one, the thought came to him that the threads used in sewing saddles might also be used as strings in the primitive instruments that were ancestors of the violin. Thus the business of making violin strings from "catgut" began, and so important did the industry become to the small town that eventually Erasmo was sainted, and St. Erasmo is not only the patron saint of the town, but also of the profession of string making.

And why, by the way, was it called catgut? The people of Salle, the La Bella Web site continues, said their strings were made from the intestines of cats because "the cat was viewed with superstition in Italy, and the slaying of a cat was supposed to be followed by a period of bad luck. The fiddle string makers of Salle reasoned that few indeed would attempt to copy their trade, if it involved slaying cats."

Steel strings illuminate the industrial revolution. They turn up in the United States in a scene that could be from Dickens, or from the first socialist reformers of the nineteenth century. In *The employments of women; a cyclopaedia of woman's work* (1863), Virginia Penny wrote that she had watched women making guitar strings in a factory in Connecticut, "and the manufacturer said they could earn as high as $9 a week. It is rather severe on the fingers, but that can be avoided to some extent by wearing a glove finger. In New York, it is done mostly by Germans and French, who have taken the trade from Americans. The preparing of catgut from the intestines of sheep and goats, and making it into strings, is carried on mostly in Germany, and some women are employed at that. Most metal strings are of steel, and covered with fine wire of other metals. Mrs Z., whose husband, when living, manufactured covered strings for musical instruments, told me, she and her daughters often assisted in covering guitar strings and the lighter piano strings. She thinks a person of good abilities could learn it in from two to four weeks, with an attentive instructor. She usually rested against a bench while employed."

As the industry develops, the issue becomes one of consistency. It's astonishing how recently string gauges have settled down to the point where you could buy a standard set of extra-lights and be sure of their widths—in the past forty years, pretty much. When the steel guitar-ists, with their nine- or eleven-string fingerboards, emerged in the thirties and forties they had a devil of a job making up a set of strings for themselves, and keeping them in tune.

Nylon strings grew out of the plastics revolution, which emerged during World War II. A classical luthier named Albert Augustine, who was getting intensely frustrated with the poor quality of gut string available during the war, started experimenting with nylon fishing line. Segovia was thinking along the same lines—and, as it happens, was staying with Augustine and his family on arriving in New York as a semipermanent resident. Working with Du Pont and Segovia, Augus-tine developed nylon strings, which were more consistent, brighter, louder, more accurately milled, and ultimately cheaper than gut. He sold them under the Augustine name, with Segovia's face and endorsement on the package.

The latest advance, of course, has to do with miniaturization: a number of makers now spray their strings with a form of Teflon coating so the minute finger slough of oil, dirt, and skin cells doesn't stick, and the string degrades much more slowly. (I used to clean my strings after every gig with alcohol or metal polish for the same reason.) The trouble is, the microcoating also stiffens the string, altering its resonating properties, and this technology is generally regarded as being promising but still a work in progress.

Rick gets out his electronic tuner, selects one string, plays the octave harmonic at the twelfth fret, which is exactly midway along the length of the string, and then depresses the string and plays the note at the same fret. If all is well the two pitches should be identical, but slightly sharp. The reason for this is simple: the string is, by an almost infinitesimal amount, too short. The leading edge of the saddle bone is still square, and Rick needs to bevel it, to shave it ever so carefully to a more rounded shape. That tiny alteration extends the length of string between saddle and nut and slightly lowers the pitch. He keeps adjusting until the string is at pitch, then moves on to the next string. This process is known as intonation, that is, "putting in tune."

The B string is a rogue, a pain in the ass. For some reason, possibly because it has a thicker core than any other string (the G, D, A, and low E strings are thicker overall, but that's because of the wire wound around their core), the B tends to be stiffer than the other strings, and so intonates differently. It's an advanced player's nightmare, almost impossible to keep in tune at both the low and high ends at the same time. Here's a tip: if you're thinking of buying a guitar, look at the saddle where the B string passes over it. Any decent guitar will have what's called a "compensated" B string, a tiny chip cut out of the saddle to compensate for the string's unhelpful behavior, or even a separate mini-saddle. If you're thinking of buying a guitar and you see it has a clean, smooth saddle, pick a different guitar.

"A cheap guitar will always have a lousy setup. If you have a thousand dollars to spend on a guitar," Rick says, "don't buy a thousand-dollar guitar. Buy a nine-hundred-dollar guitar and pay your local repair guy a hundred dollars to set it up."

A factory looking to reduce its labor costs is always likely to be weak on setup. "You can't make a machine that does setup. You need a guy who sits there with a bunch of files." All a factory can do is make the action as low as it dares and hope for the best.

This is also an advantage of buying a guitar at what he calls a mom-and-pop guitar store rather than at one of the new giant guitar chains. "Almost every mom-and-pop guitar store will spend *some* time working on setup."

Finally, cosmetic stuff. "Make sure all the polishing compound's cleaned off. Maker sure the tuners aren't too tight. Make sure the bridge pins are all the same height—that kind of crap. I can't believe I waste time with that." Rick shakes his head, then adds dryly, "Putting the label in. That's an important part."

# Once and Future

At the beginning of the twenty-first century the guitar is in a curious and unfamiliar situation. On the one hand, it is by far the most popular instrument in the United States. Despite the popularity of pop divas, boy bands, rap, techno, hip-hop, Gregorian chants, and whale sounds, more than half the top one hundred albums of the year feature guitar-dominated music, and the guitar has become the essential instrument in heavy metal, country, and classic rock. Sales of acoustic guitars, electric guitars, amps, stomp boxes, and guitar strings have all recovered from the malaise of the eighties. In the past decade the dollar value of total sales has more than doubled. In 2003 acoustic guitar sales rose 20 percent to 1,168,237 units. Electrics sold even better, moving up 21 percent to 1,173,314 units.

On the other hand, the identity of the guitar has changed even more radically. Here's the year-end summary of NAMM, the International Music Products Association: "In the late '40s, folksinger and social activist Woody Guthrie once described his battered Martin guitar as a 'tool of subversion and dissent.' In the ultimate twist of irony, the guitar has become totally mainstreamed—equally at home at a church service or a nightclub, or in a television commercial hawking dishwasher detergent. Message to all those baby boomers who once used the guitar in their protests against the establishment: You are the establishment, and so is your preferred instrument."

It's true. The guitar has become domesticated. The long, screaming guitar-god solos and the ambitious concept albums went out with the mullet; instead, the guitar presents a broad palette of sounds, a familiar landscape of old, green hills instead of a new upthrusting of jagged peaks. Top 40 songs routinely use tiny decorations played on steel-string acoustic. Some new age music uses a kind of diluted flamenco. The guitar turns up, often very skillfully, in Celtic and bluegrass, even though traditionally it wasn't a major instrument in either. At the same time, other instruments, especially folk instruments, are withering, their playing becoming less common. The guitar is in danger of becoming the default instrument, the path of least resistance.

Something else has been happening to the guitar over the past fifteen years. Possibly arising from the if-you-can't-beat-'em principle, more and more music schools and university music departments are offering guitar classes, guitar programs, degrees in guitar. Formerly, individual colleges had individual starving adjunct guitarists who took on students, but now we're talking accredited programs, with actual curricula. Nobody seems to have accurate figures but the number bandied around is that there are about sixteen hundred colleges in the United States and Canada that offer some kind of guitar program. The first were classical programs, though even these were very recent, the first guitar degree being awarded by the Mannes School of Music in New York in 1960. Then came jazz, starting at the Berklee School of Music in Boston, and most recently even rock and other subspecialties, as they say in medical school.

This flies in the face of tradition, not to mention common sense. Not one outstanding guitarist from the first four hundred years of the instrument's history in this country ever got a degree in guitar. Almost none even got a degree. Most never took lessons. It was a point of pride—it was a reason for taking up guitar, even—that you taught yourself. Picking up chords or licks from the black guy down the block, perhaps, but always being your own boss. As for flying in the face of common sense, well, classical music and jazz each make up perhaps 3 percent of the total market of music sales, and promoters in the classical field in particular seem to have decided that the world needs only about sixteen concert guitarists. Come to think of it, with the brilliant young Ana Vidovic coming up, someone's going to have to retire. As for jazz, the idea seems rather too cerebral to me. How many kids at eighteen have already been through so much music that they're ready for something this complex? It reminds me of writing literary criticism at sixteen, being told to discuss the immaturity of Keats's love poetry—at sixteen, and never been kissed.

I'm mulling this over when, to my surprise, I get a chance to visit the Future Guitarists of America. A friend tells me that a local high school offers a guitar class. This is very unusual; there are good school guitar programs in the United States, but they are few and far between. One of the main reasons why the guitar remains cool, in the face of all its recent mainstreaming, is that it isn't generally taught in schools. What kids are offered instead are the two most conservative elements of the American curriculum, band and drama, both of which are firmly stuck in the fifties, at best. Broadway revivals, in this day and age? In England a whole subgenre of school rock musicals has sprung up over the past thirty years or so that are written to be fun for the kids and scored for electric guitar and bass, drums, sax, the whole caboodle. In the United States you sometimes find a guitar in the school jazz band, but if so it's often played by a teacher because jazz guitar is just damn hard. Many school music programs, I'm sorry to say, remain seriously geeky. In Vermont maybe half a dozen schools have any kind of guitar class, and it's just as well that there's not more interest because the company that rents instruments to schools wouldn't have any more guitars.

With all this in mind I set out for Mount Mansfield Union High School, very curious.

The class is being held in a corner of the seating in the auditorium, about as low an investment in physical plant as possible, but the kids, draped over the seats in that high school way, don't seem fazed.

"Nice overalls," one boy says sarcastically to a girl, who grins and gives him the finger. Another girl, coming in through the stage door, slips coming down the steps, yelps, and like a born guitarist instinctively holds her instrument above her head as she slides down on her butt. Several kids cheer her but most barely glance up, because they're already getting their guitars out and starting to play. They're learning the way guitarists learn: by themselves, from one another, in their own ways. It's probably the least orderly class that takes place in the entire school all week, but every moment is spent practicing or learning.

I ask you, in what other class do the students start work before the teacher even shows up? One boy is playing the guitar part of the *Deliverance* duet. A couple of girls are showing each other some chords and one is singing quietly to the other. This, they agree, is a rule: girls sing, guys don't. The guys are mostly into their own fingerboards, bent over, attacking this or that, exploring. The girls are more social. After a while the same two girls are singing a Dar Williams song together. "She went to my summer camp."

They've been told not to bring their electrics in and they all have cheap classicals or steel-string acoustics—and I do mean cheap. Several were made in China, one was bought at Wal-Mart. Brands I've never heard of, mostly. Plus a Yamaha. The only moderately fancy guitar is a Washburn, but in terms of sound it's one of the worst guitars there.

The teacher turns up, grinning cheerfully. He's wearing a woolen hat, and a rowdy kid with a baseball cap on backwards tells him he looks like a Keebler elf. It turns out he's the chorus director—he doesn't even *play* the guitar, yet he was smart enough to recognize the interest, and the need. Now he has twenty kids in this class, kids he would normally never see in chorus, probably never even see anywhere in school, and another twenty or so in a more advanced class. While he's talking they pay him barely any attention; they just want to play their guitars. One is even playing scales.

He passes out the chord sheet and words for "Let It Be," which nobody groans at, and asks them to work on it in class for an ensemble performance in twenty minutes or so. I go around watching and chatting. They tell me they want to play classic rock, mostly, and the Beatles, but others like Blink 182, a couple like jazz. They're very well aware of the difference between guitar and a classical instrument such as violin. They want to play the guitar because the violin is kinda nerdy while the guitar is cool; more important, they agree, the guitar allows you to play what you want. One kid with shaven sidies and foot-long hair, sitting at the back, explains articulately that the guitar enables you to play any kind of music—and he's interested in all kinds.

I've brought along my Fylde and a borrowed steel guitar from the late forties. A couple recognize what it is, to my surprise, and they line up to try it. The rowdy kid with the backwards baseball cap is the first down, vaulting over seats. One kid takes a flying leap over my open guitar case with the Fylde in it. I raise an eyebrow. "You do realize you just nearly put your foot through two thousand dollars' worth of guitar?" I say, a slight exaggeration. He grins and shrugs. He knew he was going to make the jump.

Probably half the class tries the steel, some setting it upright like a Spanish, some strumming on strings on the wrong side of the steel, all making interesting and quasi-musical noises. Can't go wrong.

One student, Elden Kelly, is flat-out amazing: he gives me his audition CD for music college. He's already got the thin, spade-shaped fingers of an experienced guitarist. He plays chords on my guitar that I don't know. Over the summer he's going to study flamenco in Spain and in the fall he'll be taking conservatory classes in improvisation. Okay, so maybe I was wrong about students not being ready for jazz at eighteen.

When the chorus director brings them all back together to play "Let It Be," at least half a dozen kids talk while he's talking, and while most of them play the chords together, a couple of them play something completely different.

There's no mistaking them: they're guitarists.

Now what I need is the other side of this odd new coin, a guitar professor, and again I get lucky. Not only do I meet such a guy, but he shows me the guitar in its maturity at the turn of the millennium, with all its strengths and weaknesses.

Randall Dollahon is professor of jazz guitar at the University of Miami, which has one of the most respected jazz guitar programs in the country. He has a slightly professorial look about him: in his late fifties, bespectacled, graying, with an air of mild, benign thoughtfulness, spreading comfortably around the middle but tall enough to carry it.

He grew up in Texas, was inspired by the Ventures and the Beatles, and started a garage band but paid his professional dues in country music, traveling throughout eastern Texas with Mickey Gilley's band when he was in high school. In the mid-sixties he went to the director of the music program at the University of Houston to see about majoring in music, only to be told, "We do not consider the electric guitar to be a musical instrument here."

Instead he went to Berklee, which had one of the first jazz programs in the country, and subsequently he played with Burt Bacharach, Placido Domingo, Bob James, Steve Morse, Jaco Pastorius, Toots Thielemans, Edgar Winter, and many other jazz, country, rock, and Latin artists and groups. He's been at the University of Miami for thirty years, hired to take over Pat Metheny's job when Metheny left to play with Gary Burton and teach at Berklee. Like any good teacher he also practices what he teaches.

Which is not all that easy. Fifty or sixty years ago Miami Beach was a jazz center. All the big ocean-front hotels had house bands. Sammy Davis Jr. and Frank Sinatra played there regularly; it was the Las Vegas of the east, the Atlantic City of the south, the Havana of the north. Now, when I ask the Latino manager of my hotel where I can go to hear live jazz, he sucks his teeth and frowns.

Randall is playing in Coconut Grove, a hip little corner of southern Miami with strings of lights in the trees and throngs of people spilling off the sidewalks into the narrow streets.

He's playing his favorite guitar, a Gibson ES-347, a variation on the classic fifties Gibson ES-335; in jazz, even the look of the instruments must suggest the music's traditions, its collective past. He was afraid he wouldn't be able to use it, because the pickup jack—the socket in the guitar where he plugs in—had worked loose, and when he tried to tighten it the thing fell through into the body of the guitar and stayed there, rattling around out of reach. Luckily, when he called the guitar shop around the corner from his house, the tech said, "Bring it round right away," fished out the jack with his dentist's around-the-corner tool, and fixed the guitar in less than an hour. These are the things guitarists talk about to each other: getting guitars fixed, having guitars stolen, seeing their guitar come out on the airport luggage belt crushed and mangled beyond recognition.

We discuss the inconvenience of sound holes and hollow bodies. Picks, pocket change—any small object nearby seems drawn to fall in through the sound hole. A vet in Vermont made a name for himself by extricating a guy's pet python that had escaped from its tank and taken up residence in his acoustic guitar. Not only that but the hollowbody electric can be something of a liability, as it can produce too much body sound and echo, causing feedback. Some early electric guitarists went so far as to stuff socks in the f-holes to cut down on the sound, thus inventing what might be called the cottonbody.

"I've seen all kinds of things stuck in there," Randall says. "Some guys use balloons . . ."

"Balloons?"

"Yeah, they push them in through the f-holes and inflate them. Anything to cut down on the sound. I've seen guys cover the f-holes with scotch tape."

The Tuscany, the Italian restaurant where he's playing, has no LIVE MUSIC TONITE signs set up outside. The sound will be the marquee. Half the restaurant is full of tables, the other half has a few tables, a small space for the band, and a dance floor the size of a dollar bill.

The Tuscany seems almost a throwback, a family-style Italian restaurant with an Italian waitress, the walls painted with bizarre, surreal versions of classic Mediterranean scenes. Next to me a sad harlequin plays a melon-back mandolin, his fingers long and dark, articulated like the legs of Dalí's ants.

The other members of the five-piece band have been around almost as many musical blocks as has Randall. The keyboard player, wearing a baseball cap over his ponytail, is a former musical director for Tito Puente. The upright bass player, with silver hair but dark eyebrows and looking like a TV pitchman for multivitamins, is a member of the Bee Gees' band. Everyone has played so much jazz it has become ingrained, like a deep tan.

The bandleader is Joe Donato, a warm guy with a powerful presence, shaven head, tanned, relaxed. He stands up behind an illuminated dais reminiscent of big bands and game shows. His name is painted on the front under a caricature of his smiling face, his bald dome. He looks around, nods, and they're off.

Joe comes in on alto sax with Randall comping chords behind him, and at once it's clear why jazz is really a horn player's form. A single note on the sax has more power than any other instrument in the combo, a power that goes beyond sheer volume; it's simply a more interesting sound, richer, more complex, somehow more human. It's as if the big guy, the man to be respected, has just turned up and said, "Listen up, you all" with the voice of one who knows he will command attention.

As soon as I think "voice" I start to understand these complicated jazz chords. Jazz is a social form, with its origins in ensembles in which several players speak up at once—unlike blues, which characteristically has one voice at a time, whether the human voice or the guitar's voice responding. (Likewise rock, the thick-necked adolescent child of the blues.) When Randall plays those chords he's hearing the small combos of the early century, swelling into the polyphonic arrangements of the big bands. It's his job to respect those voices, because they are what makes jazz different from, and arguably more interesting than, other traditions. The social setting and the history play out on the fingerboard. The chords echo the organized anarchy of a bunch o' guys having fun kicking a song around between them, like good soccer players on their day off, playing in a park league. Simple two-voice counterpoint has nothing on this. No wonder those chords are so bloody hard.

One more thing. The Tuscany gig is a sign that people play jazz for pleasure, not because it's the only music they like but because it keeps them alive. This is the paradox of improvisation: the roots of the music go so deep into tradition that it will fall into cliché unless each player constantly refreshes it. Every player has to understand the past but reach with each phrase into the future. What Randall is playing is in a sense the mature compilation of much of American musical culture of the twentieth century. When he teaches his students jazz guitar, he's also teaching them America, once and future.

Joe brings the song to a close. Some applause from the three tables nearest the band, all groups of people in, shall we say, late middle age, like the audience at the Guitar Marathon. Along with George Gruhn, I worry that the devoted, discerning guitar audience reached its heyday in the late sixties and doesn't get around so much anymore.

All the same, I'm starting to get the fun of this, the social intimacy, the dynamic. These aren't stars, or even musicians, necessarily; they're a bunch of guys who come here every Thursday to play jazz. It makes a concert performance seem like a transaction between strangers, stiff and a little artificial. Here the atmosphere is constantly under revision, and the audience is very much a contributing partner. Almost everyone sitting at the tables is talking, except five people—again, none of them spring chickens—sitting at a rail to Joe's left, a foot or so above the playing area. One of them has his reading glasses down at the end of his nose and the row of spectators looks much like a panel of judges, though not hanging judges.

As the set goes on Randall breaks out the skills of a lifetime, or of the guitar's lifetime, playing sometimes with pick, sometimes with fingers, sometimes with the side of his thumb, sometimes using an odd circular motion, like a drummer with a brush, as if he were rubbing the strings instead of playing them. Every so often he goes into Wes Montgomery mode, playing the melody in parallel octaves, or into Freddie Greene mode, playing traditional eight-to-the-bar rhythm guitar, or into Instant Arthritis mode, playing the melody in chords, which takes a phenomenal knowledge of the fingerboard and the shapes of the chords. Lead guitar is hard, rhythm guitar isn't easy, but together, well, that's one of the special challenges of jazz. When they go into an R&B-flavored piece with a strong backbeat and a steady four-on-the-floor rhythm, Randall adjusts his tone controls so he has more of a lean, yearning B. B. King sound and holds his blues phrases longer, reminding me of something that Jim Hall said of B. B. King—that he'd rather hear him play one note than anyone else play a hundred.

I can't help wishing his guitar sound had just a little more attack, a little less of that velvet tux sound. Yet at the same time I know this is the sound of a guitar that, unlike the rock instrument, has social skills, has learned how to play nicely with others. As Jorma Kaukonen has said, "The first sign of maturity is the discovery that the volume knob also turns to the left."

After half a dozen songs they're really cooking. Nobody is sitting back politely. Joe is wailing, the bass player and drummer are flailing, and Randall has turned himself up and is doing his Mickey Baker's Book of One Thousand Chords. This is jazz in the sense that people used the word in 1935—something with enough zip and rhythm to grab you by the shirtfront. A couple stands up in the narrow squeeze-space between the bar and the upper tables and is dancing with a formal sexiness.

The guys play three sets, heavily laced with requests, mostly Tin Pan Alley standards, Latin pieces, and show tunes, songs as much as sixty years old refreshed with contemporary phrasings. A flower seller goes table to table and does brisk business. One of the judges drums on the counter, his left hand flat and steady on the beat, his right hand knuckling a little off-the-beat excursion.

Someone's son sits in for Randall on one song and plays respectably—on a Fender, in defiance of tradition. He must be one of these college guitarists I've been hearing about. He has Charlie Christian bop lines, but he's a little stiff. He can play but he can't yet swing.

When I ask Randall where the kid will find work when he graduates with his jazz guitar degree he points out mildly that I've made the schoolboy mistake of assuming that people study guitar like they study dentistry. Some of Randall's former students are freelance club jazz musicians, but others are touring with big-name pop singers, playing Broadway and touring shows, teaching at various levels, owning recording studios, or doing something completely different. One is a popular novelist. Maybe this kid will never play out again but spend his life happily playing with friends on Thursday nights in the den. Maybe he'll teach his daughter.

The Tuscany is now packed, half loud dinner chatter, half dancing for sardines, so close to the musicians that the artificial wall is down: everyone's swinging together. This is what a night out ought to be.

Randall and the boys wrap up shortly after 11 P.M. on a warm velvet south Florida night. The Tuscany is a middle-aged musician's dream gig.

Next door, a large bar called Senor Frog's is packed with young people and there's a line maybe fifty long at the door. A sound system is pounding but nobody's dancing.

# Gluing the Nut

On August 6, Rick calls. "I just finished gluing the nut," he says elliptically.

I'm not sure what that means, but when I get to his shop it becomes clear: the guitar is finished. I'm caught off balance. There it is on the bench, bridge on, tuners in, frets in, strings on. A guitar.

It's amazing. The depth and richness of the golden body strike me all over again, leave me breathless. The black tuners make the face-plate glow between them. All over the guitar, in fact, the black outline framing the lighter woods gives the whole instrument a photo-negative look, given that guitars traditionally have dark backs and sides with light binding, and even though I sort of planned it this way it's still a small jolt of surprise. The inlaid falling maple leaves actually look right now—not what I wanted but just fine. The fingerboard, which I was afraid would look pale and dusty without the ebony dye, is dark and rich; Rick has oiled it and that's quite enough. The eccentric sound hole and the cutaway don't look gimmicky or even especially unusual. This is their guitar, their natural habitat.

When I pick it up I'm struck by how light it is compared to the Fylde, a good eight ounces lighter, I'm guessing. The neck, though as broad as the Fylde's to allow for all those fingers on it, is much less thick, and with its stripe up the back it feels like a racing neck. The box, too, is fractionally shallower, which feels good. The whole thing is stepping away from the dreadnought, which by now is seeming almost unbearably dull, a blunt instrument.

Playing it is a series of revelations. I barely notice the fat frets: my fingers slide around freely. The action is already lower than the Fylde's (and due to be lowered still more) and my fingers find themselves falling into chords I have been used to fighting my way into. I've already forgotten about the cutaway, and when I get to a high passage in "Nuages" I'm baffled by how easy it is.

The sound is completely different from the Fylde. Rick was right; it isn't as rich and mellow, but it isn't wimpy or tinny, either. It has a youthful strength, bright and unafraid. I bang on it a bit and it doesn't buzz or hollow out; I play way up high; I play jazz chords in the middle range.

My third and fourth strings between the eighth and twelfth frets have a particularly appealing timbre, especially when played with the side of the thumb, but with no nail. It's a strong, round, but resonant sound, with excellent sustain—hardly metallic at all. I've barely thought about this question. How can I best use the sounds of the guitar, and even of this particular guitar? I try playing the tenth fret of the fourth string, a C, and it swells out into the room with no apparent effort from the body of the guitar at all. When I move down and play the same string at the fourth fret, I feel the top of the guitar vibrate against the skin of my right forearm and the back vibrate against my abs. Yet in this sweet patch higher up the fingerboard it's as if the entire construction of the guitar comes together, wasting not an iota of energy, converting the entire motion of strings and wood into harmonic sound, the ethereal alchemy of music.

Rick twangs a string and listens. The note reaches out, grows, seems to spread through the whole body of the guitar, then through the air in the box and above the sound hole until it seems to have had nothing to do with the act of playing the string and hovers independent of the materials, the spirit of the note. It takes a good fifteen seconds to settle, like the settling of acoustic dust, back to nothing. A fifteen-second decay is a good sign.

I can't stop playing; then I put it down and I can't stop looking at it.

This is a greyhound, lean, light, ready.

Now it's my turn.

# Chapter Notes

This book is intended primarily for the general reader rather than the scholar, but there's so much about the guitar worth reading that I'm glad to offer these chapter notes as a form of annotated selected bibliography. Anyone with more detailed questions should feel free to contact me at brookes@champlain.edu.

## The First Guitar

Gregg Miner's amazing collection, and a cornucopia of materials about the harp-guitar builder Christian Knutsen, can be viewed at www.minermusic.com. For some photos of astonishing modern instruments in the spirit of sixteenth-, seventeenth-, and eighteenth-century guitar and lute family instruments, see www.lutesandguitars.co.uk. The history of the European guitar can be found in abundance in James Tyler and Paul Sparks's *The Guitar and its Music: From the Renaissance to the Classical Era.* The authority on guitar music in New Spain is John Koegel of the Department of Music, California State University, Fullerton. Craig Russell's work is also well worth exploring, as are Marta Weigle and Peter White's *The Lore of New Mexico,*

Robert Stevenson's *Spanish Music in the Age of Columbus* and *Music in Mexico*, Eleanor Hague's *Latin American Music*, Harry W. Crosby's *Antigua California*, and *Music in Puerto Rico*, edited by Donald Thompson.

## Other Colonists: French and English Guitars

The sad story of Fort Caroline is from Wiley Housewright's fine book *A History of Music and Dance in Florida, 1565–1865*. Colonial America and its guitar music are chronicled by Oscar Sonneck in *Early Concert-Life in America (1731–1880)*, which is a pleasure to read not least because of the odd places that were used for concerts before purpose-built palaces of art were constructed for formal music at the end of the nineteenth century.

## Evanescence

A great deal of the material in this chapter is from the searchable databases of the American Memory collections of the Library of Congress, at http://memory.loc.gov/, which leads to hundreds of references to the guitar, far more than I've been able to do justice to here. The searchable online *New York Times* database is another wonderful source. Check out Strenuous Lifer, a turn-of-the-century pig whose obituary mentions his ability to play the guitar. Excellent background and parallel material turn up in Craig H. Roell's *The Piano in America, 1890–1940*, one of the most thoughtful books on music I have ever read. And the trenchant, slightly bitter coda on the maligned importance of parlor music came from Edith Boroff's article "An American Parlor at the Turn of the Century," published in *American Music*, Fall 1986. The definitive work on the bizarre history of the guitar and the BMG (banjo, mandolin, and guitar) movement is Jeffrey J. Noonan's, *The Guitar in America as Reflected in Topical Periodicals, 1882–1933* (Ph.D. dissertation, Washington University in St. Louis, May 2004), xv, 748.

## The Hawaiians Have Landed

The expert on Hawaiian music on the mainland is Lorene Ruymar, whose book *Hawaiian Steel Guitar* contains most of what is good in this chapter. George Kanahele's magisterial *Hawaiian Music and Musicians: An Illustrated History* is also required reading.

## The Starvation Box

More books have been written on blues and the guitar than any other genre; in fact, the blues writers of the late fifties and early sixties such as Paul Oliver were probably the first writers to take American folk music, its personalities, its stories, and its complex energies, seriously. (Among later writers, Peter Guralnick stands out.) This chapter steals from most of them, especially W. C. Handy's *Father of the Blues* and Charles Schaar Murray's *Crosstown Traffic*, a life of Jimi Hendrix.

## Desperadoes

*New Orleans Jazz: A Family Album* by Al Rose and Edmond Souchon includes probably the most interesting and informative group of photographs of musicians I have come across.

## Radio Castles in the Air

The Nick Lucas story comes from James Sallis, whose *The Guitar Players* and *Jazz Guitars* are among the few books from as early as the eighties to take jazz guitar, and guitar in general, seriously. Nolan Porterfield is a genuine scholar, and his books *Jimmie Rodgers: The Life and Times of America's Blue Yodeler* and *The Last Cavalier: The Life and Times of John A. Lomax* were both useful and inspiring.

## The Guitar Breaks In

To find out more about the fascinating and diverse muscial activities in Whitesburg, Kentucky, which range from old-time to punk, go to www.appalshop.org. Eddie Pennington can tell you everything about thumbpicking and Appalachian guitar in general; track him down at www.eddiepennington.com.

## Bargaining with the Devil

The high (and deceptive) hopes occasioned by the invention of the phonograph are well documented by Mark Katz in "Making America More Musical through the Phonograph, 1900–1930," in *American Music*, Winter 1998. The steady decline and fall of those hopes is documented all over the place, in books such as Tony Palmer's *All You Need Is Love*, Charles Schaar Murray's *Boogie Man*, Francis Davis's *History of the Blues*, Colin Escott's *Hank Williams*, Chuck Berry's *Chuck Berry: The Autobiography*, Sandra Tooze's *Muddy Waters*, Mark Zwonitzer's and Charles Hirshberg's *Will You Miss Me When I'm Gone?: The Carter Family and Their Legacy in American Music*, Richard K. Spottswood's *Ethnic Recordings in America*, Benjamin Filene's *Romancing the Folk*, Buddy Guy's *Damn Right I've Got the Blues*, Alan Lomax's *Land Where the Blues Began*, and Nolan Porterfield's biographies of Jimmie Rodgers and John Lomax (see above).

## The Modern Age

In addition to more material from the online *New York Times* and Sallis's two books (see above), the principal sources for this potpourri of research are: Steven Loza's *Barrio Rhythm: Mexican American Music in Los Angeles*, Douglas Green's *Singing in the Saddle*, Duncan McLean's *Lone Star Swing*, Cary Ginell's *Milton Brown and the Founding of Western Swing*, Ann Allen Savoy's *Cajun Music*, Jerry Byrd's *It Was a Trip . . . On Wings of Music*, Charles Delaunay's *Django Reinhardt*, Whitney Balliett's *Collected Works: A Journal of Jazz 1954–2001*, Mary Alice

Shaughnessy's *Les Paul: An American Original,* and John Schroeter's collection *Between the Strings: The Secret Lives of Guitars.* Lydia Mendoza's story, and many other insights into American music in the early twentieth century, can be found in *Ethnic Recordings in America,* edited by Richard Spottswood.

## Postwar Ennui

*Guitar Review* is the best source for classical guitar activity at this time, as well as for Ron Purcell's articles on the fascinating Vahdah Olcott Bickford and Laurindo Almeida. Some of my observations on the differences in playing technique between the acoustic guitar and the electric, and the effect those differences had on jazz playing, are lifted from Norman Mongan's *The History of the Guitar in Jazz.*

## Killing for a Dime

Harley Cokliss's documentary *Chicago Blues,* grimy and sad, is well worth renting. The Ernest Withers photograph can be found in Daniel Wolff's stunning book *Ernest C. Withers: The Memphis Blues Again.*

## Love Me Tender/The Worst Trip

Any book by Peter Guralnick is worth reading (elsewhere I quote from *Lost Highway* and *Feel Like Going Home*); this material is from *Last Train to Memphis: The Rise of Elvis Presley.* Women rockers turn up in profusion in Lucy O'Brien's *She Bop: The Definitive History of Women in Rock, Pop, and Soul,* Gillian Gaar's *She's a Rebel,* and perhaps most thoughtfully in an article in *American Music* by Susan Fast entitled "Rethinking Issues of Gender and Sexuality in Led Zeppelin." The almost incredible details of Buddy Holly's last road tour are from Ellis Amburn's *Buddy Holly: A Biography.* Material on B. B. King is from *Blues Boy: The Life and Music of B. B. King,* by Sebastian Danchin.

## The Guitar Just Grabbed Me

An unusual and interesting view behind the scenes of the folk aspects of the British Invasion turns up in Colin Harper's *Dazzling Stranger*, a biography of Bert Jansch. Bill Wyman's *Rolling with the Stones* is full of interesting and unexpected documents.

## Something Is Happening

Fans of surf and rockabilly should subscribe to Dick Stewart's Web letter *The Lance Monthly* via www.lancerecords.com. Other sources: Filene's *Romancing the Folk* (see above) and David Hajdu's interesting, waspish *Positively 4th Street: The Lives and Times of Joan Baez, Bob Dylan, Mimi Baez Fariña, and Richard Fariña.*

## Inlay

Essential reading: Larry Robinson's *The Art of Inlay* and William "Grit" Laskin's *A Guitarmaker's Canvas: The Inlay Art of Grit Laskin.*

## Satisfaction

More from *Hispanic Music in the Twentieth Century,* and Paul Burlison's story is another from Schroeter's *Between the Strings* (see above). *Standing in the Shadows of Motown* is well worth renting. The El Monte Legion Stadium scene is from Steven Loza's fine book *Barrio Rhythm: Mexican American Music in Los Angeles.*

## Guitar Rock Takes Over

The best source for new instrument sales is NAMM, which confusingly now calls itself the International Music Products Association, though their Web site is www.namm.com. Some useful information is to be found in David P. Szatmary's surprisingly pedestrian *Rockin' in Time: A Social History of Rock-and-Roll.* Andrew Neill and Matthew Kent's delightfully self-mocking *Anyway, Anyhow, Anywhere: The Complete Chronicle of the Who, 1958–1978* is anything but pedestrian. Michael Wright has done sterling research, much of it for *Vintage Guitar*, in a field where the principals often can't remember or agree on what they were doing as recently as the previous evening. Material about studio musicians comes from Robert R. Faulkner's *Hollywood Studio Musicians*, based on interviews conducted between July 1966 and August 1967.

## "Vintage" Guitars

Drool over used guitars at www.mandoweb.com; the cheaper and perhaps more eccentric end of the range can be seen at www.bernunzio. com.

## Sound Check

For more information about the New York Guitar Festival, including photos, schedules, and its CD recordings, go to www.newyorkguitar festival.org.

# Appendices

## Top Ten Recordings

All music writing, according to Nick Hornby, boils down to a list of personal favorites. Here, in no particular order, are the ten guitar CDs or albums I listened to most often while writing this book.

Sergio and Odair Assad, *Sergio and Odair Assad Play Piazzola*
  (Brazilian guitar duo play Argentine tango rock and roll)
Eddie Pennington, *Just My Style*
  (Chet Atkins-style thumbpicking jazz)
*Django Reinhardt and Stéphane Grappelli with the Quintet of the Hot Club of France*
  (The Ace of Clubs album recorded before and after the war)
Richard and Linda Thompson, *I Want to See the Bright Lights Tonight*
  (Songs of hope and pain)
Mark O'Connor, Frank Vignola, Jon Burr, *Hot Swing*
  (Hot Club trio swing, uptempo and lyrical)
Stefano Grondona, *Lo Cant dels Aucells*
  (Spanish and classical pieces played on period instruments)

Fountains of Wayne, *Welcome Interstate Managers*
  (Ironic killer two-minute singles)
Roy Rogers, *Slideways*
  (Amazing slide guitar)
Fapy Lafertin, *Fine and Dandy*
  (Django-style gypsy jazz)
Kaki King, *Everybody Loves You*
  (Guitar percussion played in the style called "tapping." An
  ear-opener)

## Revivals I Wish I Could Start

If I could start one revival, I'd bring back the fun jazz school of forgotten hip, black guitar acts, late thirties precursors to both R&B and
rock and roll but with a crucial difference: they had a cabaret sophistication and a vaudevillian sense of humor.

In the thirties the guitarist Teddy Bunn played with (among others) the hilarious Spirits of Rhythm, probably the only jazz band to
make extensive use of the tiple, a Hispanic instrument that looks like
the outcome of a happy mating between a guitar and a mandolin. The
band's three-tiple attack gave a wonderful no-pie-in-our-pants rhythmic foundation with swinging tiple and guitar parts, which went hand
in hand with high-spirited nonsense, scat, and Harlem jive lyrics. The
band was a regular and popular feature of the live New York jazz scene
around 52nd Street until well into the forties.

In much the same vein were Slim and Slam—that is, the bassist Slam
Stewart and the guitarist Bulee "Slim" Gaillard, who first made a name
for himself in vaudeville by playing the guitar while tap dancing. They
had a 1938 hit with "Flat Foot Floogie"; Gaillard could also play the piano
with his hands upside down and had a hit with a song whose lyrics were
from the menu of an Armenian restaurant, but he wasn't only a joker:
he recorded with Charlie Parker and Dizzie Gillespie.

Another jazz-nonsense-highjinks-tiple band of the late thirties was
Cats and the Fiddle, with the excellent Lloyd "Tiny" Grimes on guitar. (Grimes also played and recorded with Art Tatum and Charlie

Parker.) One reviewer described some of the band's work as "noisy and meaningless vocal jam stuff that lacks imagination and everything else to make it appeal to anyone but those whose passion for swing is such that they feel as long as it's hot it's good." Whatever happened to bands like these?

## Woods

Here's Dick Boak, head of artist relations at Martin Guitars, lovingly describing some of the more and less common guitar tonewoods. (The woods marked with an asterisk are not genuine members of the rosewood family, though they're sometimes passed off as such.

AFRICAN BLACKWOOD    Dark purple to black in color.

COCOBOLO    Brilliant orange, rust, purple, and yellow with distinctive superimposed lines of purple and black.

EAST INDIAN ROSEWOOD    Predominantly light to dark purple, with occasional red and brown streaks.

HONDURAS ROSEWOOD    Pinkish brown to salmon red with dark irregular grain lines.

KINGWOOD    Often referred to as violetwood, brownish purple with fine stripes of black and luminous violet that can approach royal blue.

TULIPWOOD    Sometimes distributed as "Brazilian pinkwood," tulipwood has a rich pinkish-golden hue with luminous salmon stripes.

BOCOTE*    Contrasting black, green, and vibrant golden yellow with tight wild figure patterns.

BUBINGA*    Often referred to as "African rosewood," bubinga is purplish pink to salmon red with dark red veining.

GRANADILLO*    Reddish brown to purplish orange.

PADAUK*    Often referred to as vermilion. Padauk varies in color according to a number of variations within species, but most varieties will display a brilliant red-orange color when freshly cut, with darker crimson grain lines.

## One Gig I Wish I Could Have Seen

If I could travel through time and space to see a single guitar concert, it would have to be one by Agustin Barrios Mangore, who has been described by no less an authority than John Williams (the classical guitarist, not the *Star Wars* composer) as the greatest guitarist of all time, and who was into the bargain either deeply eccentric, or deeply spiritual, or both.

Barrios was born in 1885 in southern Paraguay and, inspired by his mother's guitar playing, began to play the guitar at a very young age. By twenty he was a successful composer, writing brilliant and idiomatic transcriptions of Bach, Beethoven, Chopin, and Schumann (but hated by Segovia, who carried out a one-man boycott of Barrios's works), yet success didn't interest him; what interested him were the cultures and musics of South America, especially the songs and dances from Argentina, Chile, and Paraguay.

In 1930 Barrios took on a new persona, Cacique (Chief) Nitsuga Mangoré, the "messenger of the Guarani race . . . the Paganini of the guitar from the jungles of Paraguay." Nitsuga, you may notice, is Agustin spelled backwards.

Barrios's compositions became increasingly profound and spiritual, and he would dress for concerts in full Guarani tribal clothing, or lack thereof: he seems to have played while stripped to the waist and wearing feathers.

After his final composition Barrios spent his remaining days in tranquillity, solitude, and meditation, preparing himself for death. He began to suffer from heart trouble, and on August 7, 1944, he went into cardiac arrest and died. The priest who attended him proclaimed, "This is the first time I have witnessed the death of a saint."

# Glossary

**Archtop:** Guitar with two f-shaped sound holes, like a cello, instead of one round one. Strings typically run over the bridge to be anchored in a tailpiece attached to the bottom of the guitar. The top, like a cello's, is typically carved in an arch—hence the name. Jazz players tend to favor archtops, mostly because jazz players have always tended to favor archtops.

**Binding:** The strip of wood (or sometimes plastic. Hiss! Hiss!) glued along the outside of the join where the top meets the sides, and the sides meet the back, intended to make the join seem intentional, even attractive. Think of it as guitar grout.

**Bluegrass:** Often defined as "three men sharing a sinus," bluegrass takes traditional rural American tunes and plays them with speed and dexterity, typically on fiddle, guitar, and mandolin, with a high harmony vocal sound sometimes described as "lonesome," with good reason.

**Blues:** Traditional form of complaint music, originally played by African-Americans for lack of any better way of earning a living, now played by Caucasians for lack of any better way of avoiding earning a living.

**Bout:** The outward-curving parts of the body of a guitar, two-thirds of its femininity. The upper bout is the shoulders of the guitar, the lower bout her hips. The inward curve between the two bouts is the waist.

**Bracing:** Struts glued to the underside of the top and back (a) to transduce the vibrations passing from the strings through the bridge into the vibrating top of the guitar, and (b) to prevent the whole damn thing from exploding.

**Course:** Pair of strings mounted close together, usually tuned in unison or an octave apart. Very common on fretted instruments before about 1800, as hitting two strings is a lot easier than hitting one, after several bottles of Rhenish and a flagon of mulled claret.

**DADGAD:** A wonderfully clever tuning that has the combined effect of making a guitarist seem not only dextrous but also emotionally complex. Deep, even. Its use is heavily protected by copyright.

**Dobro:** An ingenious form of acoustic guitar designed to sound as if the player is trapped inside a cookie tin.

**Fingerstyle:** Playing a guitar with the tools God gave you: your digits. Viewed by flatpickers (q.v.) as sissy.

**Flattop:** Just like an archtop except that the top is flat, the sound hole is round, and the strings are usually attached to the bridge. Not favored by jazz players.

**Flatpicking:** Playing a guitar with a piece of plastic, a nickel, the tooth of a comb, or, if you're a European gypsy, even a small flat stone. Viewed by fingerpickers (q.v.) as Neanderthal.

**G, C, D, A7:** All the chords a guitarist needs to know in order to make money.

**Guitar, acoustic:** Traditional hollow seduction device. Acoustic means, "Drop it and it breaks."

**Guitar, bass:** Low-end instrument, in every sense, to which a guitarist is banished when the band hires someone better than him to take over lead.

**Guitar, classical:** Instrument played by socially phobic overachiever under a brutal regime of constant discipline until the results begin to approach what a guitar is truly capable of. By then, all but a few of the players are broken men and women.

**Guitar, electric:** Inert lump of wood wired for sound.

**Guitar, rhythm:** In jazz, an amazingly demanding style of guitar playing that demands incredibly dextrous fingers, an encyclopedic knowledge of the fingerboard, and a subtle and far-ranging understanding of rhythm. In every other kind of music, exactly the opposite.

**Guitar, steel:** The most complex and demanding form of guitar, burdened with an almost infinite number of strings set in algebraically complex tunings in an effort to make the instrument sound sweet and simple.

**Guitar, tenor:** Guitar built with only four strings so even banjo players could navigate it.

**Guitar maker:** Luthier (q.v.) who charges less than $1,000 per guitar.

**Hammer-on** (see Pull-off): Tricks that involve adding notes by left-hand movements only, thereby making the guitarist seem much faster than is really the case, and also delaying the onset of right-wrist arthritis.

**Inlay:** Decorations, sometimes in marquetry but usually in the nacreous shells of certain molluscs, that adds individuality and several hundred dollars to the price of the guitar. Country guitarists like to have their names inlaid along the fingerboard—a smart move, as guitars are among the most frequently stolen commodities.

**Lining:** Like binding (q.v.) but on the inside angle of the join, where it can't be seen and thus doesn't need to be made of some expensive rain-forest wood.

**Luthier:** Guitarmaker (q.v.) who charges more than $1,000 per guitar.

**Nut:** (a) Chunk of wood, plastic, or bone nicked with six slots that anchor the strings in place as they pass from the tuners to the fingerboard. (b) Anyone who pays more than $250 for a used guitar.

**Nut width:** Width of the fingerboard at the nut. Classical guitarists like a broad nut width of more than two inches because they play so many strings at once, and need plenty of room to park all those left-hand fingers. Bluegrass guitarists like skinny necks because they only ever play one string at a time.

**Old-Time:** Traditional rural American music, especially of the region spanning the Appalachians, drawing heavily on adaptations of British Isles songs, tunes, and ballads. The pop music of an era before electricity.

**Open-string:** A technique used by most stringed-instrument players whereby in addition to plucking or picking strings on which your left-hand fingers are parked, you also pluck or pick ones devoid of fingers, preferably when the resulting note is in the same key as the tune you're trying to play.

**Position marker:** Dot, square, or other small inlaid design inlaid on the fingerboard at certain frets so an electric guitarist knows where to start.

**Pull-off:** See hammer-on.

**Rock:** Suitable article to throw at any electric guitarist whose solo exceeds seven minutes.

**Rockabilly:** Rock and roll played by hillbillies, that deep twangy sound out of the Sun studios in Memphis and Clovis, New Mexico. Think Duane Eddy, whose own first name echoes the bent low strings of an early electric. More recently picked up by Brian Setzer and the Stray Cats. Leather jacket essential.

**Rock and roll:** A Western adaptation of traditional trance music in which the electric guitar hits the chord, the electric bass hits the root note, the drummer hits the drum, and the listener's forehead hits the wall at the same repeated interval.

**Scale length:** Distance from nut (q.v.) to saddle. Basically, the vibrating length of the strings, usually about twenty-five inches.

**Skiffle:** In the United States, African-American rent-party music. In the UK, American folk songs played at high tempo with wild enthusiasm on instruments that called for the minimum of skill and financial investment.

**Tonewood:** Wood used for the top, back, and sides of an acoustic guitar. In the case of the back and sides in particular, chosen in theory for its tone but in practice for its looks. Often a highly colorful endangered species, exported from its native land by shady characters making a quick profit.

**Western swing:** Thirties jazz played by a string band dressed as cowboys.

**X-bracing:** Bracing in the shape of an X.

**Zither:** Guitar gone bad.

# Acknowledgments

This project began with its author in a state of confusion and almost complete ignorance, and I'd still be there but for the help of:

Paul Asbell, Tom Ayres of the Flynn Center for the Performing Arts, Dennis Boutsikaris, Richard Bruné, Al Carruth, Walter Carter, Randall Dollahon, Vic Flick, Ed Gerhard, Doug Green, George Gruhn, Amy Hartman, Chris Herrod, Sharon Isbin, Stan Jay, Bill Kinzie, Rich Kirby, Dennis Koster, Gregg Miner, Doug Morier, Aaron and Michael Newman, Dave Nichols, Laura Oltman, Jay Orr, Rik Palieri, Eddie Pennington, Jeff Rice, Roy and Gaynell Rogers, Lorene Ruymar, Colin Sillence, David Spelman, David Starobin, Dick Stewart, Rick Turner, Ben Verdery, and the library research staff at the University of Vermont.

Special thanks to Jeff Noonan for being a diligent and sympathetic reader who has actually done real research, to Joan Bingham, my editor at Grove/Atlantic, Inc., for believing in the idea, to her assistant, Lindsay Sagnette, who cared for this book as if it were her own, my daughter Zoe for art direction, and my wife, Barbara, whose generosity and insight started everything off.